AF560357

Women, Peace and Security
Implementation of the UNSCR 1325 in South Asia

Women, Peace and Security

Implementation of the UNSCR 1325 in South Asia

DR. SEEMA THAKUR

REGAL PUBLICATIONS
New Delhi

WOMEN, PEACE AND SECURITY
Implementation of the UNSCR 1325 in South Asia

ISBN 978-81-8484-462-7

Typeset by
RAHUL COMPOSERS
New Highway Apartments, Lakshmi Niwas
760, Pocket-D, Lok Nayak Puram, New Delhi - 110 041

Printed in India at
MAYUR ENTERPRISES
WZ Plot No. 3, Gujjar Market, Tihar Village, New Delhi - 110 018

Published by
REGAL PUBLICATIONS
F-159, Rajouri Garden, New Delhi - 110 027
Phone : 45546396, 25435369
E-mail : regalbookspub@yahoo.com, regaldeepbooks@yahoo.com

Contents

Preface

The first International Women's Day of the millennium would be remembered as historic as it is on this day that the President of the United Nations Security Council on behalf of the Council recognized that peace is inextricably linked with equality between women and men, a splendid recognition of the promise and premise of the United Nations Charter. This was followed by the adoption of the Resolution 1325 on Women, Peace and Security by the Security Council on October 31, 2000.

History of humankind is replete with instances of criminal violence against women during war and armed conflicts and perpetrators enjoying impunity in as much as its being oblivious of the role of women pacifists and their contribution to conflict resolution and peace processes. Resolution 1325 is a landmark development in International Law and the UN history that recognizes the gendered nature of war and peace processes. It takes cognizance of gender-based violence and lays down a normative framework for women's role in peace and security.

Resolution 1325 and the subsequent Resolutions 1820, 1888, 1889, 1960 and 2106 have established a legal regime that has opened the way for women to bring a qualitative improvement in negotiating and peace structuring. With its enormous potential and implications, the Resolution has rightly been declared by its architect—Anwarul Karim Chowdhury "a common heritage of humanity" wherein the global objectives of peace, equality and development are reflected.

With all the laudable objectives has the Resolution in reality made any impact since its adoption? This is a question that is being raised by the advocates of the Resolution and by the women peace activists who have lobbied over the years for its passage. The author in the present book has attempted to examine the impact of Resolution 1325 in South Asia in terms of its implementation in the region. The book has added significance as the region is affected with ongoing inter and intra-state conflicts. This perhaps is the first study of its kind that focuses on the implementation of Resolution 1325 on Women, Peace and Security in South Asia.

During the exciting and stimulating work, I was privileged to have guidance of Professor Manohar Lal Sharma, Chairperson, Department of Gandhian and Peace Studies, Panjab University Chandigarh. I was equally fortunate to have frequent interactions with Dr. Pam Rajput, Former Professor of Political Science and Founder Director of Centre for Women's Studies and Development, Panjab University Chandigarh who gave the benefit of her expertise and also access to her library and I wish to thank her for going through my manuscript and giving me insightful suggestions. I owe her my eternal gratitude.

My sincere thanks are due to my respondents from Afghanistan, Bangladesh, India, Nepal, Pakistan and Sri Lanka for their cooperation and cordiality.

I thank the Global Action to Prevent War (GAPW) for the internship experience that facilitated my field research in and around the United Nations (UN) Headquarters in New York. A special thank is also due to Waverly de Bruijn, International Coordinator of GAPW, who provided a window into the work of the NGO Working Group on Women, Peace and Security, and shared her experience of advocacy at the UN Security Council. She also introduced me to many of the practitioners I interviewed for my work.

I would also like to express my gratitude to my family for the support they provided me throughout and in particular, I must acknowledge my Mother, without whose love and encouragement I would not have finished this work.

Above all I am grateful to the Almighty who gave me strength and wisdom to write this book.

DR. SEEMA THAKUR

Abbreviations

AFSPA	Armed Forces Special Power Act
ANBP	Afghanistan New Beginnings Programme
APDP	Association of Parents of Disappeared Persons
APWW	Asia Pacific Women's Watch
AWAW	Association of War Affected Women
BBC	Beyond Beijing Committee
BONUCA	United Nations Peace-building Support Mission in the Central African Republic
CAFI	Control Arms Foundation of India
CAP	Consolidated Appeals Process
CARE	Cooperative for Assistance and Relief Everywhere
CCA	Common Country Assessment
CEDAW	Convention on the Elimination of All Forms of Discrimination against Women
CENWOR	Centre for Women's Research
CPA	Comprehensive Peace Agreement
CVA	Capacities and Vulnerabilities Analysis
DAW	Division for the Advancement of Women
DDA	Department for Disarmament Affairs
DDR	Disarmament, Demobilization and Reintegration
DESA	Department of Economic and Social Affairs
DESC	Division for Economic and Social Council Support and Coordination
DFAIT	Canadian Department of Foreign Affairs and

	International Trade
DFID	United Kingdom Department for International Development
DPA	Department of Political Affairs
DPADM	Division for Public Administration
DPI	Department of Public Information
DPKO	Department of Peacekeeping Operations
ECA	Economic Commission for Africa
ECE	Economic Commission for Europe
ECHA	Executive Committee on Humanitarian Affairs
ECOWAS	Economic Community of West African States
ECPS	Executive Committee for Peace and Security
ESCAP	Economic and Social Commission for Asia and the Pacific
ESCWA	Economic and Social Commission for Western Asia
FAO	Food and Agriculture Organization of the United Nations
FMLN	Farabundo Marti National Liberation (El Salvador)
FOWSIA	Forum on Women in Security and International Affairs
GDI	Gender Development Index
GII	Gender Inequality Index
GOS	Guild of Service
HDI	Human Development Index
HDRs	Human Development Reports
HIV/AIDS	Human Immunodeficiency Virus/Acquired Immunodeficiency Syndrome
IANWGE	Inter-Agency Network on Women and Gender Equality
IASC	Inter-Agency Standing Committee
ICC	International Criminal Court
ICES	International Centre for Ethnic Studies
ICRC	International Committee of the Red Cross
ICTR	International Criminal Tribunal for Rwanda
ICTY	International Criminal Tribunal for the former Yugoslavia
IDPs	Internally Displaced Persons

IFAD	International Fund for Agricultural Development
IFP	In Focus Programme
IFRC	International Federation of Red Cross and Red Crescent Societies
IHRICON	Institute of Human Rights Communication, Nepal Forum for Women, Law and Development
ILO	International Labour Organization
INSTRAW	United Nations International Research and Training Institute for the Advancement of Women
IOM	International Organization for Migration
ISAF	International Security Assistance Force (in Afghanistan)
JCYCN	Jagriti Children and Youth Concern Nepal
MAS	Mine Action Service
MDL	Mothers and Daughters of Lanka (MDL)
MINURSO	UN Mission for the Referendum in Western Sahara
MINUSTAH	UN Stabilization Mission in Haiti
MONUC	United Nations Mission in the Democratic Republic of the Congo
MONUSCO	UN Organization Stabilization Mission in the Democratic Republic of the Congo
MWRAF	Muslim Women's Research and Action Forum
NATO	North Atlantic Treaty Oganization
NAWO	National Alliance of Women
NEN	North East Network
NGO	Non-governmental Organization
NMA	Naga Mother's Association
NPC	National Peace Campaign
NSCN(I-M)	Nationalist Socialist Council of Nagaland (Issac-Muivah)
OCHA	Office for the Coordination of Humanitarian Affairs
OHCHR	Office of the High Commissioner for Human Rights
OHRM	Office of Human Resources Management
OLA	Office of Legal Affairs

OSAGI	Office of the Special Adviser on Gender Issues and Advancement of Women
OSCE	Organization for Security and Co-operation in Europe
OSRSG/CAC	Office of the Special Representative of the Secretary-General for Children and Armed Conflict
OXFAM	Oxford Committee for Famine Relief
PRST	Presidential Statements
SANGAT	South Asian Network of Gender Activists and Trainers
SAWW	South Asia Women's Watch
SG	Secretary General
SGBV	Sexual and Gender-based Violence
SLWNGOF	Sri Lanka Women's NGO Forum
SOP	Standard Operating Procedure
SRSG	Special Representative of the Secretary-General
STI	Sexually Transmitted Infection
STOP	Special Trafficking Operations Programme
STRWN	Sinhala Tamil Rural Women's Network
TES	Training and Evaluation Service
UNAIDS	Joint United Nations Programme on HIV/AIDS
UNAMA	United Nations Assistance Mission in Afghanistan
UNAMA	UN Assistance Mission in Afghanistan
UNAMID	African Union-UN Hybrid Operation in Darfur
UNAMSIL	United Nations Assistance Mission in Sierra Leone
UNAVEM II	United Nations Angola Verification Mission II
UNDAF	United Nations Development Assistance Framework
UNDG	United Nations Development Group
UNDOF	UN Disengagement Observer Force
UNDP	United Nations Development Programme
UNEP	United Nations Environment Programme
UNESCO	United Nations Educational, Scientific and Cultural Organization
UNFICYP	UN Peacekeeping Force in Cyprus

UNFIP	United Nations Fund for International Partnerships
UNFPA	United Nations Population Fund
UN-HABITAT	United Nations Human Settlements Programme
UNHCR	Office of the United Nations High Commissioner for Refugees
UNICEF	United Nations Children's Fund
UNICRI	United Nations Interregional Crime and Justice Research Institute
UNIDIR	United Nations Institute for Disarmament Research
UNIFEM	United Nations Development Fund for Women
UNIFIL	United Nations Interim Force in Lebanon
UNITAR	United Nations Institute for Training and Research
UNMEE	United Nations Missions in Ethiopia and Eritrea
UNMIBH	United Nations Mission to Bosnia and Herzegovina
UNMIK	UN Interim Administration Mission in Kosovo
UNMIL	UN Mission in Liberia
UNMIS	UN Mission in the Sudan
UNMIT	UN Integrated Mission in Timor-Leste
UNMOGIP	United Nations Military Observer Group in India and Pakistan
UNOCI	UN Operation in Côte d'Ivoire
UNOGBIS	United Nations Peace-building Support Office in Guinea-Bissau
UNOL	United Nations Peace-building Support Office in Liberia
UNOMIG	United Nations Observer Mission in Georgia
UNOPS	United Nations Office for Project Services
UNRWA	United Nations Relief and Works Agency for Palestine Refugees in the Near East
UNTAET	United Nations Transitional Administration in East Timor
UNTOP	United Nations Tajikistan Office of Peace-building
UNTSO	UN Truce Supervision Organization
UNU	United Nations University

URNG	Universidad Revolucionaria Nacional Guatemalteca
VMLR	Verified Minor Late Recruit
WAC	Women's Action Committee
WAF	Women'Action Forum
WAP	Women's Action for Peace
WFP	World Food Programme
WHO	World Health Organization
WHR	Woman for Human Right
WILPF	Women's International League for Peace and Freedom
WIPSA	Women's Initiative for Peace in South Asia
WISCOMP	Women in Security, Conflict Management and Peace
WOREC	Women's Rehabilitation Center

1

Introduction

We can no longer afford to minimize or ignore the contributions of women and girls to all stages of conflict resolution, peace-making, peace-building, peace-keeping and reconstruction processes. Sustainable peace will not be achieved without the full and equal participation of women and men.

—United Nations Secretary-General Kofi A. Annan (2002)

War is a regular and recurring feature of human history. The 20th Century alone has seen over 250 wars including the two World Wars, the Second World War bordering almost on annihilation of humanity. Nearly three times as many people were killed in this century due to conflict as in the previous four centuries combined.[1] It is realized that contemporary armed conflicts increasingly targeted civilian population. If during the First World War, only five per cent causalities were of civilians, it rose to 65 per cent by the end of the World War II and during 1990s civilians accounted for up to 90 per cent of the causalities.[2] These conflicts are characterized by a total breakdown of law, security and community structures, with gross human rights violations perpetrated against civilian populations. The most vulnerable are women and children.[3]

War has traditionally been regarded as an exclusively male activity and women are often seen as merely the passive victims of war. Both women and men suffer multiple forms of violence during the war but sexual and gender-based violence have become defining characteristics of modern warfare, and women, often seen as the vessels of cultural identity, are increasingly considered legitimate strategic targets by armed forces, especially where conflicts revolve around identity politics.[4] Women's rights issues are often labeled as "soft" issues or low priority issues by policy-makers all over the world. In spite of women's history of activism for their long fight against war and advocacy for pacifism, their perspectives and issues have been constantly ignored in armed conflict situations.

Women supported the establishment of the United Nations to maintain international peace and save the succeeding generations from the scourge of war. However, as Diane Otto observes, the UN system has developed into a state-centered, militaristic and male dominated organization, very far from women's initial ideas of peace.[5] In the 90s, the trend changed with the United Nations becoming more responsive to the need to incorporate a deeper understanding of the differentiated needs and capacities, interests of local populations in conflict-affected regions.[6] Increased number of policies and programmes were formulated by the United Nations that aimed to address human security issues as threats to international peace and security and consequently adopted resolutions in this field.

Related to this change, the Security Council, previously a gender-blind institution, also began to realise that securing durable peace depends on an inclusive approach to peace-building and security, particularly the full participation of women in all decision-making to prevent violent conflict and to protect all civilians. Consequent to this the Beijing Platform for Action was adopted in 1995. It emphasised that "*The equal access and full participation of women in power structures and their full involvement in all efforts for the prevention and resolution of conflicts are essential for the maintenance and promotion of peace and security... If women are to play an equal part in securing and maintaining peace, they must be empowered politically and economically and represented adequately at all levels of decision-making.*"[7]

Such commitments were reinforced five years later by the UN Secretary-General, Kofi A. Annan, in the open debate on the Security Council Resolution 1325, Women, Peace and Security, on October 24, 2000. He stated that "*peace is inextricably linked to equality between women and men . . . maintaining and promoting peace and security requires women's equal participation in decision-making.*"[8] And on October 31, 2000, the importance of women's engagement in peace processes was finally recognized through the unanimous adoption of the historic Security Council Resolution (SCR) 1325 on Women, Peace and Security.

The SCR 1325 is the first instrument of International Law which explicitly addresses the role of women in peace processes and the particular challenges faced by them during conflict and post-conflict situations. The Resolution is a landmark development for women around the world. This was the culmination of a long process of advocacy, research and activism by civil society organisations from around the world in collaboration with the key UN agencies and Member-States on the Security Council.

UNDERSTANDING THE ARMED CONFLICT AND GENDER

Armed conflict has been present in all societies throughout the history of humankind. According to the UN Office for the Coordination of Humanitarian Affairs (OCHA) an *armed conflict* is defined as : A dispute involving the use of armed force between two or more parties. International humanitarian law distinguishes between international or non-international armed conflicts.

- *International armed conflict:* A war involving two or more States, regardless of whether a declaration of war has been made or whether the parties recognize that there is a state of war.[9]
- *Non-international Armed Conflict:* A conflict in which government forces are fighting with armed insurgents, or armed groups are fighting amongst themselves.[10]

War or armed conflict has a gender face. It is therefore very important to define and understand what is *gender* and what are the gender dimensions of conflict. Feminist theorists argue that men and women are socialized from birth to perform specific gender roles. [11] The term *gender* denotes all the qualities of what it is to be a man or a woman which are socially and culturally, rather than biologically, determined. Gender includes the way in which society differentiates appropriate behaviour and access to power for women and men and, in practice, this refers to patterns in which women are generally disadvantaged over men. Consequently, gender leads to the introduction of a category challenging power structures which insisted on the recognition of subordination and suppression.

Elaborating it, Ann J. Tickner writes that gender is a set of culturally shaped and defined characteristics associated with masculinity and femininity and subsequently applied to men and women. The gender characteristics are assigned to a person at birth according to one's biological identity, hence the traditional assumption that sex and gender is one and the same thing.[12] Persons who are born as biological males or females are expected to naturally develop 'masculine' or 'feminine' character traits and to then behave in ways appropriate to their assigned gender.[13] The terms masculine and feminine therefore do not describe natural characteristics, but are rather gender terms. Furthermore, Tickner argues that biology is used to justify practices, institutions and choices that could under another system have been different from what they are.[14]

Feminists like Goldstein explain that "sex" refers to what is biological and "gender" to what is cultural.[15] Consequently, it is argued that one's sex is determined by one's genitalia, whereas one's gender is the result of a lifelong process of socialisation, which starts at birth. Goldstein argues ."We *are* a certain sex but we *learn* or *perform* certain gender roles which are not predetermined or tied rigidly to biological sex".[16] On the other hand, Simone de Beauvoir famously claimed that 'one is not born', but 'rather *becomes* a woman', and that "social discrimination produces in women moral and intellectual effects so profound that they appear to be caused by nature".[17]

One way to interpret Beauvoir's claim that one is not born but rather becomes a woman is to take it as a claim about gender socialisation or gender roles assigned to a person in accordance with their gender characteristics by the society. As Steans argues, "the real target is gender: not the anatomical difference between the female and the male sex but the complicated aspect of social being known as gender. When tradition teaches that those of the female gender perform certain tasks in society while those of the male gender perform others, the separation is not made between specific, individual women and men. Gender roles are archetypal models of how human function in society."[18]

Joshua Goldstein writes that "war is among the most consistently gendered of human activities".[19] Feminists argue that socially constructed gender differences between men and women shape not only how both genders understand their own experiences, but also how these gender differences have multifaceted effects on gender relations.

The Impact of Armed Conflicts on Gender Roles and Relations

Gender roles and relations are often altered during and after an armed conflict. These gender roles determine not only how men and women are expected to act in times of peace, but also guide their actions in times of armed conflicts. Throughout history and in many cultures gender roles during wartime show a stereotypical division : men fight with weapons and women do not—with few exceptions. Women are often seen as merely the passive victims of war and conflict struggling to cope with the effects of war on their lives. Writing on gender roles during the war, Elshstain in her famous work on Women and War observes:

> "Men fight as avatars of a nation's sanctioned violence. Women work and weep and sometimes protest within the frame of discursive practices that turn one out, militant mother and pacifist protestor alike, as the collective "other" to the male warrior. These identities are underpinnings for decision and action..."[20]

Traditional understandings of warfare regard men as the warriors and defenders of a nation, while women are considered to be the auxiliaries; they provide logistical support in the war effort, or in the domestic sphere, since they are often confined to the home front as the wives and mothers of soldiers.[21] Jean Elshtain suggests that women have been confined to their traditional gender roles in war because of their socialised caring natures and their potential for motherhood, which essentially deems them life givers and not life takers.[22]

Similar views are expressed by Logwe that :

> "War is a foolish game, invented by men and played by men. It should be stopped by women. War is a game which men enjoy—more aggressive, more uncompromising and more destructive than football. They like the uniforms, they like to the marching up and down, and waving flags. They like saluting each other. Most of all they like killing."[23]

Women are expected to continue fulfilling their traditional gender roles during armed conflict and not to overstep any gender boundaries that could challenge established male supremacy.[24] Women have subsequently been confined to wartime roles that have been deemed appropriate to their gender and rather than participating in the processes of war, women have been treated as outsiders. Elshstain writes,

> "Men see edifying tales of courage, duty, honour, glory as they engage in acts of protection and defence and daring: heroic deed doing. Women see edifying stories of nobility, sacrifice, duty, quite immortality as they themselves engage in defensive acts of protection, the non-heroics of taking care of.[25]

Another role that women traditionally fulfill in war is to boost men's morale by enhancing a man's identification of himself as a warrior.[26] Simultaneously, women also serve to shame men into persisting in their soldiering efforts.[27] The closest women have come to the battlefront as non-combatants in the 20th Century have been as nurses in nursing the injured and sick soldiers. As argued by D'Antonio, "nursing gave them the chance to participate as few other women could in the tumultuous events of their times".[28]

In armed conflict or post-conflict situations men and women's gender roles inevitably shift to accommodate wartime circumstances. Sometimes, women are not only passive observers to war but, they have become active agents and direct participants in conflict situations. In Sri Lanka, for example, the induction of women into Liberation Tigers of Tamil Eelam's (LTTE) military ranks radically transformed the Tamil women's self-image.[29] However, the LTTE allowed its female militants freedom of movement and equality of social and political commitments and consequently, challenged the rituals and practices that oppressed Tamil women in a social system characterised by caste, dowry, the seclusion of the unmarried women and sequestration of menstruating women.[30] The LTTE also encouraged its women cadres to form a separate political wing.[31] These new roles and subsequent autonomy liberated many Tamil women participating in the LTTE and also set an example for many younger women hoping to enjoy the same freedoms.[32]

Another example is that of Nepal, where women had been key players in the conflict comprising 40 per cent of cadres in combatant roles. In some of the villages, leaders and fighters of various Guerilla fighter units were women.[33] Women's participation as combatants in armed conflict both challenges gender stereotyping and empowers women. Many women who fight in wars can turn the experience into a successful endeavour. The experience of participating in war may also give women an added advantage in terms of changed behaviour, as many women gain confidence and hope to improve their status in society following their experience as armed combatants

In most situations of armed conflict for those women who do not join the armed forces, the majority of the burden of raising children, managing households, and caring for aging relatives is on women's shoulders as men go off to fight in the war. During conflicts, women become more visible within the family and community as men are absent for long periods of time. Women may become breadwinners and primary decision-makers in the home and in the community. In addition, women may fill other roles within the conflict including supporting pro- or anti-war movements. However, these new roles also challenge norms about gender roles and about the participation of women in decision-making capacities in their households, civil society, and the formal economy.

Another significant role which women play in armed conflict situations is that of an active agents of peace. Although predominantly excluded from formal peace negotiations, many women engage in peace activism. They play a critical role in mediation and conflict resolution in these situations. It is said to be true that whether victims or active agents in the conflict, nearly all women have an interest in the peace process. The former United Nations Secretary General, Kofi Annan, argues that women's interest in becoming involved in peace processes often stems from their experiences of armed conflict, whether as victims or as armed participants.[34]

It is observed that the gender roles always change in armed conflict situations. Women at times make significant gains from the changed gender relations. However, it has also been noted that gains made are often temporary in nature and that gender equality seen during the conflict may be illusory that might vanish with the end of the conflict.

Impact of Armed Conflict on Women and Girls

Gender inequalities are exacerbated during periods of armed conflict and continue during post-conflict reconstruction. Both women and men suffer war abuses and traumas, disruptions and loss of resources, the impact of these losses is experienced in different ways and women are often disproportionately affected. The gendered impact of war on women and men varies. Women and girls do share similar experiences to that of men and boys in the sense that they are as much targeted with the same weapons and suffer social and economic dislocation, the loss of shelter, and shortage of medical, food and water; they suffer the psychosocial impact of the loss of family members or witnessing violence against their families and neighbours, the loss of their possessions and homes, and the effects of violence prior to, during and after armed conflict; they are at risk of certain diseases, including increased exposure to diseases and sexually transmitted infections (STIs), including HIV/AIDS. Like men and boys, they are also affected by the environmental damage and resource depletion that results from armed conflict.

However, women and girls experience armed conflict differently than men and boys. Armed conflicts exacerbate existing gender inequalities, placing women at a heightened risk of various forms of sexual and gender-based violence perpetrated by various actors in the conflict and that this form of sexual violence persists even after the cessation of hostilities. In armed conflict, gender-based violence, especially sexual violence against women and girls, is used as a weapon of war to achieve military objectives such as ethnic cleansing, spreading political terror and intimidation, and breaking down communities. As Usta note, "women's bodies can become battle grounds where sexual violence becomes a weapon of war to be used to express power and to humiliate, dominate or disrupt."[35]

Gender-based and sexual violence has come to be seen as weapon of war in contemporary conflicts. The violence experience during war is often an escalation of violence that women experienc prior to the war and is expected to further increase in the aftermath of war. According to a UNIFEM report, "violence against women in wartime is a reflection of violence against women in peacetime, as long as violence against women is pervasive and accepted, stress, small arms proliferation and a culture of violence push violence against women to epidemic proportions, especially when civilians are the main targets of warfare."[36]

Sexual violence was perpetrated by all sides to the conflict. Consequently, it was difficult for one party to make allegations against the other at the conclusion of hostilities. Moreover, sexual violence had long been accepted as an inevitable, albeit unfortunate, reality of armed conflict.

Earlier the sexual and gender-based crimes in armed conflicts were not discussed easily or openly, and there was no strong, mobilized women's movement to exert pressure for redress. However, it has only recently been defined as a crime in international law. Although Article 4(2)(e) of the 1997 Additional Protocol II of the

Geneva Convention includes rape among the list of 'outrages upon human dignity' that it prohibits, there was no provision that made rape and other forms of sexual violence during conflicts as specific crimes.[37] Current legal definitions of sexual violence, particularly rape, in conflict were established in legal decisions by the International Criminal Tribunal for Rwanda (ICTR) and the International Criminal Tribunal for the former Yugoslavia (ICTY) that make it a crime. And under the Rome Statute of the International Criminal Court (ICC), rape, sexual slavery, enforced prostitution, forced pregnancy, enforced sterilization and any other form of sexual violence of comparable gravity are recognized both as crimes against humanity and as war crimes.[38] Despite internationally coordinated efforts to combat sexual violence against women during armed conflict, the use of rape and other forms of sexual violence persists.

FORMS OF VIOLENCE AGAINST WOMEN IN ARMED CONFLICT

Women are victims of systematic violence during war. Moreover, the violence against women does not end once the conflict comes to an end, but in most cases it continues into the aftermath. The Secretary General's reports on Women, Peace and Security gives a comprehensive account of how women and girls suffer in multiple ways in the armed conflict and post-conflict situations. The violence against women can take on many forms and these are :

Rape as a Weapon of War

Rape in warfare is deep rooted in world history and well established in modern warfare. Since times immemorial, women have been raped during armed conflicts. Women and girls have been primarily targeted in armed conflict and post-conflict situations. They are often targeted of sexual violence because they belong to particular ethnic, national, or religious group.[39] The use of rape as a weapon is one of the most violent and humiliating act on the enemy. Rape as a weapon is intended to humiliate, dehumanize and control and dominate women, their families and their communities. It has been used as a tool for "ethnic cleansing" or genocide. Until recently, rape and sexual abuse of women were seen as natural and inevitable though unfortunate by-products of armed conflict.

Around the world, women have long been attributed the role of transmitters of culture and symbols of nation or community. Rape of a woman in armed conflict is often considered as an attack against the values or 'honour' of a society.[40] As Nordstrom argued, "Rape, as with all terror-warfare, is not exclusively an attack on the body—it is an attack on the 'body-politic'. It's goal is not to maim or kill one person but to control an entire socio-political process by crippling it. It is an attack directed equally against personal identity and cultural integrity".[41]

War rape has a severe impact on women and may be systematic in nature or an isolated act of sexual violence.[42] The victims of rape are re-victimized and abused by the society because rape is especially stigmatizing in cultures with strong customs and taboos regarding virginity, sex and sexuality. Thus, a victim may be viewed by society as being: unfaithful, dirty/unclean, traitor, damaged, and what not. Often victims suffer isolation, disownment, are prohibited from marrying, divorced, abandoned, abused, neglected and even killed.

Victims are often raped multiple times and gang raped, which can cause a much higher degree of physical and physiological injuries, and even lead to death. Due to unwanted pregnancies, many women who undergo abortions through non-sterile procedures, non-medical methods, risk death, infection, scarring or sterilization. Physical injuries may include gynecologic, rectal, and internal hemorrhaging. The long-term physical effects of rape can include pregnancy and sexually transmitted diseases including HIV/AIDS.

International Alert's report, Women's Bodies as a Battlefield (2004) noted that the violence and brutality of the use of rape as weapon of war does not begin or end with the rape itself, victims are most often beaten, and in many cases physically mutilated. Horrific acts are often carried out in front of family members, such as the torture and mutilation. One mother as per the report witnessed:

> "...My daughter refused to obey the order to get undressed. So they ordered her to choose between rape and death. She choose death. So they started to torture her, cutting-off her breasts one at a time with a knife, then her ears and then they completely cut open her belly...after a time, my daughter breathed her last...I was powerless, I wasn't able to protect her. Since then I haven't been able to do anything..."[43]

Rape is both a weapon and a strategy of war. As a weapon, it "attacks women's physical and emotional sense of security while simultaneously launching an assault, through women's bodies, upon the genealogy of security as constructed by the body politic".[44] As a strategy, it is a sanctioned, systematic means of attaining specific political objectives. Achieved by using war rape as an instrument of terror, domination, political repression, torture, intimidation, and humiliation, these objectives have at their heart control, compliance of civilians, and even genocide. Political ends include inciting ethnic hatred to accomplish ethnic cleansing and 'genetic imperialism' as well as to destroy an enemy's cohesion, spirit, and identity.

Radhika Coomaraswamy, the former UN Special Rapporteur on Violence Against Women, opines :

> "rape is one of the most widely used types of violence against women and girls, it remains the least condemned war crime; throughout history, the rape of hundreds of thousands of women and children in all regions of the world has been a bitter reality".[45]

Despite the progress in setting standards, it is argued that very little has changed in the lives of most women, as both state and non-state actors continue to commit acts of GBV with impunity. It was noted that during the 14-year conflict in Liberia, an estimated 40 per cent of the population was affected by sexual violence. An average of 40 women are raped every day in South Kivu in the context of the armed conflict in the Democratic Republic of the Congo.[46] In Northeast Sri Lanka more than 12,500 women were raped or killed.[47] During Bangladesh's 9-month war for independence in 1971, between 250,000 and 400,000 girls and women were raped, leading to an estimated 25,000 pregnancies.[48] In Rwanda, at least 250,000 women were raped in the 1994 genocide.[49] It is estimated that between 20,000 and 50,000 women were raped as part of an ethnic cleansing campaign in during the war in Bosnia and Herzegovina in the early 1990s.[50]

Children Born of Rape and Sexual Exploitation

The long lasting effect of rape as a weapon of war is the number of children born as a result of rapes. Forced pregnancy is very commonly used as a form of ethnic cleansing.

There are no definite statistics on the number of children born as a result of rape in the armed conflicts. In Bosnia and Herzegovina, many women were imprisoned until their children were born to ensure that the pregnancy was not terminated. In many cases in Bosnia women who had been raped repeatedly and became pregnant had little choice but to continue with the pregnancy to give birth to a Serbian child.[51] In Liberia and Sierra Leone thousands of babies were born to women and girls who had been abducted and forced to accompany combatants into the bush, where many gave birth without medical help. In Rwanda after the 1994 genocide, as many as 5000 children were born to women as a result of rape.[52]

Kosovo and East Timor conflicts record the same situation. Up to 20,000 women are believed to have been raped during the fighting in Kosovo, and many of them bore children. In one month alone, January 2000, the International Red Cross estimated that 100 babies conceived in rape were born in Kosovo, and that many other women gave birth to children born of rape but decided not to identify them as such.[53] Many women are forced to bear multiple pregnancies. In a testimony recorded in East Timor, a woman testified that she had four children, all born of rape.[54] The mother of a child born of rape faces a lifetime of turmoil over the conception, regardless of her decision to raise the child, give the child up for adoption or terminate the pregnancy. It is noted that a mother who keeps a child is often tormented and pulled between feelings of love and hate. Many children are never adopted and orphanages in conflict zones are often flooded with "rape babies". These offsprings came to be known as *enfants mauvais souvenir*, or children of bad memories. Many women had difficulty in caring for these children, and there have been reports of abandonment and infanticide.[55] Orphanages in conflict zones are often flooded with "rape babies".

Sexual Slavery

Sexual slavery is another form of gender-based violence that is experienced by women and girls during armed conflict. This is a inextricably linked to conflict. Women are abducted by armed groups and forced to accompany them on raids and to provide everything from food to sexual services. Among the prominent examples of sexual slavery, was the system of rape camps organized by the Japanese Imperial Army during the World War II, where more than 200,000 women and girls were enslaved as "comfort women" throughout Asia.[56]

Based on these estimates, young women were recruited or kidnapped by soldiers to serve in Japanese military brothels where they were victims of coercion, rape and abuse day and night. Most of the comfort women were between fourteen and eighteen years of age, and most were Korean.[57] And the most unfortunate part is, to date, only one Japanese woman has published her testimony. This was done in 1971, when a former "comfort woman" forced to work for showa soldiers in Taiwan, published her memoirs under the pseudonym of Suzuko Shirota.[58] On October 12, 2011 South Korea presented the issue to the General Assembly of the United Nations to seek recognition of the legal responsibility of Japan.

Trafficking in Women and Girls

Trafficking of women and girls is another threat of violence in armed conflict situations. According to UNIFEM, there is increasing evidence that a significant incidents of this activity is associated with armed conflict. It increases the risk of women and girls being trafficked across international borders to be used in forced labour schemes that often include sexual labour and/or forced prostitution.[59]

INTERNALLY DISPLACED PERSONS AND REFUGEES

Displacement is the most common consequence of armed conflict and women and children are the most affected. The majority of the people fleeing armed conflict situations are women and children. Armed conflict, political violence and civil unrest forcibly uproot hundreds of thousands of civilians every year. According to the report of the Secretary General, of the 40 million people—an estimated 80 per cent are women and children—they fled their homes because of armed conflict and human rights violations.[60] Without a viable social or economic support network and often without male protection, the displaced women are highly vulnerable to violence.

The displaced persons find shelter in refugee camps in desperate situations. These camps can become extremely dangerous places for women. In most camps there are not enough protection officers or female staff. The unique types of persecutions that women are subjected to and which may compel them to flee their countries of origin, are not enumerated as grounds for prosecution in the international legal instruments that define refugees. The 1951 Convention relating to the Status of Refugees does not provide for a separate category for women who face gender-specific persecution or human rights abuses, which often occur in the private sphere and the sanctity of the home. In other words, as Gadam and Charlesworth observe, these women also face distinctive problems that are largely unacknowledged as they attempt to rebuild their lives as refugees in a new country.[61]

Women can be subject to many other types of *violence in camps*. The physical structure and location of the camp itself can undermine the safety of refugee women and contribute to the increase of sexual violence. For example, refugee camps are generally located in areas with serious crime problems; they can be geographically isolated from local populations, making police protection difficult. Simple problems like poor lighting can compound the risk of sexual attacks at night. Women are also targeted when they leave the camp to collect water, firewood or simply when they have to use the facilities, which may be located away from the security cordons of the camp.

Refugee and internally displaced women, especially those in camp situations, are also particularly vulnerable to human trafficking and other forms of exploitation. As noted by the United Nations SG Report, 2002, both the refugee and internally displaced women and girls may become victims of hostage-taking for purposes of enslavement and trafficking into slavery, coerced or enforced prostitution, abduction and forced military recruitment for participation in hostilities or support of combatants.[62]

Impact of Armed Conflict on Health

The fatalities, injuries and disabilities suffered on the battlefield are obviously the direct effects of conflict. The destruction of health care facilities and drug supplies as well as the lack of qualified medical staff are most prevalent in conflict situations. Furthermore, sexual violence has always led to direct physical harm, emotional trauma, stigma, and social ostracism for women. It also carries an additional risk of sexually transmitted infections (STIs) and increasingly, of acquiring HIV infections. Sexually transmitted diseases are a lasting consequence of GBV and are a major health concern for women in conflict areas.

Violence, especially coerced sex, increased a woman or child's vulnerability to becoming infected with HIV infection. Men who are aware that they are carriers of disease, especially HIV/AIDS, may be encouraged to rape local women in areas which are suspected to support their opposition in an effort to exterminate the local population.[63] The United Nations Secretary General's Report recognises that use of sexual violence as a strategic and tactical weapon of war contributes to the spread of Sexually Transmitted Infections (STIs), the most dangerous of which is HIV/AIDS.[64] Physical harms such as injury to reproductive organs, traumatic fistulas, and infertility often accompany brutal or repeated rapes.[65]

Lack of obstetrical care, write Thomas Pluemper and Eric Neumayer, expose women to an increased risk of maternal mortality, clandestine and spontaneous abortions as well as miscarriages.[66] In addition to these physical effects, GBV also has serious psychological consequences, including depression, anxiety, post-traumatic stress disorder, shock, memory loss, and sexual dysfunction.[67] Rape trauma syndrome, a syndrome used to describe emotional responses to sexual assault including hopelessness, loss of control, anger, guilt, and phobias, is common, although the root cause of such symptoms may often go undiagnosed and untreated.[68]

FEMINIST PERSPECTIVES ON PEACE AND SECURITY

Feminist analysis looks at the world by gathering and interpreting information through the eyes and experiences of women as subjects. Feminist peace theorists and activists argue that the inclusion of women's perspectives in formal peace processes would lead to a more peaceful world. Linking peace with the absence of every type of structural violence is the main goal of the feminists. They have challenged narrow concepts of war and peace. For many years, the feminist peace researchers have been highlighting the gender discrimination that continues through political exclusion, economic marginalization, and sexual violence during and after conflict, denying women their human rights and constraining the potential for development.[69] In terms of *women, peace and security,* feminist analysis identifies women's specific concerns and approaches to violence and peace-building from women's perspectives. They always support *positive peace rather than negative peace in the society.*[70] Gender-based violence is the primary human security concern for women. They focus both on direct and indirect violence in armed conflict situations.

Charlotte Bunch and Roxanna Carillo describe direct violence as.

> "Women in both the [global] North and South live with the constant risk of physical harm. The experience and fear of violence is an underlying threat in women's lives that intertwines with their most basic security needs at all levels—personal, community, economic, and political. In virtually every nation, violence (or the threat of it) shrinks the range of choices open to women and girls, limiting their mobility and even their ability to imagine having control over their lives".[71]

However, structural violence is usually given limited attention despite its major effects on women's lives. In addition to the importance of preventing and reducing direct violence, women point to the insecurity of structural (indirect) violence. Deborah DuNann Winter and Dana Leighton define structural violence as follows:

> "[structural violence is] embedded in ubiquitous social structures, normalized by stable institutions and regular experiences. Structural violence occurs whenever people are disadvantaged by political, legal, economic, or cultural traditions. Because they are longstanding, structural inequities usually seem ordinary—the way things are and always have been. But structural violence produces suffering and death as often as direct violence does, though the damage is slower, more subtle, more common, and more difficult to repair."[72]

Such an understanding was already included in Galtung's early discussions. He looked at concern of peace in broader perspective by defining that peace was not only as the absence of war but more universally as the absence of *all* violence.

As Galtung wrote :

> "It will soon be clear why we are rejecting the narrow concept of violence—according to which violence is *somatic* incapacitation, or deprivation of health, alone (with killing as the extreme form), at the hands of an *actor* who *intends* this to be the consequence. If this were all violence is about, and peace is seen as its negation, then too little is rejected when peace is held up as anideal. Highly unacceptable social orders would still be compatible with peace."[73]

Given this hypothesis Galtung was led inevitably to add another element to the notion of peace, namely, peace also as the absence of structural violence. He states :

> "Violence becomes two-sided, and so does peace conceived as the absence of violence. An extended concept of violence leads to an expended concept of peace...Peace also has two sides: absence of personal violence, and absence of structural violence...We shall refer to them as negative peace and positive peace respectively."[74]

Birgit Brock-Utne, pushes beyond Galtung's distinction between negative peace and positive peace when she writes:

> "negative peace exists when there is absence of personal, physical

and direct violence, while positive peace exists where there is the absence of indirect or structural violence."[75]

Elaborating the perspectives of the feminist peace theorists, Linda Groff writes in 70s and 80s the feminist peace researchers extended both negative and positive peace to include eliminating both physical and structural violence down to the individual level. "The new definition of peace", Linda writes, " includes not only abolishing macro level organized violence, such as war, but also eliminating micro level unorganized violence, such as rape or domestic violence in war or in the home. The concept of structural violence includes personal/micro and macro-level structures that harm or discriminate opportunities available to other groups. This feminist peace model came to include the elimination of all types of violence (physical and structural) on all levels, from the individual, family, and community levels on upto transnational level, as well as the elimination of patriarchal values, attitudes and institutions on all levels, as necessary conditions for a more peaceful planet that provides increasing opportunities for all its citizens."[76]

From 1990s onwards, the feminist theorists in the field of international relations challenged the conventional discourse around peace and conflict. Writers critiqued the myth of the warrior hero and the militaristic patriarchal state, and analysed the meaning of 'security' from a feminist viewpoint. They see peace as Michelle Malsbury points out, as a by-product of social/economic equality, ecological balance, and justice.[77] Betty Reardon sees peace as condition of social justice and equality while Judith Ann Tickner talks of gender justice. In her book on Gender in International relations she observes, "The achievement of peace, social justice and ecological sustainability is inseparable from overcoming social relations of domination and subordination". She continue, "genuine security requires not only the absence of war, but also the elimination of unjust social relations including unequal gender relations".[78]

On the whole, it could be said that the feminist concepts are premised on the universal integration of a gender perspective into all spheres, as well as on the equal participation of women and men at all levels and in all processes, but especially in the context of security and peace policy. This clear shift in the 90s onwards helped the feminists, in particular the NGOs to move from 'oppositional criticism' to strategising and lobbying and finally influencing the UN Conferences, particularly the Fourth UN World Conference on

Women held in Beijing in 1995. The Beijing Platform for Action adopted at this Conference not only dealt with the issue of Women and Armed Conflict as a Critical Area but also called upon the States to "support mainstreaming of a gender justice perspective in all policy areas and all levels of government".

This was further strengthen by the Outcome Document of Beijing +5, the Windhoek Declaration and the Namibia Plan of Action on Mainstreaming a Gender Perspective on Multidimensional Peace Support Operations, the 1997 United Nations Economic and Social Council's call for gender mainstreaming, and the 1998 recommendations of the Commission on the Status of Women for increasing women's participation in conflict prevention, peace-keeping, and post-conflict peace building and reconstruction. These resolutions and conferences had built the momentum for the passage of the UN Security Council Resolution 1325 on Women, Peace and Security. The Resolution adopted in October 2000 addresses the impact of armed conflict on women as well as their undervalued contribution to conflict prevention and peace-building. However, none of these developments, would have been possible, without sustained campaigning and lobbying by the women peace activists all over the world.

The Resolution has been lauded as ground breaking for it recognizes that " women need to be at the peace table, women need to be involved in decision making and in peace-keeping teams, particularly as civilians, to make a real difference in transitioning from the cult of war to the culture of peace".[79] Is there a movement in that direction? Has the Resolution made any impact, are the critical questions that need to be studies. There are some studies conducted on this in Africa, Middle-East and Central America but there is no such study on the Resolution in the context of South Asia. The present study is an attempt to examine how responsive have been the South Asian countries to the mandates of the Resolution and what impact has it made in the conflict-ridden region since its adoption.

Notes and References

1. United Nations Development Programme, (2005), *Human Development Report, 2005,* New York, Oxford University Press, p. 153.
2. United Nations Security Council, (2002), *Report of the Secretary-General on Women, Peace and Security*, (S/2002/1154), United Nations, New York, p. 2.

3. Sherrill Whittington, (2005), *The Impact of Conflict on Women and Girls in West and Central Africa and the UNICEF Response*, New York, UNICEF, p. 1.
4. Sanam, B. Naraghi-Anderlini, 2001, *Women, Peace and Security: A Policy Audit*, International Alert, p. 12.
5. Diane Otto, 2004, *Securing the Gender Legitimacy of the UN Security Council: Prising Gender from its Historical Meanings, Issue 92. Melbourne,* The University of Melbourne Faculty of Law Legal Studies Research
6. In 1994, the Human Development Report from United Nations Development Program (UNDP) officially launched the concept of *human security* as a viable alternative.
7. United Nations (1995), *Beijing Declaration and Platform for Action*, (A/ CONF.177/20), New York, UN/Division for the Advancement of Women, para 134.
8. Statement made by the UN Secretary-General, Kofi, A. Annan, Security Council Resolution 1325 on Women, Peace and Security on October 24, 2000.
9. United Nations Office for the Coordination of Humanitarian Affairs (OCHA), (2003), *Glossary of Humanitarian Terms in Relation to the Protection of Civilians in Armed Conflict*, New York, United Nations Office for the Coordination of Humanitarian Affairs (OCHA), p. 7.
10. *Ibid.*
11. The term gender first introduced by Ann Oakley in her book, *Sex, Gender, and Society* (1972).
12. Ann, J. Tickner, (1992), *Gender in International Relations: Feminist Perspectives on National Security*, New York, Columbia University Press, p. 7.
13. *Ibid.*, p. 7.
14. *Ibid.*, p. 11.
15. Joshua S. Goldstein (2001), *War and Gender: How Gender Shapes the War System and vice versa* Cambridge, Cambridge University Press, p. 2.
16. *Ibid.*
17. Simone de Beauvoir, 1949), *The Second Sex*, New York, Alfred A. Knopf, Inc, p. 18.
18. Jill Steans, (1998), *Gender and International Relations: An Introduction,* New Brunswick, Rutgers, p. 12.
19. Josuah, S. Goldstein, (2001), *War and Gender: How Gender Shapes the War System and vice versa,* Cambridge, Cambridge University Press, p. 172.
20. Jean, B. Elshtain, (1987), *Women and War*, New York, Basic Books, p. 3.
21. Pillay Meintjies, and Turshen M. (eds.), (2001), *The Aftermath: Women in Post-Conflict Transformation*, London, Zed Books, p. 63.
22. Elshtain, *op. cit.*, p. 4.
23. H.S. Longwe, (1995), *Men and Women, War and Peace*', in African Woman, Issue 10, London, Akin Mama wa Africa, p. 6.
24. Penny Summerfield, (1997),*Gender and War in the Twentieth Century*, The *International History Review*, Vol. 19, No. 1, pp. 2-15, p. 4.
25. Jean, B. Elshtain (1987), *Women and War*, New York, Basic Books, p. 165.

26. Joshua, S. Goldstein (2001), *War and Gender: How Gender Shapes the War System and Vice Versa* Cambridge, Cambridge University Press, p. 307.
27. *Ibid.*
28. D'Antonio Patricia (2002), *Nurses in War,* The Lancet, Supplement 360, pp. 7-8.
29. Rita Manchanda (2001), *Ambivalent Gains in South Asian Conflicts.* In S. Meintjies, A. Pillay and M. Turshen (eds.), The Aftermath: Women in Post-conflict Transformation, London, Zed Books, pp. 97-120, p. 115.
30. *Ibid.*
31. *Ibid.*
32. *Ibid.*
33. http://samarmagazine.org/archive/articles/198.
34. United Nations Security Council, (2002), *Report of the Secretary-General on Women, Peace and Security,* (S/2002/1154), New York, United Nations, p. 54.
35. Farver Usta and Zain Lama, (2008), *Women, War and Violence: Surviving the Experience,* Journal of Women's Health 17, Issue 5, pp. 793-804, p. 793
36. http//www.womenwarpeace.org
37. *Geneva Convention IV: Protection of Civilian Persons in Times of War*, 12 August, 1949, Part I, Article 18 and Part II, Article 27.
38. Rome Statute of the International Criminal Court, 17 July 1998, The Hague.
39. http://www.amnestyusa.org/women/rapeinwartime.html
40. http://www.amnestyusa.org/women/rapeinwartime.html
41. Carolyn Nordstrom, (1991), *Women and War: Observations from the Field,* Minerva Quarterly Report on Women and the Military, Volume 9, No. 1, p. 9.
42. Dorothy Q. Thomas and Ralph Regan, (1994), *Rape in War: Challenging the Tradition of Impunity,* SAIS Review Baltimore, Johns Hopkins University Press, pp. 82-99.
43. International Alert, (2004), *Women's Bodies as a Battleground: Sexual Violence Against Women and Girls During the War in the Democratic Republic of Congo,* United Kingdom, International Alert, p. 35.
44. K. Koo, (2002), *Confronting a Disciplinary Blindness: Women, War and Rape in the International Politics of Security,* Australian Journal of Political Science, Volume 37, pp. 525-36.
45. Radhika Coomaraswamy, (1998), *Report of the Special Rapporteur on Violence Against Wcmen, its Causes and Consequences,* UN. Doc E/CN.4/1998/54, New York, United Nations para, 263.
46. United Nations Development Fund for Women (UNIFEM), (2007), *Facts and Figures on Violence Against Women and Girls in Situations of Armed Conflict,* New York, United Nations Fund for Women http://www.unifem.org/gender_issues/violence_against_women/facts_figures.php?page=5.
47. http://www.asianruralwomen.net
48. Ferdousi Priyabhashini (1999), *Ekattorer Duhsaha Smriti,* Ekattorer Ghatok Dalal Nirmul Committee, Dhaka.

49. United Nations Economic and Social Council, Commission on Human Rights, (1996), *Report on the situation of human rights in Rwanda submitted by Mr. René Degni-Ségui*, Special Rapporteur of the Commission on Human Rights, under paragraph 20 of resolution S-3/1 of 25 May 1994, (E/CN.4/1996/68), New York, United Nations, para 16.
50. Jeanne Ward (2002), *If Not Now, When? Addressing Gender-Based Violence in Refugee, Internally Displaced, and Post-Conflict Settings: A Global Overview*, New York.
51. Ritu Menon and Kamla Bhasin (1998), *Borders & Boundaries : Women in India's Partition*, Piscataway, N.J. Rutgers University Press, p. 42.
52. L. Shanks and M.J. Schull, (2000), *Rape in War: The Humanitarian Response*, Canadian Medical Association Journal, Volume, 163, Issue 9, pp. 1152-56.
53. Helena Smith (2000), *Rape Victims Babies Pay the Price of War,* The Observer, April 16. http://www.newsunlimited.co.uk/Kosovo/0,2759, 45613,00.html
54. Louise Williams, and Leonie, Lamont (1999), *Rape Used Over and Over as a Systematic Torture*, The Sydney Morning Herald, 1999, p. 10.
55. *Ibid.*
56. Tessa Morris-Suzuki (2007), *Japan's Comfort Women: It's Time for the Truth (in the Ordinary Everyday sense of the Word, Japan Focus*, 8 March, The Asia-Pacific Journal, Japan Focus http://japanfocus.org
57. Chung Hyun-Kyung (2000),*Your Comfort versus My Death': Korean Comfort Women*, In Anne Llewellyn Barstow (ed.), War's Dirty Secret: Rape, Prostitution, and Other Crimes against Women, Cleveland, Ohio: Pilgrim Press, pp. 17-19, p. 17.
58. China Daily 2007-07-06. http://www.chinadaily.com.cn/world/2007-07/06/content_911759.htm
59. http//www.womenwarpeace.org
60. United Nations Security Council (1999), *Report of the Secretary-General to the Security Council on the Protection of Civilians in Armed Conflict, (S/1999/957),* New York, United Nations, p. 4.
61. Judith Gadam and Hilary Charlesworth (2000), *Protection of Women in Armed Conflict*, Human Rights Quarterly, Vol. 22, pp. 148-66.
62. United Nations Security Council, (2002), *Report of the Secretary-General on Women, Peace and Security*, (S/2002/1154), New York, United Nations, p. 26.
63. Elisabeth Rehn and Ellen Johnson Sirleaf (2002), *Women, War and Peace: The Independent Expert's Assessment on the Impact of Armed Conflict on Women and Women's Role in Peace-building—Progress of the World's Women 2002*, Vol. 1, New York, United Nations Development Fund for Women (UNIFEM), p. 52.
64. United Nations Security Council, *op. cit.*, p. 20.
65. Jeanne Ward (2005), *Broken Bodies, Broken Dreams, Violence Against Women Exposed*, Nairobi, United Nations Office for the Coordination of Humanitarian Affairs (UN OCHA), p. 190.

66. Thomas Pluemper and Eric Neumayer (2006), *The Unequal Burden of War: The Effect of Armed Conflict on the Gender Gap in Life Expectancy*, International Organisation, Vol. 60, No. 3, pp. 723-54, p. 730.
67. *Ibid.*
68. http://www.stopvaw.org/consequences_of_sexual_assault.html
69. Richard Strickland and Nata Duvvury, (2003), *Gender Equity and Peace Building, From Rhetoric to Reality: Finding the Way*, Gender Equity and Peace-building Workshop, International Centre for Research on Women, p. 1.
70. *Positive peace refers*, a society in which there is no indirect or structural violence such as gender inequality. *Negative peace* occurs when personal, physical, and direct violence such as armed conflict, rape, and spousal battering are absent.
71. Charlotte Bunch and Roxanna Carillo (1998), *Global Violence against Women: The Challenge to Human Rights and Development*, In Michael Klare and Yogesh Chandrani (eds.), World Security: Challenges for a New Century, New York, St. Martin's Press, p. 230.
72. Deborah DuNann Winter and Dana Leighton (2001), Structural Violence: Introduction, In Daniel Christie, Richard Wagner and Deborah DuNann Winter (eds.), Peace, Conflict, and Violence: Peace Psychology for the 21st Century, Upper Saddle River, NJ, Prentice Hall, p. 99.
73. Johan Galtung (1969), *Violence, Peace, and Peace Research*, Journal of Peace Research, Vol. 6, No. 3, pp. 167-91, p. 168.
74. *Ibid.*, p. 168.
75. Birgitt Brock-Utne (2004), *Peace Education in an Era of Globalization, Transcend,* p. 5.
76. Groff, Linda (2008), *Contributions of Different Cultural-Religious Traditions to Different Aspects of Peace, Leading to a Holistic, Integrative View of Peace for a 21st Century, Interdependent World,* Future takes Transcultural Magazine, Vol. 7, No. 1, pp. 27-34, p. 32.
77. Michelle Malsbury (2009), *Peace and Security from a Feminist Perspective*, American Chronicle http://www.americanchronicle.com/articles/view/113193.
78. Ann Judith Tickner (1992), *Gender in International Relations: Feminist Perspectives on Achieving Global Security*, New York, Columbia University Press, p. 127.
79. Anwarul Chowdhury (2011), *The Intrinsic Role of Women in Peace and Security—Genesis and Follow-up of UNSCR 1325,* Palestine-Israel Journal, Vol. 17. No. 3, p. 2.

2

Genesis of the United Nations Security Council Resolution on Women, Peace and Security 1325 (2000)

The United Nations Security Council unanimously adopted an historic Resolution on Women, Peace and Security 1325 at its 4213th meeting on October 31, 2000. The Resolution was passed during the Presidency of Namibia, but it is Ambassador *Anwarul K. Chowdhury* of Bangladesh who is credited with this Resolution as it was he who pursued it vigorously during his Presidency of the Council. In his landmark speech on International Women's Day, that is, March 8, 2000, he said, "peace is inextricably linked with equality between women and men" and highlighted the importance of women's full participation and involvement in all efforts for the prevention and resolution of conflicts.[1] Initially, there was reluctance on the part of the permanent members of the Security Council to accept the Resolution. Ambassador Chowdhury records that five permanent members of the Council resisted stubbornly through procedural and substantive maneuvers and had decided not to connect women, peace and security.[2] To them, perhaps it was diluting the mandate of the Council. However, later they conceded and the Resolution was passed unanimously.

It took 55 years to the UN Security Council, which has the primary responsibility of maintenance of international peace and security, to take cognizance of and make visible women's perspective and concerns on war, peace and security. While in the past, there are some scattered references made by the Security Council in which the Council had condemned atrocities against women and taken note of women's plight and suffering in armed conflicts, and had urged the states to take special measures to protect women and girls from rape and other forms of gender-based violence during conflict and post-conflict situations, but unfortunately, the women's issues related to armed conflict had not been integrated consistently in the Council's activities; nor did the Council officially recognize women's role as agents of peace. In adopting SCR 1325, the Security Council for the first time in its history formally recognized the distinct roles and experiences of women in the context of armed conflict, peacebuilding, peace-keeping and conflict resolution. The forty one speeches made in the Security Council chamber at the time of adoption of the Resolution, articulated fairly the sufferings of women in war, the under-valued and under-utilized conflict prevention and peace building work of women and the leadership they show in building war torn societies.[3] Speaking in the Open Debate (2000), the then, Secretary-General of United Nations, Kofi Annan said: the theme of "Women, Peace and Security" is an important step in bridging together the multiple goals of the UN Charter, namely, saving future generations from the scourge of war and proclaiming equality between men and women.[4] Furthermore, he acknowledged that "Women, who know the price of conflict so well, are also often better equipped than men to prevent or resolve it. For generations, women have served as peace educators, both in their families and in their societies. They have proved instrumental in building bridges rather than walls. They have been crucial in preserving social order when communities have collapsed."[5]

MILESTONES ON THE ROAD TO SCR 1325

The Resolution 1325 was not an overnight development. Many efforts had gone into creating the setting for the Resolution. The landmark adoption of the SCR 1325 was largely due to the advocacy and lobbying of non-governmental organizations (NGOs) with the United Nations and its Member-States. But this outstanding achievement was built upon many other documents and treaty texts throughout the UN's history. A reference to these may be in order.

It is pertinent to note that violence against women during war and armed conflicts drew little attention until the Twentieth Century. Even the Hague Conferences of 1899 and 1907, popularly known as Peace Conferences, did not make any reference to the situation of women. The Conferences were organized with the objective of bringing together the principal nations of the world to discuss and resolve the problem of maintaining universal peace, reducing armaments and ameliorating the conditions of warfare and were the first effort in the direction of establishing normative principles based on the laws of humanity [6] but the issue of impact of war on women did not figure at all.

It was equally true of the Paris Peace Conference of 1919 convened after the First World War that had as much witnessed horrifying instances of heinous acts of rapes and other brutalities which are well documented by a British historian Arnold Joseph Toynbee.[7] Belligerents often capitalized upon the abuse of their women, writes Susan Brownmiller, to garner sympathy and support for their side and to strengthen their resolve against the enemy. But the apparent concern for these women vanished when the propaganda value of their sufferings diminished and they were left without any prospects of redress.[8]

The Peace Conference resulted in the foundation of the League of Nations, the first intergovernmental body of nations. In another significant development a parallel NGO Conference—the first one, was also organized in Paris to raise their voices and give proposals regarding the Covenant of League of Nations. A few women organizations founded the Inter-Allied Suffrage Conference and its delegates participated certain Commissions of the Conference with aim to make women's voices heard in the official discussions.[9] The League was formally established in 1919 with the objective to promote international cooperation and peace. Women were quite hopeful and looking to the fact that League will promote women's rights, will reflect on the impact of war on women and their role as peace agents but expectations were belied. The League took limited steps to enhance women's rights.[10]

Be that as it may, women's inter-governmental groups became very active, founded the Liaison Committee of Women's International Organisations in Geneva and participated in the dialogues between IGO and INGOs and pursued their pacifist and feminist aims, that is, disarmament, peace and equality.

1899, 1907	The Hague Conventions and Treaty of Versailles
1919	League of Nations
1945	The United Nations Charter
1946	Establishment of the Commission on the Status of Women
1948	Universal Declaration on Human Rights (UDHR)
1949, 1977	The Geneva Conventions and its Two Additional Protocols
1951	United Nations Convention relating to the Status of Refugees
1974	Declaration on the Protection of Women and Children in Emergency and Armed Conflict

The international women's organistions that were active on the scene at that time were mainly based in Europe and the United States of America. Reference may particularly be made to organizations such as the International Council of Women (ICW), International Alliance of Women (IAW), International Cooperative Women's Guild (ICWG), International Federation of Business and Professional Women (IFBPW), International Federation of University Women (IFUW), World Young Women's Christian Association (WYWCA), and the Women's International League for Peace and Freedom (WILPF).[11]

According to Carol Miller, there were two major achievements of these organizations that were crucial for women's equality agenda. The *first* was the recognition that women's status was an issue to be addressed at the international level. The *second* was the establishment in 1937 of the League of Nations Committee of Experts on the Legal Status of Women, which laid the foundations for the United Nations Commission on the Status of Women (CSW).[12] These achievements paved the way for their further efforts to promote the rights of women at the international level.

The failure of the League of Nations led to the breaking out of the Second World War and as noted earlier this war was the most devastating one. The world suffered unprecedented devastation especially due to bombings of Hiroshima and Nagasaki. Over 70 millions people were killed—a majority of them being civilians and mass of people were rendered homeless and refugees. Women and children were affected in large number. The history of violence to women was repeated with vengeance during the Second World War.[13] The misogynist philosophy of the Fascists came to the fore—'Men should be trained for war and women for the recreation of the warrior'.[14] In the backdrop of sexualized violence, sexual humiliation and sexual slavery perpetrated on women, women all over the world launched an unprecedented international movement for the recognition of women's role in peace building and equality in decision-making processes before the founding of the United Nations.

THE UNITED NATIONS CHARTER (1945)

The United Nations was founded on October 24, 1945 as a successor to the League of Nations with the purpose to save the future generations from the scourge of war, encourage and respect for human rights, create conditions under which justice and respect for International Laws and Treaties can be achieved, and promote social progress and better standards of living throughout the world. Of the 160 signatories, only four were women[15]—but they succeeded in inscribing women's rights in the founding document of the United Nations, which reaffirms in its preamble "faith in fundamental human rights, in the dignity of the human person, in the equal rights of men and women and of Nations large and small".[16]

For the women present at the birth of the United Nations, the provisions of the Charter on women's equality offered a clear and compelling basis for the assertion of international law to advance the political and legal status of women. Although international and intergovernmental bodies had begun working to advance the status of women long before, no previous legal document had so forcefully affirmed the equality of all human beings, or specifically outlawed sex as a basis of discrimination.[17]

Eleanor Roosevelt and 16 other women attending the inaugural session of the UN General Assembly had drafted an Open Letter that reflects the spirit and aspirations of the women of that era. The Open Letter read in that session by Eleanor addressed to " the women of the World". She said that :

> "To this end, we call on the Governments of the world to encourage women everywhere to take a more active part in national and international affairs, and on women who are conscious of their opportunities to come forward and share in the work of peace and reconstruction as they did in war and resistance."[18]

This letter was the first formal articulation of women's voices in the UN. It hailed the coming of peace to a democratic world and pointed out the joint efforts of men and women.[19]

The UN is credited with advancing women's agenda, promoting and protecting equal rights of women and proclaiming gender equality as a fundamental human right. "Few causes promoted by the United Nations" opines Boutros Boutros—Ghali "have generated more intense and widespread support than the campaign to promote and protect the equal rights of women."[20] It is beyond the scope of the present study to deal with all initiatives of the UN at length yet it is pertinent to highlight some of the developments as precursor to the passage of the SCR 1325.

The Preamble of the Charter of the UN affirms that:

> "We the Peoples of the United Nations determined to reaffirm faith in fundamental human rights, in the dignity and worth of the human person, in the equal rights of men and women and of nations large and small to promote social progress and better standards of life in larger freedom to unite our strength to maintain international peace and security and to ensure that armed force shall not be used, save in the common interest to maintain international peace and security, and to that end: to take effective collective measures for the prevention and removal of threats to the peace, and for the suppression of acts of aggression or other breaches of the peace, and to bring about by peaceful means, and in conformity with the principles of justice and international law, adjustment or settlement of international disputes or situations which might lead to a breach of the peace."[21]

It urged the governments 'to encourage women everywhere to take a more active part in national and international affairs' and expressed the hope that the involvement of women in the United Nations may grow and may increase in insight and skill.[22]

Responding to the voices of these women, the newly established organization provided a prominent space to the women issues, concerning economic and social development, codification and advancement and monitoring of human rights. However, the understanding of the impact of armed conflict on women and girls and the role of women in conflict resolution and peace-building developed slowly within the United Nations. It took several decades to develop a strong normative framework and strengthen operational policies and procedures and make the UN system increasingly responsive to the needs and priorities of women and girls in countries in conflict.

Equality of rights is further recognized in three of the Articles of the Charter. It must be stated here that earlier drafts of the Charter did not provide for equality on the basis of sex.[23] The passages of outlawing discrimination on the on the basis of sex introduced at the insistence of women delegates and representative

Some of the significant developments that paved the way for the SCR 1325 and need to be taken cognizance are :

Establishment of the Commission on the Status of Women (1946)

The United Nations took a major step towards integrating women in development in 1946 when it set up a Sub-Commission on the Status of Women under the Commission on Human Rights to monitor the situation of women and promote their rights. The Sub-Commission was mandated to submit the recommendations and reports to the Commission on Human Rights regarding the status of women. But the Chair of the Sub-Commission soon communicated to the Economic and Social Council that Sub-Commission should be made a separate independent Commission.[24]

The Council responded favourably and on 21 June 1946, the Sub-Commission formally became the Commission on the Status of Women (CSW), a full-fledged Commission dedicated to ensuring women's equality and to promoting women's rights. Its mandate was to "prepare recommendations and reports to the Economic and Social Council on promoting women's rights in political, economic, civil, social and educational fields" and to make recommendations "on urgent problems requiring immediate attention in the field of women's rights."[25]

The mandate of the CSW was expanded in 1987 to include activities like advocacy of equality, development and peace, monitoring the implementation of internationally agreed measures for the advancement of women, and reviewing and appraising progress at the national, sub-regional, regional, sectoral and global level.[26]

Universal Declaration on Human Rights (1948)

Another historic effort made by the United Nations was to adopt the Universal Declaration of Human Rights (UDHR) in 1948. The Declaration enshrines the principle of equality between women and men and prohibits discrimination against women. Although the

Universal Declaration of Human Rights is not legally binding, its main principles have acquired the status of standards which are to be respected by all States.

The Universal Declaration of Human Rights adopted on December 10, 1948 by the General Assembly affirms :

> "The inherent dignity and of the equal and inalienable rights of all members of the human family is the foundation of freedom, justice and peace in the world ... the peoples of the United Nations have in the Charter reaffirmed their faith in fundamental human rights, in the dignity and worth of the human person and in the equal rights of men and women and have determined to promote social progress and better standards of life in larger freedom, In addition, Article 3 of the Declaration defines that Everyone has the right to life, liberty and security of person.[27]

The UDHR spelt out for the first time a global agreement that every woman, man and child had certain rights merely because they were human beings. It had affirmed the principle of the inadmissibility of discrimination and proclaimed that all human beings are born free and equal in dignity and rights and that everyone is entitled to all the rights and freedoms set forth therein, without distinction of any kind, including distinction based on sex.

The International Covenants on Civil and Political Rights (ICCPR) and Economic, Social and Cultural Rights (ICESCR) adopted in 1966 also provide for equality among women and men. It must however, be stated that neither the UDHR nor the Covenants recognize gender equality firmly.[28] It is only lately that the Committees on ICCPR and ICESCR have started focusing and questioning the State parties as they present their periodic reports on women's position *vis-à-vis* the rights envisaged in theses Covenants. The Human Rights Council has also been emphasizing upon integration of gender in Universal Periodic Review (UPR). This noticeable change is because of the lobby by women's networks and shadow reports being presented by the NGOs that reflect on situation of women's human rights including the conflict zones.

The Geneva Conventions and its Two Additional Protocols (1949 and 1977)

During the Second World War shocking crimes were committed against humanity. The neglect to codify International Law on armed conflict continued even after the end of the War. While the Charter of the United Nations explicitly condemned war and defined the war of aggression as a crime against international peace and humanity, attempts to revise existing standards adopted by the laws on war did not take place in a promising way. The horrors of war led the nations to realize the inadequacy of rules of warfare and that resulted in the Four Geneva Conventions (1949) at the initiative of the International Committee of the Red Cross (ICRC).

The Geneva Conventions together provided a substantive framework of the laws on war, and their significance was gradually realized. These were signed at Geneva on August 12, 1949 and are as follows:

1. Convention (I) for the Amelioration of the Condition of the Wounded and Sick in Armed Forces in the Field
2. Convention (II) for the Amelioration of the Condition of the Wounded, Sick and Shipwrecked Members of Armed Forces at Sea
3. Convention (III) Relative to the Treatment of Prisoners of War
4. Convention (IV) Relative to the Protection of Civilian Persons in the War

Each Convention lists a number of "grave breaches", which include willful killing, torture or inhuman treatment, and the causing of great suffering or serious injury to body or health. States party to the Conventions undertook to enact legislation to try those suspected of grave breaches and to search for such persons. But the Fourth Geneva Convention *Relative to the Protection of Civilian Persons in the War* explicitly covers all individuals "who do not belong to the armed forces, take no part in the hostilities and find themselves in the hands of the Enemy or an Occupying Power".[29]

The International Law of armed conflicts developed before 1949 was only concerned with combatants, not with the civilians. The atrocities and cruelties suffered by the civilian population during the World War II also provided a background for adoption of this Convention. The events of World War II showed the disastrous consequences of the absence of a Convention for the protection of civilians in wartime.

The Fourth Convention includes many provisions which are significant to women that protect expectant mothers and nursing mothers from effect of war, treatment of female prisoners, etc. In addition, Article 27 explicitly deals with sexual violence during armed conflict. "Women shall be especially protected against any attack on their honor, in particular against rape, enforced prostitution, or any form of indecent assault." It further denounces these actions based upon "nationality, race, religious beliefs, age, marital status or social condition."[30]

Subsequently to expand and strengthen the protection provided in the Geneva Convention, two Additional Protocols were adopted in 1977. Article 76(1) of the Additional Protocol I (1977) to the Conventions states "Women shall be the object of special respect and shall be protected in particular against rape, forced prostitution and any other form of indecent assault."[31] Furthermore, Article 4(2)(e) of the Additional Protocol II of 1977 prohibits "Outrages upon personal dignity, in particular humiliating and degrading treatment, rape, enforced prostitution and any form of indecent assault."[32]

The Fourth Geneva Convention of 1949 and its two Additional Protocols are considered to be the main source of international humanitarian law. Though the Conventions contain many provisions for women, yet these suffer from certain weaknesses. In the 1949 Geneva Conventions and Additional Protocol I, certain crimes are designated as "grave breaches". Sexual violence is not expressly designated as a grave breach, although the view that sexual violence fits within other categories of grave breaches, such as "willfully causing great suffering or serious injury to body or health", and "torture or inhuman treatment", has gained acceptance.

Another problem with the provisions of the Geneva Conventions and Additional Protocols is that they characterize rape and other forms of sexual violence as attacks against the "honour" of women, or at the most as an outrage upon personal dignity. The implication that the "honour" (or dignity) is something lent to women by men, and that a raped woman is thereby dishonored. Failure of these instruments to categorize sexual violence as a crime that violates bodily integrity, presents a serious obstacle to addressing crimes of sexual violence against women. It directly reflects and reinforces the trivialization of such offences. Gardam rightly opines that the provisions are protective rather than prohibitive.[33] Overall, the approach to women remains unchanged in the provisions of the Protocols. The focus continues to be on the protection for pregnant women and mothers.

United Nations Convention Relating to the Status of Refugees (1951)

The United Nations in the beginning adopted a number of conventions on the matter relating to war and peace but women's issues and concerns were never seriously discussed. One of such Conventions is the United Nations Convention Relating to the Status of Refugees adopted on July 28, 1951[34] that provides the most comprehensive codification of the rights of refugees at international level with an equally comprehensive definition of refugees. However, it is drafted in the framework of male experiences and completely ignores the women's perspectives. It goes without saying that majority of the refugee population in the world is that of women and children. Women refugees faced gender specific persecution and violation of human rights but the Convention does not address these and they are not covered as a separate category. Accordingly women refugees find it difficult to establish their claims and get relief.

Declaration on the Protection of Women and Children in Emergency and Armed Conflict (1974)

The UN concern about women in armed conflict really begins with the Commission on the Status of Women (CSW) taking up this issue. The Commission expressed its concerns first in 1966 on the special protection of women and children during armed conflict and emergency situations. Following this, the Economic and Social Council (ECOSOC) recommended to the UN General Assembly to adopt a declaration on this issue. Consequently, the General Assembly adopted a *Declaration on the Protection of Women and Children in Emergency and Armed Conflict* in 1974.[35]

The Declaration expressed a deep concern over the sufferings of women and children belonging to the civilian population who in periods of emergency and armed conflict in the struggle for peace, self-determination, national liberation and independence are too often the victims of inhuman acts and consequently suffer serious harm.[36]

The Declaration stated that "all efforts shall be made by States involved in armed conflicts, military operations in foreign territories or military operations in territories still under colonial domination to spare women and children from the ravages of war. All the necessary steps shall be taken to ensure the prohibition of measures such as persecution, torture, punitive measures, degrading treatment and violence, particularly against that part of the civilian population that consists of women and children."[37]

Furthermore, it stated that women and children belonging to the civilian population and finding themselves in circumstances of emergency and armed conflict in the struggle for peace, self-determination, national liberation and independence, or who live in occupied territories, shall not be deprived of shelter, food, medical aid or other inalienable rights.[38]

The Journey towards Development and Peace for Women in the UN (1975-85): From Mexico to Copenhagen to Nairobi

Notwithstanding the ideology and structural acknowledgements of gender equality and concerns through the UN Charter, the UDHR, the Covenants and even the establishment of the Commission of the Status of Women, it may not be wrong to say that the condition of women worldwide was never a priority for action in any part of the United Nations system. From its founding until 1970s and the declaration of the International Women's Year (IWY), the United Nations did little to advance the cause of women's rights.

In the beginning, the work of the United Nations primarily on the codification of women's legal and civil rights, and the gathering of data on the status of women around the world. With time, however, it became increasingly apparent that laws, in and of themselves, were not enough to ensure the equal rights of women.[39] A critical change in the attitude and approach of the United Nations and Member-States concerning the status of women began in the 1970s. This was a time when the feminist movement was also growing strong and active around the world and a shift was taking place in the approach from welfare to development. The UN Decade for Women (1975-85) witnessed that noticeable change.

It was an eventful decade that witnessed the happening of three International Forums and Conferences: in Mexico City in 1975 to inaugurate the Decade; in Copenhagen in 1980 to give a mid-Decade report; in Nairobi in 1985 to formulate strategies and goals for the future and the adoption of the Convention on All Forms of Discrimination Against Women (CEDAW) (1979), have been instrumental in elevating the cause of gender equality to the very centre of the global agenda. The Conferences united the international community behind a set of common objectives with an effective plan of action for the advancement of women everywhere, in all spheres of public and private life.

1975	First UN World Conference on Women, Mexico
1976-85	United Nations Decade for Women
1979	Adoption of Convention on Elimination of All Forms of Discrimination Against Women (CEDAW)
1980	Second UN World Conference on Women, Copenhagen
1985	Third UN World Conference on Women, Nairobi

First UN World Conference on Women, Mexico (19 June-2 July 1975)

The first UN World Conference on the status of women was convened in Mexico City to coincide with the 1975 International Women's Year. It was indeed to remind the international community that discrimination against women continued to be a persistent problem in the world. The Conference, along with the United Nations Decade for Women (1976-85) proclaimed by the General Assembly, launched a new era in global effort to promote the advancement of women by opening a worldwide dialogue on gender equality. The Mexico City Conference was called for by the United Nations General Assembly to focus international attention on the need to develop future oriented goals, effective strategies and plans of action for the advancement of women. To this end, the General Assembly identified three key objectives that would become the basis for the work of the United Nations on behalf of women:

- Full gender *equality* and the elimination of gender discrimination;
- The integration and full participation of women in *development*; and
- An increased contribution by women in the strengthening of world *peace*.

Delegations from 133 Member-States attended the Conference, 113 of these were headed by women.[40] The Conference began a process to articulate the women's peace discourse through the United Nations to reconceptualize women's issues regarding development and peace through feminist perspectives. Women also organised a parallel NGO Forum, the International Women's Year Tribune (IWT), which attracted approximately 6,000 participants.[41] The Forum played an important role in bringing together women and men from different cultures and backgrounds to share information and opinions and to set in motion a process that would help unite the women's movement. The Forum was also instrumental in opening up the United Nations to NGOs, who provided access for the voices of women to the Organization's policy-making process.[42]

Though the Conference was organized to link the three themes simultaneously on gender equality, development and peace but only one Panel on Disarmament was included in the *Tribune* on the request and advocacy of some women's peace groups.[43] It was a great achievement, since women were not considered to be competent to discuss the issues of disarmament.[44]

The Declaration of the World Conference recognized that :

> "women of the entire world, whatever differences exist between them, share the painful experience of receiving or having received unequal treatment, and that as their awareness of this phenomenon increases they will become natural allies in the struggle against any form of oppression, such as is practiced under colonialism, neo-colonialism, zionism, racial discrimination and apartheid, thereby constituting an enormous revolutionary potential for economic and social change in the world today."[45]

In addition, the Conference also recognized :

> "the urgency of improving the status of women and finding more effective methods and strategies which will enable them to have the same opportunities as men to participate actively in the development of their countries and to contribute to the attainment of world peace."[46]

The Declaration further stated that :

> "women must play an important role in the promotion, achievement and maintenance of international peace, and that it is necessary to encourage their efforts towards peace, through their full participation in the national and international organizations that exist for this purpose, and furthermore, the Conference also convinced that women have a vital role to play in the promotion of peace in all spheres of life: in the family, the community, the nations and the world. As such, women must participate equally with men in the decision-making processes which help to promote peace at all levels and Women as well as men should promote real, general and complete disarmament under effective international control, starting with nuclear disarmament. Until genuine disarmament is achieved, women and men throughout the world must maintain their

> vigilance and do their utmost to achieve and maintain international peace."[47]

A World Plan of Action was adopted at the end of the Conference that offered guidelines for governments and the international community to follow for the next ten years in pursuit of the three key objectives set by the General Assembly.[48]

The Plan of Action set minimum targets, to be met by 1980, that focused on securing equal access for women to resources such as education, employment opportunities, political participation, health services, housing, nutrition and family planning. To strengthen the role of women in peace-building the World Plan of Action for the Implementation of the Objectives in the Advancement of Women at the International Women's Year for the forthcoming decade urged that :

> "the primary objective of development being to bring about sustained improvement in the well-being of the individual and of society and to bestow benefits on all, development should be seen not only as a desirable goal in itself but also as the most important means for furthering equality of the sexes and the maintenance of peace."[49]

It further stated :

> "for essential condition for the maintenance and strengthening of international co-operation and peace is the promotion and protection of human rights for all in conditions of equity among and within nations. In order to involve more women in the promotion of international co-operation, the development of friendly relations among nations, the strengthening of international peace and disarmament, the peace efforts of women as individuals and in groups, and in national and international organizations should be recognized and encouraged."[50]

Furthermore, the World Plan of Action "desired that women should have equal opportunity with men to represent their countries in all international forums where the above questions are discussed, and in particular at meetings of the organization of the United Nations system, including the Security Council and all conferences on disarmament and international peace, and other regional bodies."[51]

The International Women's Year (IWY) rightly observes Hilkka, "worked as an engine to change the situation of Women".[52] The General Assembly, endorsed the Declaration of Mexico and the World Plan of Action. Within the United Nations system, in addition to the already existing Division for the Advancement of Women (Now UN Women), the Mexico Conference led to the establishment of the International Research and Training Institute for the Advancement of Women (INSTRAW) in 1983 and the United Nations Development Fund for Women (UNIFEM) in 1984 to provide the institutional framework for research, training and operational activities in the area of women and development.

The World Conference also gave impetus to the drafting of an international treaty to eliminate discrimination against women. In time for the Copenhagen Conference, the Convention on the Elimination of All Forms of Discrimination against Women (CEDAW), often referred to as women's bill of rights, was adopted by the General Assembly in 1979 that came into force in 1981.

Convention on the Elimination of All Forms of Discrimination Against Women (CEDAW), 1979

The Convention on the Elimination of All Forms of Discrimination Against Women (CEDAW) is one of the founding international treaty that provides a starting point on which Resolution 1325 has been built. The CEDAW adopted by the General Assembly in 1979 is a milestone for women around the world.[53] The Convention is known as a charter of women's rights. Women's perspectives and issues were ignored in early human rights documents. The Convention in that respect was a great achievement. It emphasizes on substantive equality rather than formal equality. It mandates the Member-States to end discrimination. The Convention is the first international legal instrument that defines discrimination against women in such broad terms as:

> "Any distinction, exclusion or restriction made on the basis of sex which has the effect or purpose of impairing or nullifying the recognition, enjoyment or exercise by women, irrespective of their marital status, on a basis of equality of men and women, of human rights and fundamental freedoms in the political, economic, social, cultural, civil or any other field."[54]

The CEDAW incorporates the principles of women's rights and gender equality into International Law. It includes all provisions aimed at the elimination of discrimination against women previously covered by separate conventions. It also contains provisions covering issues that had been omitted from earlier conventions. But the major weakness of the Convention is that it has no specific provision on violence against women and on women and armed conflict. To rectify this, the CEDAW Committee has adopted two General Recommendations on "Violence against Women" in 1992 (GR 19)[55] and on "Women and Health" in 1999 (GR 24).[56]

The General Recommendation 19 on *"Violence Against Women"*, recognizes that wars, armed conflicts and the occupation of territories often lead to increased prostitution, trafficking in women and sexual assault of women, which requires specific protective and punitive measures.[57]

Similarly, the General Recommendation 24 adopted by the CEDAW Committee at its 20th Session, 1999, makes recommendations on Article 12 : *Women and Health*. Under this the CEDAW Committee has emphasized the need to give special attention to the health needs and rights of women belonging to vulnerable and disadvantaged groups, such as refugee and internally displaced women, the girl child and older women, women in prostitution and women with physical and mental disabilities.[58]

It further urges that the state parties should provide adequate health services, including trauma treatment and counseling, for women trapped in situations of armed conflict and women refugees.[59] Furthermore, it obligates the state parties to provide sexual health information, education and services to women and girls, including those who have been trafficked.[60]

There is a great demand for another General Recommendation on Women in Conflict and Post-Conflict Situations. The Committee is currently engaged with that. It had its general discussion on 11-29 July, 2011 in New York on the protection of women in conflict and post-conflict situations. The purpose of the general discussion was to commence the Committee's process of elaborating a *"General Recommendation on Women in Conflict and Post-conflict Situations"* and also to provide appropriate and authoritative guidance to State Parties on the measures to be adopted to ensure full compliance with their obligations to protect, respect and fulfill women's human rights during times of armed conflict and in all peace-building processes, which includes the immediate aftermath of conflict and long-term post-conflict reconstruction.[61]

In the general discussion, the *Women and Media Collective (Sri Lanka) and Forum for Women, Law and Development (Nepal)* from South Asia participated and made statements. Both the NGOs highlighted the different types of vulnerabilities that exist as a result of the militarization and displacement during conflict. They demanded that the Committee must take into account: the social stigma experienced by women combatants; the need to include preventative measures and mechanisms to hold states accountable; implement gender sensitive demilitarization, demobilization and reintegration plan (DDR); temporary special measures to prevent the exploitation that arise out of post-conflict trafficking and exploitative relationships; and reconciliation initiatives that are participatory and inclusive to address the concerns of marginalized and non-majority communities, including political rights/issues.[62]

Once the General Recommendation is there, it will be obligatory on the part of the State Parties to report on that. However, it needs to be emphasized that the UNSCR 1325 and CEDAW share a common gender equality agenda that the two can be used together to broaden, strengthen and operationalise gender equality in the context of conflict, peace building and post conflict reconstruction.

There is a "synergy between the two sets of standards that can be used to greatly enhance their implementation and impact".[63] A UNIFEM publication *CEDAW and Security Council Resolution 1325* demonstrates the areas which CEDAW standards and 1325 provisions can strengthen each other.[64] There is an attempt to link CEDAW and Resolution 1325 and see how the Resolution can expand the reach of CEDAW and conversely the way CEDAW can be used to deepen the impact and effectiveness of Resolution 1325.

Second UN World Conference on Women, Copenhagen (14 July-30 July 1980)

The Mexico Conference was followed by the Copenhagen Conference in 1980. The Conference was convened to have the first five year review and appraisal of the implementation of the Mexico World Plan of Action and to update it.[65] The Conference was attended by approximately 2000 delegates from 145 States and the NGO Forum in Copenhagen brought together some 7,000 participants.[66] Despite the progress made, the Copenhagen Conference recognized that signs of disparity were beginning to emerge between rights secured and women's ability to exercise these rights. To address this concern, the Conference focused on only three areas which included equal access to education, employment opportunities and adequate health care services rather than broad goals of equality, development and peace, identified by the Mexico Conference.

There are only a few paragraphs which mentioned the need to increase the role of women in armed conflict situations in the Report of the World Conference and the impact of violence and role of women in conflict resolution and peace building largely remained unrecognized in the Conference.

The Para 33 of the Report states:

> "The obligations under the Charter to maintain peace and security and to achieve international cooperation in promoting and encouraging respect for human rights and fundamental freedoms, bearing in mind, in this respect, the right to live in peace, States should help women to participate in promoting international cooperation for the sake of the preparation of societies for a life in peace."[67]

Likewise, Para 76 states :

> "Women of the entire world should participate in the broadest way in the struggle to strengthen international peace and security, to broaden international cooperation and develop friendly relations among nations, to achieve detente in international relations and disarmament, to establish a new economic order in international relations, to promote guarantees of fundamental freedoms and human rights." [68]

Furthermore, Para 77 of the Report states:

> "Solidarity campaigns with women struggling against colonialism, neo-colonialism, racism, racial discrimination and apartheid and for national independence and liberation should be intensified; such women should receive all possible assistance, including support from agencies of the United Nations system as well as other organizations."[69]

And Para 78 states:

> "The efforts of inter-governmental and non-governmental organizations to strengthen international peace and security should be intensified in every way. The active participation of women in the activities of such organizations should be supported."[70]

A Programme of Action and 48 Resolutions were adopted for the advancement of women. The Programme of Action called for stronger national measures to ensure women's ownership and control of property, as well as improvements in women's rights to inheritance, child custody and loss of nationality. Delegates at the Conference also urged an end to stereotyped attitudes towards women.

It is pertinent to note here that throughout 1980s, the UN continued with its endeavors to advance women's equality and development, but still without any reference to the impact of violence on women in conflict situations or women as an agents of peace. Peace received cursory attention at the mid-decade Conference in Copenhagen.

However, soon after the Copenhagen, Conference, on December 3, 1982, the UN General Assembly adopted a Declaration on the *Participation of Women in Promoting International Peace and Cooperation.*[71]

Article 1 of the Declaration recognized that women and men have an equal and vital interest in contributing to international peace and cooperation. To this end, women must be enabled to exercise their right to participate in the economic, social, cultural, civil and political affairs of society on an equal footing with men.[72]

Article 12 of the Declaration emphasized that all appropriate measures shall be taken to provide practical opportunities for the effective participation of women in promoting international peace and cooperation, economic development and social progress including, to that end:

a) The promotion of an equitable representation of women in governmental and non-governmental functions;
b) The promotion of equality of opportunities for women to enter diplomatic service;
c) The appointment or nomination of women, on an equal basis with men, as members of delegations to national, regional or international meetings; and
d) Support for increased employment of women at all levels in the secretariats of the United Nations and the specialized agencies, in conformity with Article 101 of the Charter of the United Nations.[73]

Third UN World Conference on Women, Nairobi (15-26 July 1985)

The movement for gender equality had gained true global recognition by the time the Third World Conference on Women was convened in Nairobi in 1985. The Conference was convened to review and appraise the achievements of the United Nations Decade for Women. The Conference was attended by 157 States and the more than 16,000 participants participated in the NGO Forum.[74]

Significantly a Peace Tent was put by women's oraganisations at the Nairobi Forum. It was the main centre of women's groups where many women from states with hostile relations had the opportunity to talk with each other the contentious issues. The Peace Tent firmly gave the message that peace was an integral part to the other two themes of the decade. Peace remained a key issue of concern for women's movements, which from the time of Nairobi maintained and extended an active global network that made many advances later possible.

The Conference represented the culmination of ten years of work on gender empowerment. A lot of information, knowledge and experience had been gathered through the process of discussion, negotiation and revision during the decade. Data gathered by the United Nations revealed that improvements in the status of women and efforts to reduce discrimination had benefited only a small minority of women and the appraisal showed that the objectives of the United Nations Decade for Women had not been met.

This realization demanded that a new approach be adopted. The Nairobi Conference was given the mandate to seek new ways to overcome the obstacles to achieving the Decade's goals for equality, development and peace. *The Nairobi Forward-looking Strategies* (NFLS) to the Year 2000 were adopted in the Conference.[75] The NFLS provided a blueprint for action until 2000 to achieve the decade goals.

Three basic categories of measures were identified:

- Constitutional and legal steps;
- Equality in social participation; and
- Equality in political participation and decision-making.

In keeping with the view that all issues were women's issues, measures were recommended by the Nairobi Forward-Looking Strategies and it urged the member states to take constitutional and legal steps to eliminate all forms of discrimination against women, and modify national strategies to facilitate the participation of women in efforts to promote peace and development. At the same time, it contained specific recommendations for gender empowerment in regard to health, education and employment.

The NFLS acknowledged the vulnerable situation of women affected by inter alia armed conflict, including the threat of physical abuse. The general vulnerability of women to sexual abuse and rape in everyday life was recognized, but sexual violence was not specifically linked to armed conflict.[76] It is disappointing to note that again the Report of Nairobi Conference and NFLS did not firmly pay much attention on the third theme of the decade, i.e peace. There were only a few paragraphs which reflected on the role of women in peace.

The Report of the Nairobi Conference declared that "the full and effective promotion of women's rights can best occur in conditions of international peace and security."[77] In addition, the Report explained that "Peace cannot be realized under conditions of economic and sexual inequality, denial of basic human rights and fundamental freedoms, deliberate exploitation of large sectors of the population, unequal development of countries, and exploitative economic relations".[78]

It is recognized that "Peace is promoted by equality of the sexes, economic equality and the universal enjoyment of basic human rights and fundamental freedoms. Its enjoyment by all requires that women be enabled to exercise their right to participate on an equal footing with men in all spheres of the political, economic and social life of their respective countries, particularly in the decision-making process, while exercising their right to freedom of opinion, expression, information and association in the promotion of international peace and cooperation."[79]

In the Section on Peace both obstacles and strategies were highlighted in the Report.

> Paragraph 232 acknowledged that "the threat to peace resulting from continuing international tension and violations of the United Nations Charter, resulting in the unabated arms raceways well as wars, armed conflicts, external domination, foreign occupation, acquisition of land by force, aggression, imperialism, colonialism, neo-colonialism, racism, apartheid, gross violation of human rights, terrorism, repression, the disappearance of persons and discrimination on the basis of sex are major obstacles to human progress, specifically to the advancement of women."[80]
>
> Paragraphs 235, 236 and 237 acknowledged
>
> "the important role of women to attain world peace. The

paragraphs mentioned that the universal and durable peace could not be attained without the full and equal participation of women in international relations, particularly in decision-making concerning peace, including the processes envisaged for the peaceful settlement of disputes under the Charter of the United Nations nor without overcoming the obstacles mentioned in paragraph 232; full equality between women and men is severely hampered by the threats to international peace and security, all obstacles at national and international levels in the way of women's participation in promoting international peace and co-operation should be removed as soon as possible."[81]

Underlying the **strategies**, the document stated that :

"In view of the fact that women are still very inadequately represented in national and international political processes dealing with peace and conflict settlement, it is essential that women support and encourage each other in their initiatives and action relating either to universal issues, such as disarmament and the development of confidence-building measures between nations and people, or to specific conflict situations between or within States."[82]

In addition :

"The strategies in this field should include the mobilization of women in favour of all acts and actions that tend to promote peace, in particular, the elimination of wars and danger of nuclear war."[83] And "Women's equal role in decision-making with respect to peace and related issues should be seen as one of their basic human rights and as such should be enhanced and encouraged at the national, regional and international levels."[84]

In the Report it was urged that to take measures for the implementation of the basic strategies at the national level[85] and women's participation in efforts for peace :[86]

"Women should be able to participate actively in the decision making process related to the promotion of international peace and co-operation. Emphasis should be given to the grass-roots participation and co-operation of women's organisations with other non-governmental organisations in this process."[87]

Further, it emphasised :

"Governments which have not done so should undertake all appropriate measures to eliminate existing discriminatory practices towards women and to provide them with equal opportunities to join, at all levels, the civil service, to enter the diplomatic service, and to represent their countries as members of delegations to national, regional and international meetings, including conferences on peace, conflict resolution, disarmament, and meetings of the Security Council and other United Nations bodies."[88]

UN Reform in the 1990s: The Evolution of Peace-building and the Development of International Concern over Sexual Violence During Armed Conflict

While the United Nations was established to maintain international peace and security, the organistaion's approach to build sustainable peace began in the early 1990s after the end of the cold war. In the1990s, the increased concentration of the Security Council on intrastate wars and their devastating effects on civilians led to the development of security concepts that no longer merely focused on possible threats to states' borders, but also on individuals.

An Agenda for Peace, Preventive Diplomacy, Peace-making and Peace-keeping

Starting after the end of the Cold War, the then United Nations Secretary-General Boutros Boutros-Ghali came out with a report—An Agenda for Peace in 1992, which quickly became a milestone in the UN's peace-building work.[89] The report set out the beginnings of a blueprint for international interventions in war torn countries. Nevertheless, the Agenda for Peace was the first stage in a shift away from traditional national security discourse towards more inclusive approaches focusing on human rights and collective action based on liberal principles.[90] The Agenda, however, suffered from gender blindness as there was no mention of it in the document. Women only featured once in their 'traditional' place of being lumped with children as the 'more vulnerable group' in society.[91]

Influenced by the horrifying experiences of sexual violence in Bosnia and Rwanda in the beginning of the 1990s, a window opened up for gender issues to enter in the UN's discourse on peace and security. Throughout the 1990s, the United Nations took many steps to incorporate a gender perspective into peace-building policy and practice. During this period, the United Nations sponsored a series of Conferences and Summit meetings to advance the status of women worldwide and referred especially to the impact of armed conflict and their role as peace-builders.

1992	An Agenda for Peace, Preventive Diplomacy, Peace-making and Peace-keeping by Boutros-Ghali, Boutros
1993	The Vienna Conference on Human Rights and the Declaration on the Elimination of Violence against Women
1993	International Criminal Tribunal for the former Yugoslavia (ICTY)
1994	International Criminal Tribunal for Rwanda (ICTR)
1995	UN Fourth World Conferences on Women
1996	Project on Women's Contribution to a Culture of Peace of (UNESCO)
1998	Rome Statute of the International Criminal Court
1998	Agreed Conclusions on women and armed conflict on 42nd Session of CSW
1999	CEDAW Committee's General Recommendations 24, on 20th Session
1999	Security Council Resolution on the Protection of civilians in armed conflict, 1265
2000	Security Council Resolution protection of civilians in armed conflict, 1296

The World Human Rights Conference in Vienna, 1993

The major precursor to the Resolution 1325 is the 1993 World Conference on Human Rights held in Vienna.[92] This Conference was a turning point for women's human rights. In response to the vigorous international campaign, there was unequivocal declaration that women's rights are human rights. The Conference provided an opportunity to strengthen the UN mechanisms for enforcing women's human rights, particularly with respect to the implementation procedures under the Convention on the Elimination of All Forms of Discrimination Against Women as well as mechanisms to eliminate violence against women, both in the private and public spheres. Previously, violence against women, such as domestic abuse, mutilation, burning, rape, etc. had been regarded as private matters, and therefore not appropriate for government or international action.

The Conference categorically stated that all human rights are universal, indivisible, interdependent and interrelated and that the human rights of women are an inalienable, integral, and indivisible part of universal human rights. It called for the elimination of all forms of discrimination against women and the eradication of all forms of violence against women which was missed in the Convention on the Elimination of All Forms of Discrimination Against Women earlier adopted in 1979.

The Conference affirmed that:

> "The human rights of women and the girl-child are an inalienable, integral and indivisible part of universal human rights. The full and equal participation of women in political, civil, economic, social and cultural life, at the national, regional and international levels, and the eradication of all forms of discrimination on grounds of sex are priority objectives of the international community."[93]

In the Conference, it was also agreed by the international community that discrimination against women and girls was not only a violation of their human rights, but it also impacted negatively on social and economic development processes. The Conference expressed its disappointment at the massive violations of human rights especially in the form of genocide, "ethnic cleansing" and systematic rape of women in war situations, creating mass exodus of refugees and displaced persons. While strongly condemning such abhorrent practices, it reiterated the call that perpetrators of such crimes be punished and such practices immediately stopped.[94]

The Conference stated explicitly that:

> "Violations of the human rights of women in situations of armed conflict are violations of the fundamental principles of international human rights and humanitarian law. All violations of this kind, including in particular murder, systematic rape, sexual slavery, and forced pregnancy, require a particularly effective response."[95]

Furthermore, the Conference urged the governments and regional and international organizations to facilitate the access of women to decision-making posts and their greater participation in the decision-making processes. It urged further steps within the United Nations Secretariat to appoint and promote women staff members in accordance with the Charter of the United Nations, and other principal and subsidiary organs of the United Nations to guarantee the participation of women under conditions of equality.[96]

At the *Vienna Conference*, a Tribunal was organized by the NGOs, that heard testimonies regarding violations of women's human rights around the world, including sexual violence during armed conflict. These testimonies included the statements from former "comfort women", Palestinian, Somali, and Peruvian women, as well as women from former Yugoslavia.[97]

Following this Conference the United Nations adopted a *Declaration on the Elimination of Violence against Women* in December 1993.[98] Although the Declaration is not binding under International Law, it recognises violence against women—even in the private sphere—as a violation of human rights and calls upon the states to take relevant measures. It is the first international human rights instrument to deal exclusively with violence against women. It was recognised that violence against women is an obstacle to the achievement of equality, development and peace. It serves as a reference point for human rights entities, other UN organisations, as well as NGOs in their efforts to combat violence against women. The Declarations provides a very comprehensive definition of violence that encompasses a physical, sexual and psychological violence in the family and society as well as violence perpetrated or condoned by the state.[99]

Article 4 of the Declaration states that States should develop, in a comprehensive way, preventive approaches and all those measures of a legal, political, administrative and cultural nature that promote the protection of women against any form of violence, and ensure that the re-victimization of women does not occur because of laws insensitive to gender considerations, enforcement practices or other interventions;[100]

And, Article 5(e) provided for coordination between organizations and bodies of the United Nations system to incorporate the issue of violence against women into ongoing programmes, especially with reference to groups of women particularly vulnerable to violence.

The Special Rapporteur on Violence against Women

Another important development has been the appointment of a Special Rapporteur on VAW including violence experienced during armed conflict. Dr. Radhika Coomaraswamy (Sri Lanka) was appointed as the first Special Rapporteur. On March 4, 1994, the

Commission on Human Rights adopted a resolution for "integrating the rights of women into the human rights mechanisms of the United Nations and the elimination of violence against women".[101] The creation of this mechanism and the scope of its mandate was a victory for women's rights movements globally.

As a result of these steps, the problem of violence against women has been drawing increasing political attention. The Special Rapporteur has a mandate to collect and analyse comprehensive data and to recommend measures aimed at eliminating violence at the international, regional and national levels. The mandate is three-fold:

- To collect information on violence against women and its causes and consequences from sources such as Governments, treaty bodies, specialised agencies and inter-governmental and non-governmental organisation, and to respond effectively to such information;
- To recommend measures and ways and means, at the national, regional and international levels, to eliminate violence against women and its causes, and to remedy its consequences; and
- To work closely with other special rapporteurs, special representatives, working groups and independent experts of the Commission on Human Rights. [102]

The Rapporteur was expected to cover violence in the following areas:

(a) Violence in the family (including domestic violence, traditional practices, infanticide, incest, etc.);

(b) Violence in the community (including rape, sexual assault, sexual harassment, commercialized violence such as trafficking in women, prostitution, labour exploitation, pornography, women migrant workers, etc.); and

(c) Violence by the State (including violence against women in detention and custodial violence, as well as violence against women in situations of armed conflict and against refugee women).[103]

Through analysis, recommendations and country visits, the Special Rapporteur has raised awareness of the causes and consequences of different forms of violence against women and has further elaborated an understanding of international standards in this area. Based on research, NGO reports and country visits, a report along with the causes of gender-based violence suggesting remedies to counteract it was presented by the Rapporteur. Violence in armed conflicts and trafficking in women have been thematic issues much in the same way as violence in the family and in state prisons.[104] In January 1998, the Special Rapporteur recommended in the context of international wars, that the Geneva Conventions be re-examined and re-evaluated so as to "incorporate developing norms against women during armed conflict".[105]

EVOLUTION OF RAPE AND SEXUAL VIOLENCE JURISPRUDENCE

Wartime sexual violence was seen as an inevitable consequence of war. It was often encouraged and rarely prosecuted. Rape was for the first time explicitly prohibited by an international instrument in the 1949 IV Geneva Convention Relative to the Protection of Civilian Persons in Time of War, and after that in the two Optional Protocols (1977) to the Geneva Conventions. However, as seen earlier the provisions treated sexual crimes as outrage upon personal dignity rather than violence to life and are not part of grave breach provisions.

Influenced by the horrifying incidents of sexual violence in Bosnia and Rwanda in the beginning of the 1990s, a window opened up for gender issues to enter in the UN's discourse on peace and security. The wars in Bosnia-Herzegovina and Rwanda were a turning point. These conflicts brought about the term "rape as a weapon of war" as rape was carried out systematically, and was strategically used as a war tactic. The Bosnian war witnessed as part of ethnic cleansing at the hands of Serbs what came to be known as 'mass rape phenomenon'.

The Rwanda Tribunal and the Yugoslavia Tribunal have been the two main engines driving the contemporary evolution of rape and sexual violence jurisprudence.[106] Prior to the establishment of the two ad hoc tribunals, the International Criminal Tribunal for the former Yugoslavia (ICTY) and the International Criminal Tribunal for Rwanda (ICTR), sexual violence was largely tolerated and rarely prosecuted by military tribunals. Though the precedent for international prosecution of sexual violence was first established in 1474 trial of Peter von Hagenbach.[107] Despite this precedent, the Nuremberg Trial and Tokyo Trial did not deal with sexual crimes committed during the Second World War. Rape was, however, included in the list of the crimes charged in the indictment, under the headings: inhuman treatment, ill-treatment and failure to respect family honour and rights.[108] However, there was little reference to sexual slavery, which was committed on an enormous scale by the Japanese.[109]

THE INTERNATIONAL CRIMINAL TRIBUNAL FOR THE FORMER YUGOSLAVIA (ICTY)

In 1993, as a response to the findings of the Commission of Experts (Yugoslavia Commission) of widespread violations of international humanitarian law in the former Yugoslavia, including rape and many other forms of sexual violence against women, the Security Council set-up the International Criminal Tribunal for the former Yugoslavia (ICTY) to prosecute persons responsible for such acts.[110] This was the first international war crimes tribunal since the Nuremberg and Tokyo Tribunals.

Although the value of the ICTY is limited both by its origin as a Security Council measure and by its geographical scope, the normative effect of these initiatives is much more widespread. This was a major development of humanitarian law, as hereafter it became difficult difficult to maintain that rape and various forms of sexual violence against women committed in international armed conflicts are not grave breaches of treaty rules. To date, there have been 29 convictions for sexual violence in this court.[111]

The International Criminal Tribunal for Rwanda (ICTR)

The International Criminal Tribunal for Rwanda (ICTR) was established in 1994 to prosecute those persons responsible for the genocide and other serious violations of International Law in Rwanda.An estimated 500,000 Rwandans, overwhelmingly Tutsi, were killed during this period. 250,000-500,000 women and girls were raped during the 1994 genocide in Rwanda.[112] Despite the widespread occurrence of rape, the Rwanda tribunal initially failed to include the charges in the indictments. Only in August 1997, after international pressure from women's non-governmental organizations (NGOs), that the prosecutor began to charge the perpetrators with crime of rape.[113]

In 1998, the Trial Chamber of the International Criminal Tribunal for Rwanda convicted Akayesu[114] of genocide and crimes against humanity for his encouragement of the rape of Tutsi women in Rwanda. Akayesu's conviction was historic because it was for the first time in history that a defendant was tried and convicted by an international tribunal for genocide.

The International Criminal Tribunal for the Former Yugoslavia prosecuted and convicted individuals with command responsibility for rape as a form of torture and as a crime against humanity. At the International Criminal Tribunal for Rwanda, both rape and systematic rape were prosecuted for the first time as acts of genocide. It marked the beginning of end to impunity. It was formalized later under the Statute of International Criminal Court (ICC). To date, there have been 11 convictions for sexual violence in this court.[115]

The Special Rapporteur on systematic rape, sexual slavery and slavery like practices during armed conflict, Gay J. Mc Dougall, in her update to the Final Report to the Sub-Commission on the Promotion and Protection of Human Rights 2000 observed that in particular, "with the conclusion of several precedent-setting cases in both tribunals, jurisprudence is increasingly confirming that sexual slavery and other forms of sexual violence, including rape, committed during armed conflict are violations of international law."[116]

The Statutes and jurisprudence of the two *ad hoc* Tribunals, and the more recent Statutes of the International Criminal Court (ICC), which entered into force in 2002 include provisions which reflect an understanding of the gender implications of armed conflict and are of great significance in the context of redress for women and girls through the international criminal law process.

The Fourth World Conference on Women, (4-15, September, 1995)—Another Milestone

The Fourth UN World Conference on Women, held in Beijing in 1995 marked another significant milestone. It recognized the seriousness of armed conflict and its impact on the lives of women.[117] The Beijing Platform for Action (BPFA) adopted at the Conference identified Women and Armed Conflict (E) as one of the twelve critical areas of concern to be addressed by the Member-States, the international community and civil society. The Platform for Action sets out measures for national and international action for the advancement of women. [118]

The Beijing Platform for Action states :

> "While entire communities suffer the consequences of armed conflict and terrorism, women and girls are particularly affected because of their status in society and their sex. Parties to the conflict often rape women with impunity sometimes using systematic rape as a tactic of war and terrorism. The impact of violence against women and violations of the human rights of

women in such situations is experienced by women of all ages, who suffer displacement, loss of home and property, loss or involuntary disappearance of close relatives, poverty and family separation and disintegration, and who are victims of acts of murder, terrorism, torture, involuntary disappearance, sexual slavery, rape, sexual abuse and forced pregnancy in situations of armed conflict, especially as a result of policies of ethnic cleansing and other new and emerging forms of violence. This is compounded by the life-long social, economic and psychologically traumatic consequences of armed conflict and foreign occupation and alien domination."[119]

[Platform for Action Critical Area E: Women and Armed Conflict]

The Beijing Conference brought a fresh vision to women's empowerment all over the world especially with its enormous contribution to human security perspectives and promotion of women as peacebuilders. Although, all the three previous World Conferences on Women were organized under the theme of Equality, Development and Peace, the previous three Conferences did not pay much attention to the theme of peace. It is the Beijing Conference that paid adequate attention to this issue by listing and dealing with it at length in the Critical Area E.

Para 18 of the BPFA states:

> "Local, national, regional and global peace is attainable and is inextricably linked with the advancement of women, who are a fundamental force for leadership, conflict resolution and the promotion of lasting peace at all levels."[120]

Likewise Para 23 of the Global Framework of the BPFA recognizes :

> "The achievement and maintenance of peace and security are a precondition for economic and social progress, women are increasingly establishing themselves as central actors in a variety of capacities in the movement of humanity for peace. Their full participation in decision-making, conflict prevention and resolution and all other peace initiatives is essential to the realization of lasting peace."[121]

In each critical area of concern, the problem is diagnosed and strategic objectives were proposed with concrete actions to be taken by various actors in order to achieve those objectives. The objectives and actions are interlinked and mutually reinforcing.

The *Strategic Objectives* of this *Critical Area*, that is, Women and Armed Conflict as laid down in the BPFA are:

Strategic Objective E.1: Increase the participation of women in conflict resolution at decision-making levels and protect women living in situations of armed and other conflicts or under foreign occupation.[122]

Strategic Objective E.2 : Reduce excessive military expenditures and control the availability of armaments.[123]

Strategic Objective E.3 : Promote non-violent forms of conflict resolution and reduce the incidence of human rights abuse in conflict situations. [124]

Strategic Objective E.4 : Promote women's contribution to fostering a culture of peace.[125]

Strategic Objective E.5 : Provide protection, assistance and training to refugee women, other displaced women in need of international protection and internally displaced women.[126]

Strategic Objective E.6 : Provide assistance to the women of the colonies and non-self-governing territories.[127]

These provisions emboldened the women's groups to continue their struggle against gender-based violence in armed conflict and recognition of women as peace-makers and builders. The Beijing Conference was a watershed for thrusting women to the forefront of peace activities. This conference provided a platform for deliberations on the role of women and peace. It was a major step in recognizing and legitimating the role of women in conflict resolution and peace making at all levels. Since Beijing, women and their participation has received special attention because, it is argued, they represent a vital resource for sustaining peace efforts at all levels.

Project on Women's Contribution to a Culture of Peace of (UNESCO), 1996

Following the Beijing Conference and the Strategic objectives especially the ones listed in Women and Armed Conflict as stated above, in 1996 the UN Economic, Social and Cultural Organisation (UNESCO) launched its "*Women's Contribution to a Culture of Peace*" project.[128] The programme, which concentrates on peace-building in specific war-affected countries also focused on the empowerment of women and support for their peace initiatives, as well as gender-sensitization with a focus on fostering an ethos of non-violence.[129] The project was based on the assumption that sustainable peace is achieved from the bottom up and that it is a pre-condition for development. The project was therefore of particular value to women at the community level; especially those involved in peace-building efforts.

Agreed Conclusion on Women and Armed Conflict of the 42nd Session of the Commission on the Status of Women

The *Commission on the Status of Women* again took up the issue of women and armed conflict as a thematic issue for discussion in its 42nd Session in 1998 and adopted *Agreed Conclusion* which reaffirmed the commitments made in the BPFA. The Agreed Conclusion urged that Member-States should take actions on gender-sensitive justice; the specific needs of women affected by armed conflict; the need to increase women's participation in all stages of peace processes, including conflict prevention, post-conflict resolution and reconstruction; and disarmament issues. [130]

In 2004, the *Commission* revisited this theme and adopted *Agreed Conclusions* on women's equal participation in conflict prevention, management and conflict resolution and in post-conflict peace-building.[131] It was recognized that peace agreements provide a vehicle for the promotion of gender equality and that a gender-sensitive constitutional and legal framework was necessary to ensure that women fully participate in such processes.

Finally, the allocation of necessary human, financial and material resources was seen as critical for specific and targeted activities to ensure gender equality at the local, national, regional and international levels, as well as for enhanced and increased international cooperation.

Security Council Resolutions on the Protection of Civilians in Armed Conflict, (S/RES/1265) and (S/RES/1296)

By the year 2000, protecting civilians in situations of armed conflicts had become a humanitarian imperative with the UN and the Security Council passed Resolutions 1265 (1999) and 1296 (2000) that condemned attacks against civilians. The Resolution 1265 recognises the direct and particular impact of armed conflict on women. Furthermore, it requests the Secretary-General to ensure that United Nations personnel involved in peace-making, peace-keeping and peace-building activities have appropriate training in international humanitarian, human rights and refugee law, including child and gender-related provisions, negotiation and communication skills, cultural awareness and civilian-military coordination. In addition, it urges Member-States and relevant international and regional organisations to ensure that appropriate training is included in their programmes for personnel involved in similar activities.[132]

Similarly, the Resolution 1296 reaffirms its grave concern at the harmful and widespread impact of armed conflict on civilians, including the particular impact that armed conflict has on women, children and other vulnerable groups, and further reaffirms in this regard the importance of fully addressing their special protection and assistance needs in the mandates of peace-making, peace-keeping and peace-building operations.[133] This pro-active role of the Security Council was in the right mode for the adoption of the SCR 1325.

Rome Statute of the International Criminal Court (ICC)

The establishment of the International Criminal Court in 2002 represents a major breakthrough in the understanding and prosecution of sexual crimes committed during conflicts, since many serious crimes were given recognition for the first time as crimes against humanity and war crimes.

The Rome Statute [134] recognises an unprecedented range of crimes of sexual and gender based violence. It prohibits "rape, sexual slavery, enforced prostitution, forced pregnancy, enforced sterilisation, and other forms of sexual violence" (Articles 7, 8) for the first time all these crimes have been enumerated in International Law, accorded full status as war crimes, and also explicitly recognised as crimes which can constitute acts of genocide (Article 6). Further to these provisions, trafficking and persecution are recognised as crimes against humanity (Article 7), gender is identified as a grounds for persecution for the first time, and the Statute specifically states that the application and interpretation of the law must be without adverse distinction on the basis of a number of grounds, including gender (Article 21). The ICC is a permanent tribunal with the power to prosecute individuals for genocide, crimes against humanity, war crimes.

Credit goes to the women's organizations especially the Women's Caucus for Gender Justice, which lobbied hard to get included provisions in the Rome Statute (the law of the ICC) regarding investigation and prosecution of gender crimes. The terms "gender" and "gender crimes" were included in the Rome Statute rather than the term "sex" and "sexual violence". As a result of the efforts of this Caucus, for the first time in history, gender crimes that had been historically omitted or disregarded were codified and recognized by an international treaty as crimes against humanity. With the establishment of the ICC, the era of impunity of perpetrators of gender crimes has come to an end.[135] To date the ICC has issued 23 indictments, 12 contain sexual violence charges.[136]

THE LEAD UP TO THE SECURITY COUNCIL RESOLUTION ON WOMEN, PEACE AND SECURITY 1325 (2000)

There are a number of important precursors provided a prominence to the issues related women, peace and security, like UN Conventions, Treaties, Resolutions, Declarations and UN World Conferences on Women which set in motion a global movement to identified the importance of increased participation of women in conflict resolution. The process of reformulating the Organization's role in terms of security, encouraged since the year 2000, also reflected the gender issue. Women's participation in peace operations was encouraged in this time. The main instruments, which constituted the basis for the approval of Security Council's Resolution 1325 in October this year, were:

March 8, 2000	The Security Council Press Statement on International Women's Day
26 May 2000	Millennium Forum Declaration and Agenda for Action Strengthening the United Nations for the 21st Century
May 31, 2000	The Windhoek Declaration and the Namibia Plan of Action
June 10, 2000	United Nations General Assembly Special Session "Women 2000: Gender Equality, Development and Peace for the Twenty-first Century."
August 21, 2000	*Report of the Panel on United Nations Peace Operations* (the "Brahimi Report")
October 23, 2000	Arria-formula Meeting
October24-25, 2000	Security Council Open Debate on Women, Peace and Security

The Security Council Press Statement on International Women's Day

The most significant development in the lead to SCR 1325 was the Press Statement of the Security Council issued on March 8, 2000 that became the forbearer of this Resolution which emphasized "that peace is inextricably linked with equality between women and men."[137] Bangladesh's Ambassador Anwarul K. Chowdhury, the then President of the Security Council, said, "he was convinced that gender equality was an important key to peace and proposed that the Council should adopt a resolution on this issue."[138] However, he was unable to get the Council support for a resolution due to the continued strong reservations of some Members of the Council though he succeeded in issuing a Press Statement on the occasion of International Women's Day, 8 March 2000 on the behalf of Security Council.[139]

The Press Statement highlighted the importance of women's full participation in power structures and the role of women in preserving social order and as peace educators. The Statement touched upon several of the elements which included full participation of women in all efforts for the prevention and resolution of conflicts, the particular effect of armed conflict on women and girls, awareness of gender-specific human rights abuses, protection for refugee and displaced women, and the importance of a visible policy of mainstreaming a gender perspective in policies and programmes while addressing armed or other conflicts.

The Press Statement further recognized that "sustainable peace can not be achieved if the women are excluded from the process of protection, prevention, participation and promotion of peace during pre and post-armed conflict situations".[140] In addition, it acknowledged that "women can play a critical role in preserving peace, if they are given adequate space at all levels of decision-making during the peace process".[141] Moreover, the Statement also recognized that "war and conflict affect women and men, boys and girls, in different ways differently and a gender perspective has to be included in all efforts towards peace and security".[142]

Millennium Forum Declaration and Agenda for Action Strengthening the United Nations for the 21st Century

Another important development was the adoption of a *Declaration and Agenda for Action Strengthening the United Nations for the 21st Century at the United Nations the Millennium Forum in May 2000.*[143] In the Forum, Peace, Security and Disarmament was one of the major areas of concern. The Forum recognized that the cycle of violence begins with cultures that glorify violence and warrior virtues, and may be manifest in domestic violence. Rape continues to be used as a weapon of war. The Forum admitted the failures of the UN in regard to elimination or to control the nuclear weapons which are dangerous to the very existence of humanity.

The Forum urged the United Nations to establish ready police and peace-keeping forces. Sensitivity and respect for civilians, especially women and children, should be included in the training of all peace-keepers.[144]

Promoting and protecting the rights of women and girls the Forum recognized the human rights of all women and girls as an unalienable, integral and indivisible part of human rights that must be promoted and realized at all stages of the life cycle.[145] The Forum called on the United Nations, governments and civil society to recognize and assure equal opportunity and full participation of women in all aspects of society, including leadership, the economy and decision-making. In addition to this the Forum called on the United Nations to ensure that gender mainstreaming effectively brings women into leadership positions throughout the system and a gender perspective into all its programmes and policies; to provide gender training; and to strengthen its mechanisms for the protection and promotion of the human rights of women and girls.[146]

The Windhoek Declaration and the Namibia Plan of Action

The *Windhoek Declaration* and the *Namibia Plan of Action* were the other critical steps leading to the adoption of the Resolution 1325 which called for the mainstreaming of gender perspectives in multidimensional peace operations. [147] Namibia on getting the Presidency of the Security Council perused the task where its predecessor (*Anwarul K. Chowdhury*) had left. The Government of Namibia also extended its support when it co-hosted a Seminar with the United Nations (UN Department of Peace-keeping Operations (DPKO) and Office of the Special Gender Advisor (OSAGI)) in May 2000 that led to the *Windhoek Declaration and the Namibia Plan of Action.*

The Plan called for the equal inclusion of women in all aspects of peace processes; the appointment of Gender Advisors to peace operations; the mainstreaming of gender perspectives in all mandates and in planning of peace operations; the appointment of more female Special Envoys and Special Representatives to peace operations; the recruitment of more women in all UN functions;[148] the development of training programmes to sensitize troops to gender issues; and the strengthening of monitoring and accountability.[149]

The Namibia Plan of Action further urged the Secretary-General to ensure that appropriate follow-up measures were taken to implement it, in consultation with the Member-States, and that periodic progress reviews are undertaken. [150]

United Nations General Assembly Special Session "Women 2000: Gender Equality, Development and Peace for the Twenty-first Century." New York, 5-9 June 2000

Another important precursor to SCR 1325 was the *23rd Special Session of the UN General Assembly "Women 2000: Gender Equality, Development and Peace for the 21st Century"* (also known as "Beijing + 5) which was held in June 2000. [151] The Session was convened in order to review and appraise what progress had been made in implementing the Nairobi Forward-Looking Strategies and the Beijing Platform for Action from the Fourth World Conference on Women, Beijing 1995.

The Special Session adopted an *Outcome Document*,[152] which included a section on Women and Armed Conflict. The Outcome Document took note of the various achievements made in the context of women and armed conflict. It was appreciated that there was world wide recognition that women face more gender based violence than men during armed conflict situations and that numerable steps had been taken to address abuses against women, including increased attention to ending impunity for crimes against women in situations of armed conflict at national and international levels, the setting up of International Criminal Tribunals for the former Yugoslavia and Rwanda, Special Court for Sierra Leone, and the adoption of the Statute of the International Criminal Court, which provides that rape, sexual slavery, enforced prostitution, forced pregnancy, enforced sterilization and other forms of sexual violence are war crimes have been established to redress the problems for women and girls through the international criminal law process.[153]

The Document called for full participation of women at all levels of decision-making in peace processes, peace-keeping and peace building. It also addressed the need to increase the protection of girls in armed conflict situations. However, the Document noted that the armed conflict situations created a number of obstacles to the advancement of women. Apart from the gender-based violence, armed conflicts create the high levels of female headed households was the major concern of the Outcome Document.[154]

Report of the Panel on the United Nations Peace Operations (Brahimi Report)

Another important Report which recognised the importance of peace-building as integral to the success of peace-keeping operations is known as Brahimi Report.[155] The Report defines peace-building as "activities undertaken on the far side of conflict to reassemble the foundations of peace and provide the tools for building on those foundations something that is more than just the absence of war"[156]

The Report contained a comprehensive set of recommendations related to peace-keeping operations in the United Nations.[157] The Report recognized the need for equitable gender representation in the leadership of peace-keeping missions and made several recommendations emphasizing that the United Nations Personnel in the field should respect local norms, culture and practices where they are deputed. In addition, it was also urged them to treat one another with respect and dignity, with particular sensitivity towards gender and cultural differences.[158]

Gender issues (especially the roles and rights of women) in peace operations were not addressed directly but these figured prominently during its implementation. The Report was criticised by Olivera Simiæ as a "gender-blind document, failing to address gender-related issues".[159]

Arria-formula Meeting

The *'off records'* dialogues commonly known as *Arria Formula,* between INGOs (International NGOs) and the Security Council members also played a critical role in the development and passing of the Resolution 1325. Before the adoption of the Resolution, the Security Council on 23 October 2000 under the Namibian Presidency held an Arria Formula meeting on women, peace and security. This meeting gave a space to the representatives of women's NGOs from Sierra Leone, Guatemala, Somalia, Tanzania and NGO Working Group on Women, Peace and Security to share their experiences, give their expert advice and submit their recommendations on women, peace and security issues.

It was an informal process that provided an opportunity to the NGOs to have an interface with the members of the Security Council. This practice later turned out to be formal when the NGOs got a slot to speak in the Open Debates of the Security Council from 2004 onwards.

A week before adopting the Resolution, the Security Council held an *Open Session* on the topic *Women, Peace and Security* (24 October 2000). It was the first thematic session on this issue ever held by the Council. An open session allows members of all governments to speak, not just the fifteen members of the Council. In this particular case, more than 40 speakers addressed the Council. NGOs lobbied with the governments and Permanent Missions in the UN. It paid its dividend and the Speakers almost with one voice recognized that war and conflict affect women and men, boys and girls, in different ways differently and a gender perspective has to be included in all efforts towards peace and security.

Kofi Annan while addressing the Session said that "for generations, women have served as peace educators, both in their families and their societies. They have been instrumental in building bridges rather than walls."[160] Annan urged the Council to do everything within its power to protect women and girls in conflict and to give them a role in peace-building.[161]

Noeleen Heyzer, the Executive Director of the UN Development Fund for Women, added that peace processes suffer when women are not included: "[If] women are half of every community, are they therefore not half of every solution?"[162]

ADOPTION OF THE RESOLUTION

All these developments paved the way for the adoption of the SCR 1325. Ambassador Anwarul K. Chowdhury had already laid the foundation stone, as stated earlier, but it was on October 31, 2000 consequent to the Open Debate in October 2000 that the Security Council passed the Resolution unanimously. It was a watershed in the evolution of international women's rights and peace and security issues. It is a ground breaking Resolution, the first formal and legal document that mandates the parties to a conflict to respect women's rights and to support their participation in peace negotiations and post-conflict reconstruction.

This was for the first time that relationship between gender and conflict was addressed specifically. Commenting on the Resolution Cohn wrote:

> "Resolution 1325 breaks new ground because it not only recognises that women have been active in peace-building and conflict prevention; it also recognizes women's right to participate—as decision-makers at all levels—in conflict prevention, conflict resolution and peace-building processes."[163]

The Resolution builds on the concepts developed in various international standards and conventions. Although the Resolution is not legally binding on the Member-States, it sends a strong message to all governments, the UN bodies and parties to armed conflict that special efforts must be made to protect the human rights of women and girls in conflict related situations and to ensure a gender perspective in all of activities related to peace building and maintenance. The Resolution, calls upon the UN Member States to ensure full participation of women and integration of gender perspective in peace and security issues to increase the representation of women at all decision-making levels.

KEY PROVISIONS OF RESOLUTION 1325

Resolution 1325 starts with 10 preambular paragraphs referring to broad normative standards proclaimed by the international community through legal principles, human rights and humanitarian law, as well as previous UN resolutions, declarations and documents, such as the Beijing Platform for Action, the United Nations Charter, the Windhoek Declaration and the Namibia Plan of Action.

In its 18 operational paragraphs, the Resolution focuses on *three* broad themes :

A. *Participation* of Women in Decision-making and Peace Processes

B. Protection *and* Prevention *of Gender-based Violence Against Women and Girls through the Promotion of Women's Rights, Accountability and Law Enforcement*

C. *Gender Mainstreaming* in Peace-keeping Operations

To address these three themes, the Resolution identifies 18 steps to be taken by the United Nations Secretary General, the Security Council, the Member-States and all the parties to armed conflict.

A. Participation of Women in Decision Making and Peace Processes

Women constitute half of the world's population and, often, the majority in war affected societies. From a democratic perspective, it should be self evident that women's equal participation should be ensured in all nation building processes. Resolution 1325 "reaffirms the important role of women in the prevention and resolution of conflicts and in peace-building, and *stressing* the importance of their equal participation and full involvement in all efforts for the maintenance and promotion of peace and security, and the need to increase their role in decision-making with regard to conflict prevention and resolution".[164]

The first *1 to 4 Articles* of the Resolution deal with increasing women's participation in decision-making on the prevention, management and resolution of conflict: in national, regional and international institutions and in the UN system.

Article I of the Resolution "urges Member-States to ensure increased representation of women at all decision-making levels in national, regional and international institutions and mechanisms for the prevention, management, and resolution of conflict".[165] While *Article 2* encourages the Secretary-General to implement his strategic plan of action (A/49/587)[166] calling for an increase in the participation of women at decision-making levels in conflict resolution and peace processes.

Article 3 urges the Secretary-General to appoint more women as special representatives and envoys to pursue good offices on his behalf, and in this regard calls on Member States to provide candidates to the Secretary-General, for inclusion in a regularly updated centralized roster.[167]

Furthermore *Article 4,* urges the Secretary-General to use his discretion to place more women staff in the UN field missions in those areas where they are traditionally under-represented, and ensure more gender balance,especially among military observers, civilian police, human rights and humanitarian personnel.[168]

B. Protection and Prevention of Gender-based Violence Against Women and Girls through the Promotion of Women's Rights, Accountability and Law Enforcement

During armed conflict, women and girls are frequently threatened by rape, domestic violence, sexual exploitation and trafficking These situations put them at great risk of sexually transmitted diseases including HIV/AIDS. The Resolution emphasizes on the need for the *protection* of women during and after conflict. The Resolution reaffirms the need to implement fully international humanitarian and human rights law that protects the rights of women and girls during and after conflicts.[169]

The Resolution further emphasizes on the Member-States to take measures that ensure the protection of and respect for human rights of women and girls, particularly as they relate to the constitution, the electoral system, the police and the judiciary.[170]

The Resolution further calls upon all parties to armed conflict to respect fully international law applicable to the rights and protection of women and girls as civilians, in particular the obligations applicable to them under the international laws.[171]

The *prevention* of violence against women through the *promotion* of women's rights, accountability and law enforcement is another important focused area of the Resolution. It reaffirms the important role of women in the prevention and resolution of conflicts and in peace-building, and stressing the importance of their equal participation and full involvement in all efforts for the maintenance and promotion of peace and security, and the need to increase their role in decision-making with regard to conflict prevention and resolution.[172]

Gender-based crimes are often unrecognised in international tribunals. Most acts of violence against women are never investigated, and perpetrators commit their crimes safe in the knowledge that they will never face arrest, prosecution or punishment. Impunity contributes to a climate where such acts are seen as normal and acceptable rather then criminal, and where women do not seek justice because they know they will not receive it.

Resolution 1325 not only recognizes the impact of armed conflict on women and girls but also calls on all states to take responsibility for putting an end to impunity, including for those responsible for committing sexual violence and other violence against women and girls.[173] In addition, it emphasizes on the need to take measures that support local women's peace initiatives and indigenous processes for conflict resolution, and that involve women in all of the implementation mechanisms of the peace agreements.[174]

Approximately 80 per cent of the people are displaced by conflict. As noted earlier, camps for displaced people offer refuge in conflict situations. But camps can become extremely dangerous places for women. This Resolution therefore mandates all the parties to armed conflict to respect the civilian and humanitarian character of refugee camps and settlements, and to take into account the particular needs of women and girls.[175] Article 13 of the Resolution encourages all those involved in the planning for disarmament, demobilization and reintegration to consider the different needs of female and male ex-combatants and to take into account the needs of their dependants.

C. Mainstreaming of Gender Perspectives in Peace Operations

Although "gender mainstreaming" has been the official UN

policy since 1997,[176] Resolution 1325 represents the first time that gender has been mainstreamed in the armed conflict and security areas of the UN.[177]

The Resolution calls for the incorporation of gender perspective into peacekeeping operations, when negotiating and implementing peace agreements, in humanitarian activities, and in planning for disarmament, demobilization and reintegration and reconstruction efforts. It urges the Secretary-General to ensure that, where appropriate, field operations include a gender component. The mandate of SCR 1325 applies both to the United Nations itself and to its Member States.

The Resolution calls on all actors involved, when negotiating and implementing peace agreements, to adopt a gender perspective on the special needs of women and girls during repatriation and resettlement and for rehabilitation, reintegration and post-conflict reconstruction.[178] Furthermore, it also requests the Secretary-General, where appropriate, to include in his reporting to the Security Council, progress on gender mainstreaming throughout peacekeeping missions and all other aspects relating to women and girls.[179]

Requests the Secretary-General to provide to Member-States training guidelines and materials on the protection, rights and the particular needs of women, as well as on the importance of involving women in all peace-keeping and peace-building measures, invites Member-States to incorporate these elements as well as HIV/AIDS awareness training into their national training programmes for military and civilian police personnel in preparation for deployment and further requests the Secretary-General to ensure that civilian personnel of peace-keeping operations receive similar training;

To *sum up* it may be said that the international community has systematically come to recognize the role of women in fostering peace in their communities. Fifty-five years prior to the adoption of United Nations Security Council Resolution 1325 in 2000, the equal rights of men and women were confirmed in the 1945 United Nations Charter. Despite this strong initial commitment to the equality of men and women, it has taken over half a century for the United Nations to adequately address the role of women and girls in conflict and post-conflict situations. In the words of Ambassador Anarwul K. Chowdhary it is an 'energizing Resolution'.[180] Cora Weiss, a peace and gender activist, rightly sums up the spirit of the Resolution that it is not to make war safe for women, but to structure the peace in a way that there is no recurrence of war and conflict. That is why women need to be at the peace tables; women need to be involved in discussion-making and in peace keeping teams, to make a real difference in transitioning from the cult of war to cult of peace.[181]

Notes and References

1. Statement made by Security Council President, H.E Anwarul Karim Chowdhury (Bangladesh) on behalf of the Security Council on the occasion of International Women's Day (March 8, 2000), (SC/6816), New York, United Nations.
2. Anwarul Chowdhury, (2011), *The Intrinsic Role of Women in Peace and Security-Genesis and Follow-up of UNSCR 1325,* Palestine-Israel Journal, Vol. 17, No. 3, p. 2, http://www.pij.org/details.php?id=1365.
3. United Nations Security Council, (2000), *Open Debate on Women, Peace and Security*, New York, United Nations, http://www.peacewomen.org/security_Council_monitor/debate-watch/all-debates/19/open-debate-on-women-peace-and-security-october-2000, India, Nepal, Pakistan, and Bangladesh were also present in this debate.
4. Statement made by United Nations Secretary-General, Kofi A. Annan to the United Nations Security Council on October 24, 2000, http://www.peacewomen.org/security_Council_monitor/debate-watch/all-debates/19/open-debate-on-women-peace-and-security-october-2000.
5. *Ibid.*
6. The two Conferences were instrumental in compiling customary international practices that had been evolved to restrain the destructive effects of war. They concentrated on war avoidance and limitation of suffering during war, this period saw a shift toward an absolute renunciation of aggressive war. The First were:
   I—Pacific Settlement of International Disputes; II—Respect to Laws and Customs of War on Land; III-—daptation to Maritime Warfare of Principles of Geneva Convention of 1864; Declaration I—On the Launching of Projectiles and Explosives from Balloons; Declaration II—On the Use of Projectiles the Object of which is the Diffusion of Asphyxiating or Deleterious Gases; Declaration III—On the Use of Bullets (dumdums) Which Expand or Flatten Easily in the Human Body; The *Second Peace Conference attempted* to expand upon the original Hague Conference.
7. For details see : Arnold J., Toynbee, (1915), *Armenian Atrocities: The Murder of a Nation*, London, Hodder and Stoughton, p. 14.
8. Susan Brownmiller, (1975), *Against Our Will, Men, Women and Rape*, Penguin, Middlesex, p. 38.
9. Hilkka Pietila, (2007), *The Unfinished Story of Women and the United Nations*, New York, United Nations Non-Governmental Liaison Service, p. 2.
10. The League adopted an International Convention for the Suppression of the Trafficking in Women and Children, 1921 and another Convention on the Suppression of Traffic in Women of Full Age in 1933 and later on, in 1937, it also established a Committee of Experts on the Legal Status of Women.

11. Pietila, *op. cit.*, p. 4.
12. Carol Miller (1994), *The Key to Equality: Inter-war Feminists and the League of Nations*, Geneva, Women's History Review, Vol. 3, No. 2, pp. 218-45, p. 223.
13. Susan, Brownmiller (1975), *Against Our Will, Men, Women and Rape*, Penguin, Middlesex, p. 48.
14. *Ibid.*
15. Minerva Bernardino (Dominican Republic), Virginia Gildersleeve (United States), Bertha Lutz (Brazil) and Wu Yi-Fang (China).
16. Hilkka Pietila (2007), *The Unfinished Story of Women and the United Nations*, New York, United Nations Non-Governmental Liaison Service, p. 10.
17. United Nations (1995), *United Nations and the Advancement of Women 1945-95*, The United Nations Blue Book Series, Volume VI, New York, United Nations, p. 10.
18. United Nations Division on the Advancement of Women (2005), *Short History of the Commission on the Status of Women*, New York, United Nations Division on the Advancement of Women, p. 1.
19. Hilkka Pietila (2007), *The Unfinished Story of Women and the United Nations*, New York, United Nations Non-Governmental Liaison Service, p. 12.
20. United Nations Division on the Advancement of Women, *op. cit.*, p. 3.
21. United Nations, (1945), *Charter of the United Nation*, San Francisco, United Nations, Article 1.
22. *Ibid.*, p. 11.
23. *Ibid.*, p. 10.
24. ECOSOC Resolution establishing the Commission on the Status of Women. E/RES/2/11, 21 June 1946.
25. *Ibid.*
26. The Division of the Advancement of Women (DAW) served as a secretariat to the CSW but now DAW has been merged into UN Women, the new gender entity in the UN that came into being in 2010 and formally launched in February, 2011.
27. The Universal Declaration of Human Rights General Assembly Resolution 217A (III) 10 December 1948, which came into force in 1950
28. The 6 of the 30 Articles within it specifically refer to 'he', 'his' and 'himself'. None refer to the female equivalent. Consequently, males are seen as the dominant, active members of society. Additionally, Articles 23 & 25 specifically refer to 'his family'. This relates to the burgeoning "welfare states" in the West who were delivering security to their populations in 1948. Articles 23 & 25 therefore reflect dominant Western views of men as breadwinners and women as their dependents. These perceptions are culturally relative, as they are not informed by the views of any African nation; it implies that 'he', 'his' and 'himself' is white. In effect, it distinguishes the rights of women and "non-white" people as being separate issues.
29. *Geneva Convention IV: Protection of Civilian Persons in Times of War*, 12 August, 1949, Part 1, Article 18.

30. *Ibid.*, Part II, Article 27.
31. Protocols Additional to the Geneva Convention of 12 August 1949, and relating to the Protection of Victims of International Armed Conflicts (Protocol I), 8 June 1977, Article 76(1).
32. Protocol Additional to the Geneva Conventions of 12 August 1949, and relating to the Protection of Victims of International Armed Conflicts (Protocol II), 8 June 1977.
33. J. Gardam (1997), *Women and the Law of Armed Conflict: Why the Silence?*, International and Comparative Law Quarterly, Vol. 46, p. 55.
34. Adopted on 28 July 1951 by the United Nations Conference of Plenipotentiaries on the Status of Refugees and Stateless Persons convened under General Assembly resolution 429 (V) of 14 December 1950, came into force on 22 April 1954.
35. Declaration on the Protection of Women and Children in Emergency and Armed Conflict by General Assembly Resolution 3318 (XXIX) of 14 December 1974.
36. *Ibid.*, para 1.
37. *Ibid.*, para 4.
38. Declaration on the Protection of Women and Children in Emergency and Armed Conflict by General Assembly resolution 3318 (XXIX) of 14 December 1974, para 6.
39. United Nations (1995), *United Nations and the Advancement of Women 1945-95,* The United Nations Blue Book Series, Volume VI, New York, United Nations, p. 8.
40. United Nations (1995), *United Nations and the Advancement of Women 1945-95,* The United Nations Blue Book Series, Volume VI, New York, United Nations, p. 34.
41. *Ibid.*, p. 34.
42. *Ibid.*
43. Betty, A. Reardon (1998), *Gender and Global Security: A Feminist Challenge to the United Nations and Peace Research*, Journal of International Co-operation Studies, Vol. 6, No. 1, pp. 29-56.
44. *Ibid.*
45. Declaration of Mexico on the Equality of Women and Their Contribution to Development and Peace, (E/CONF.66/34), *[Adopted at the World Conference of the International Women's Year, Mexico City, Mexico, 19 June-2 July 1975].*
46. *Ibid.*
47. *Ibid.*
48. *Ibid.*
49. *Ibid.*
50. *Ibid.*
51. *Ibid.*
52. Hilkka Pietila (2007), *The Unfinished Story of Women and the United Nations,* New York, United Nations Non-Governmental Liaison Service, p. 38.
53. Convention on the Elimination of All Forms of Discrimination Against Women (CEDAW) General Assembly Resolution, 34/180 of 18 December 1979.

The CEDAW was adopted by the United Nations General Assembly in 1979. It entered into force on 3 September 1981, and as of December 2011, State parties have ratified the Convention. It consist of a Preamble and 30 Articles.

54. *Ibid.*, Article 1.
55. United Nations Committee on the Elimination of Discrimination Against Women, (1992), *Eleventh Session, General Recommendation 19 (CEDAW/C/1992/L.1/Add.15)*, New York, United Nations.
56. United Nations Committee on the Elimination of Discrimination Against Women, (1999), *Twentieth Session, General Recommendation 24 (A/54/38/Rev.1, chap. I)*, New York, United Nations.
57. United Nations Committee on the Elimination of Discrimination Against Women, *op. cit.*, Article 16.
58. United Nations Committee on the Elimination of Discrimination Against Women, (1999), *Twentieth Session, General Recommendation 24 (A/54/38/Rev.1, chap. I)*, New York, United Nations, Article 24.
59. *Ibid.*, Article 16.
60. *Ibid.*, Article 19.
61. http://www.un.org/womenwatch/daw/cedaw/reporting.htm.
62. *Ibid.*
63. United Nations Fund for Women (UNIFEM), (2006), *CEDAW and Security Council Resolution 1325: A Quick Guide*, New York, UNIFEM.
64. For details see : United Nations Fund for Women (UNIFEM), (2006), *CEDAW and Security Council Resolution 1325: A Quick Guide*, New York, UNIFEM.
65. *Report* of the World Conference of the United Nations Decade for Women: Equality, Development and Peace, held in Copenhagen from 14 to 30 July 1980, (A/CONF.94/35).
66. Hilkka Pietila, (2007), *The Unfinished Story of Women and the United Nations*, New York, United Nations Non-Governmental Liaison Service, p. 41.
67. *Op. cit.*, para 33.
68. *Ibid.*, para 76.
69. *Ibid.*, para 77.
70. *Ibid.*, para 78.
71. General Assembly Declaration on the Participation of Women in Promoting International Peace and Cooperation of 3 December 1982, (A/RES/37/63).
72. *Ibid.*
73. *Ibid.*
74. United Nations, (1995), *United Nations and the Advancement of Women 1945-95*, The United Nations Blue Book Series, Volume VI, New York, United Nations, p. 14.
75. The Nairobi Forward-looking Strategies for the Advancement of Women from the World Conference to Review and Appraise the Achievements of the United Nations Decade for Women: Equality, Development and Peace, held in Nairobi from 15 to 26 July 1985, A/Conf.116/28/Rev. 1, 1986.

76. United Nations, Report of the World Conference to Review and Appraise the Achievements of the United Nations Decade for Women: Equality, Development and Peace, held in Nairobi from 16 to 26 July 1985; including the Agenda and Nairobi Forward Looking Strategies for the Advancement of Women, (A/CONF.116/28/Rev.1), 1986, para. 41. See also Part III Peace, para. 243 (recognizing women as one of the most vulnerable groups affected by armed conflict), para. 258 (violence against women), para. 261 (the threat posed to women and children by armed conflict), para. 232 (the obstacle armed conflict poses to the advancement of women) and para. 262 (compliance with international treaties providing protection to women and children during armed conflict).
77. *Ibid.*
78. *Ibid.*
79. *Ibid.*
80. *Ibid.*
81. *Ibid.*, Paragraph 235, 236 & 237.
82. *Ibid.*, paragraph 241.
83. *Ibid.*, paragraph 244.
84. *Ibid.*, paragraph 253.
85. *Ibid.*, paragraph F.
86. *Ibid.*, paragraph I.
87. *Ibid.*, paragraph 266.
88. *Ibid.*, paragraph 267.
89. United Nations, (1992), *Report of the Secretary-General, An Agenda for Peace, Preventive Diplomacy, Peace-making and Peace-keeping*, (UN Doc. A/47/277-S/24111), New York, United Nations.
90. Peou Sorpong, (2002), *The UN, Peacekeeping and Collective Human Security: From An Agenda for Peace to the Brahimi Report, International Peace-keeping,* Special Issue on Recovering from Civil Conflict, Vol. 9, No. 2, pp. 52-54.
91. United Nations, *op. cit.*, New York, United Nations, para. 81.
92. United Nations, Vienna Declaration and Programme of Action adopted by the World Conference on Human Rights held in Vienna from 14 to 25 June 1993 (A/CONF.157/23).
93. *Ibid.*, para 18.
94. *Ibid.*, para 28.
95. Ibid., para II.B.38.
96. *Ibid.*, para II.B.43.
97. N. Reilly, (ed.), (1993), Testimonies of the Global Tribunal on Violations of Women's Human Rights at the United Nations World Conference on Human Rights, Vienna (A video of the Tribunal produced by Augusta Productions in collaboration with the Center for Women's Global Leadership).
98. United Nations, Vienna Declaration and Programme of Action adopted by the World Conference on Human Rights held in Vienna from 14 to 25 June 1993, (A/CONF.157/24), 13 October 1993.
99. *Article 1* provides the term "violence against women" means any act of gender-based violence that results in, or is likely to result in, physical,

sexual or psychological harm or suffering to women, including threats of such acts, coercion or arbitrary deprivation of liberty, whether occurring in public or in private life.

Article 2 further states,

"Violence against women shall be understood to encompass, but not be limited to, the following:

(a) Physical, sexual and psychological violence occurring in the family, including battering, sexual abuse of female children in the household, dowry-related violence, marital rape, female genital mutilation and other traditional practices harmful to women, non-spousal violence and violence related to exploitation;

(b) Physical, sexual and psychological violence occurring within the general community, including rape, sexual abuse, sexual harassment and intimidation at work, in educational institutions and elsewhere, trafficking in women and forced prostitution; and

(c) Physical, sexual and psychological violence perpetrated or condoned by the State, wherever it occurs."

100. United Nations, Vienna Declaration and Programme of Action adopted by the World Conference on Human Rights held in Vienna from 14 to 25 June 1993, (A/CONF.157/24), 13 October 1993.

101. United Nation's Commission on Human Rights (1994), *Question of Integrating the Rights of Women into the Human Rights Mechanism of the United Nations and the Elimination of Violence Against Women*, E/CN.4/ RES/1994/45), New York, United Nation's Commission on Human Rights.

102. United Nations Economic and Social Council (1994), Preliminary Report Submitted by the Special Rapporteur on Violence against Women, its Causes and Consequences, Ms. Radhika Coomaraswamy, in Accordance with the Commission on Human Rights Resolution 1994/45,(E/CN. 4/ 1995/42), New York, United Nations Economic and Social Council, para 8, 9 and 10.

103. *Ibid.*, para 13.

104. *Ibid.*

105. Radhika Coomaraswamy (1998), *Report of the Special Rapporteur on Violence Against Women, Its Causes and Consequences*, (UN Doc. E/CN.4/ 1998/54), New York, United Nations Economic and Social Council.

106. David, S. Mitchell (2005), *The Prohibition of Rape in International Humanitarian Law as a Norm of Jus Cogens: Clarifying the Doctrine*, Duke Journal of International and Comparative Law, Vol. 15, pp. 219-57.

107. Trial of Peter von Hagenbach is the first recorded international trial. Von Hagenbach was tried before a tribunal of 28 judges from the allied states of the Holy Roman Empire for having instituted a reign of terror in the town of Braisach. He was convicted of, *inter alia*, rapes committed by his troops. However, the charges against him were .that he had instituted terror without first declaring war. If he had declared war, his acts would be proper.. If the war had been declared, .the rape of women in the case of cities which had refused to surrender when surrender had been demanded would have been legal.

See K.D. Askin, *War Crimes against Women: Prosecution in International War Crimes Tribunals*, The Hague, Kluwer Law International, p. 29.

108. R. Pritchard and S. Zaide, (eds.), (1981), *The Tokyo War Crimes Trial: Complete Transcripts of the proceedings of the International Military Tribunal for the Far East*, London, Taylor and Francis, p. 10.
109. R. Gabriel, (1990), *The Culture of War: Intervention and Early Development*, Westport, CT, Greenwood Press, p. 222.
110. According to a 1996 indictment by prosecutors at the International Criminal Tribunal for the former Yugoslavia (ICTY), eight Bosnian Serb police and military officers raped and sexually assaulted fourteen Bosnian Muslim women in the town of Foca, a bucolic village in southeastern Bosnia-Herzegovina. The eight officers, all men, detained and enslaved the women in houses and apartments that they maintained as brothels for paramilitary troops. All of the women, including some girls as young as twelve years old, were subjected to "almost constant rape, sexual assault, and torture." The impact of these attacks was both psychologically and physically devastating. Specifically, *Kunarac* was charged with rape, enslavement, torture and the commitment of outrages upon personal dignity; *Kovac* was charged with rape, enslavement and the commitment of outrages upon personal dignity; and *Vukovic* was charged with torture and rape. On February 22, 2001, the ICTY's Trial Chamber announced its decision convicting Kunarac, Kovac, and Vukovic of both war crimes and crimes against humanity.
    See generally Prosecutor v. Kunarac, Judgment, Nos. IT-96-23-T & IT-96-23/1-T (ICTY, Feb. 22, 2001), *available at* http://www.un.org/icty/foca/trialc2/judgement/index.htm
111. United Nations UNwomen, (2012), *Executive Summary, Progress of the World's Women; In pursuit of Justice*, New York, UN Women, p. 6.
112. UN Special Rapporteur to the Commission on Human Rights, (1996), *Report on the Situation of Human Rights in Rwanda,* (E/CN.4/1996/68), New York, United Nations Commission on Human Rights, para 16.
113. Report of the Special Rapporteur on Violence against Women, its Causes and Consequences, Ms. Radhika Coomaraswamy, submitted in accordance with Commission Resolution 1997/ 44, U.N. Doc. E/CN.4/1998/54, 26 January (1998), at para 52.
114. Jean-Paul Akayesu was a Mayor of Taba commune in Rwanda in1994. He was charged with genocide; complicity in genocide; direct and public incitement to commit genocide; and extermination, murder, torture, rape, inhumane acts (crimes against humanity); and murder, cruel treatment and outrages upon personal dignity including rape (violations of the laws and customs of war).
115. *Ibid.*
116. Systematic Rape, Sexual Slavery and Slavery-like Practices During Armed Conflict, Update to the final report submitted by Ms. Gay J. McDougall, Special Rapporteur, U.N. Doc. E/ CN.4/Sub.2/2000/21, 6 June (2000), at para 8.
117. The Beijing Conference is regarded as a one of the largest global conferences organized by UN for women. The Conference had

approximately 17,000 participants from 189 countries, over 4,000 accredited NGOs, a host of international civil servants and about 4,000 media representatives. The NGO Forum had the largest gathering as ever participated. The total number of participants in the Beijing Conference and Huairou forum reached 50,000.

118. United Nations (1995), *Beijing Declaration and Platform for Action.* (A/CONF.177/20), New York, UN/Division for the Advancement of Women.
119. United Nations (1995), *Beijing Declaration and Platform for Action.* (A/CONF.177/20), New York, UN Division for the Advancement of Women, para, 135.
120. *Ibid.*, para 18.
121. United Nations (1995), *Beijing Declaration and Platform for Action.* (A/CONF.177/20), New York, UN Division for the Advancement of Women, para 23.
122. United Nations (1995), *Beijing Declaration and Platform for Action*, (A/CONF.177/20), New York, UN/Division for the Advancement of Women, Strategic Objective E.1.
123. Ibid., Strategic Objective E.2.
124. *Ibid.*, Strategic Objective E.3.
125. *Ibid.*, Strategic Objective E.4.
126. *Ibid.*, Strategic Objective E.5.
127. *Ibid.*, Strategic Objective E.6.
128. United Nations Economic, Social and Cultural Organisation (UNESCO), (1995), *Women's Contribution to a Culture of Peace—Expert Group Meeting Report*, Manila, United Nations Economic, Social and Cultural Organisation.
129. *Ibid.*
130. The Commission on the Status of Women, (1998), *Agreed Outcomes on Women and Armed Conflict: Report on the Forty-Second Session (2-13 March 1998)*, New York, UN Economic and Social Council.
131. The Commission on the Status of Women, (2004), *Agreed Outcomes on Women and Armed Conflict: Report on the Forty-eighth Session (1-12 March 2004)*, New York, UN Economic and Social Council.
132. United Nations Security Council Resolution on the Protection of Civilians in Armed Conflict, (S/RES/1265) adopted on 17 September 1999.
133. United Nations Security Council Resolution on the Protection of Civilians in Armed (S/RES/1296) adopted on 19 April 2000.
134. Rome Statute of the International Criminal Court, U.N. Diplomatic Conference of Plenipotentiaries on the Establishment of an International Criminal Court, July 17, 1998, UN Doc. A/CONF.183/9, *reprinted* at 37 ILM 998 (1998).

    On July 17, 1998, 120 Member-States adopted the Rome Statute, the legal basis for establishing the permanent International Criminal Court. The Rome Statute entered into force on 1 July 2002.

    7(g) Rape, sexual slavery, enforced prostitution, forced pregnancy, enforced sterilization, or any other form of sexual violence of comparable gravity;

8(xxii) Committing rape, sexual slavery, enforced prostitution, forced pregnancy, as defined in article 7, paragraph 2 (f), enforced sterilization, or any other form of sexual violence also constituting a grave breach of the Geneva Conventions;

Article 33. The application and interpretation of law pursuant to this article must be consistent with internationally recognized human rights, and be without any adverse distinction founded on grounds such as gender as defined in article 7, paragraph 3, age, race, colour, language, religion or belief, political or other opinion, national, ethnic or social origin, wealth, birth or other status.

Article 68: (1) The Court shall take appropriate measures to protect the safety, physical and psychological well-being, dignity and privacy of victims and witnesses. In so doing, the Court shall have regard to all relevant factors, including age, gender as defined in article 7, paragraph 3, and health, and the nature of the crime, in particular, but not limited to, where the crime involves sexual or gender violence or violence against children. The Prosecutor shall take such measures particularly during the investigation and prosecution of such crimes. These measures shall not be prejudicial to or inconsistent with the rights of the accused and a fair and impartial trial.

Article 36(8)(a) : The States Parties shall, in the selection of judges, take into account the need, within the membership of the Court, for:

(iii) A fair representation of female and male judges and (b) States Parties shall also take into account the need to include judges with legal expertise on specific issues, including, but not limited to, violence against women or children

135. Nicole Eva Erb (1998), *Gender-Based Crimes Under the Draft Statute for the Permanent International Criminal Court*, Human Rights Law Review, Vol. 29, pp. 401-25.

 The women's Caucus was created in February 1997 and represented approximately three hundred NGOs.

136. United Nations UNwomen (2012), *Executive Summary, Progress of the World's Women; In pursuit of Justice*, New York, UN Women, p. 6.

137. Statement made by Security Council President, H.E Anwarul Karim Chowdhury (Bangladesh), on behalf of the Security Council on the occasion of International Women's Day (March 8, 2000), (SC/6816).

138. *Ibid.*

139. *Ibid.*

140. *Ibid.*

141. *Ibid.*

142. *Ibid.*

143. The Peoples Millennium Forum Declaration and Agenda for Action Strengthening the United Nations for the 21st Century (May 2000), (A/54/959), para B.

144. *Ibid.*, para B.11.

145. *Ibid.*, para 6.

146. *Ibid.*

147. United Nations Department of Peace-keeping Operations, *Windhoek Declaration and Namibia Plan of Action on Mainstreaming a Gender Perspective in Multidimensional Peace Support Operations,* (A/55/138-S/2000/693), (May 31st, 2000), para 3.
148. *Ibid.*, para 7.
149. *Ibid.*, para 8.
150. *Ibid.*, para 10.
151. General Assembly, (2010), *Further actions and initiatives to implement the Beijing Declaration and Platform for Action, (A/S-23/10/Rev.1- A/RES/S-23/3),* New York, United Nations, para 33.
152. United Nations, Beijing + 5 Outcome Document, June 10, 2000, Report of the Ad Hoc Committee of the Whole of the Twenty-third Special Session of the General Assembly.
153. *Ibid.*
154. *Ibid.*
155. United Nations, (2000), *Report on the Panel on United Nations Peace Operations,* (A/55/305-S/2000/809), New York, United Nations, para 272.
156. *Ibid.*, p. 3.
157. *Ibid.*
158. *Ibid.*, para 96.
159. Olivera Simiæ, (2010), *Does the Presence of Women Really Matter? Towards Combating Male Sexual Violence in Peacekeeping Operations, International Peacekeeping,* Vol. 17, No. 2, pp. 188-99, p. 191.
160. http://www.peacewomen.org/security_Council_monitor/debate-watch/all-debates/19/open-debate-on-women-peace-and-security-october-2000.
161. *Ibid.*
162. http://www.peacewomen.org/assets/file/SecurityCouncilMonitor/Debates/WPS/WPS2000/Statements/unifem_wps_2000.pdf
163. Carol Cohn, (2004), *Feminist Peacemaking,* The Women's Review of Books, Vol. 21, No. 5, pp. 8-9, p. 8.
164. United Nations Security Council, (2000), *United Nations Security Council Resolution 1325 on Women, Peace and Security* (S/RES/1325), New York, United Nations, Preparatory para 6.
165. *Ibid.*, Artcle 1.
166. The main goal of the 1999 Secretary General's strategic plan of action (A/49/587) is to achieve gender equality within the United Nations by the beginning of the twenty-first century, through a gradual, phased and focused strategy based on attrition and on targeting vacancies for the promotion and recruitment of women. An important feature of the strategic plan of action is its integrated approach. The plan sets out strategies as well as specific objectives and targets, and identifies simultaneous and interrelated actions required to achieve them. Corrective or new measures envisaged in the plan relate to career development, management training and management culture change, including implementation of a new performance appraisal system, review and improvement of recruitment processes, including the application of technological innovation to increase the access of qualified women worldwide, support for women's training; the introduction of more

effective systems to deal with mobility and spousal employment and measures and procedures to prevent sexual harassment. The strategy includes planning and database development, development of a specific roster of external candidates, a Secretariat-wide network of departmental focal points, broad advertising and communication, targeted recruitment missions, and review of the processes of recruitment and promotion and involvement of the departmental focal points in those processes.

167. United Nations Security Council, (2000), *United Nations Security Council Resolution 1325 on Women, Peace and Security* (S/RES/1325), New York, United Nations, Article 3.
168. United Nations Security Council, (2000), *United Nations Security Council Resolution 1325 on Women, Peace and Security* (S/RES/1325), New York, United Nations, Article 4.
169. *Ibid.*, preparatory para 6.
170. *Ibid.*, Article 8(c).
171. *Ibid.*, Article 9.
172. *Ibid.*, preparatory para, 5.
173. *Ibid.*, Article 11.
174. *Ibid.*, Article 8 (b).
175. *Ibid.*, Article 12.
176. The 1997 ECOSOC Agreed Conclusion emphasize the need to incorporate gender perspectives into the mainstream of all areas of the United Nations' work, including macro-economic questions, operational activities for development, poverty eradication, human rights, humanitarian assistance, budgeting, disarmament, peace and security and legal affairs. The concept of gender mainstreaming was defined as "... the process of assessing the implications for women and men of any planned action, including legislation, policies or programmes, in any area and at all levels. It is a strategy for making the concerns and experiences of women as well as of men an integral part of the design, implementation, monitoring and evaluation of policies and programmes in all political, economic and societal spheres, so that women and men benefit equally, and inequality is not perpetuated. The ultimate goal of mainstreaming is to achieve gender equality." E/1997/L.30, 14 July 1997.
177. Gender mainstreaming grew out of women activists' efforts to ensure that women would be included in and benefit from the programs and projects of international development agencies. When they saw that Women in Development programs too often resulted in the addition of small, marginal projects for women, while the major development projects proceeded unchanged, they sought a new strategy that would bring women into the mainstream of development activities. By 1995, the Beijing Platform for Action (BPfA) established gender mainstreaming as a global strategy for achieving gender quality. While the BPA addresses peace and security issues, in the early years of gender mainstreaming attention was much more focused on development, and then human rights issues. Until 1325's passage, there was no concentrated effort to apply gender mainstreaming in the security realm.

178. United Nations Security Council, (2000), *United Nations Security Council Resolution 1325 on Women, Peace and Security* (S/RES/1325), New York, United Nations, Article 8(a).
179. *Ibid.*, Article 17.
180. Anwarul Chowdhury, (2011), *The Intrinsic Role of Women in Peace and Security-Genesis and Follow-up of UNSCR 1325*, Palestine-Israel Journal, Vol. 17. No. 3, p. 2, http://www.pij.org/details.php?id=1365.
181. http://www.opendemocracy.net/5050/cora-weiss/we-must-not-make-war-safe-for-women.

3

The UN Security Council Resolution on Women, Peace and Security 1325 in Operation : A Ten Year Review

The year 2010 marked the 10th anniversary of the UN Security Resolution 1325 on Women, Peace and Security. The Resolution is the first instrument of International Law which highlights the link between women's issues and armed conflict, bridging the effects of conflict on women with their active participation in peace and security policies.[1] Since its adoption, there has been an apparent shift in the international understanding regarding the multifaceted impact of armed conflict on women and girls and their significant roles in all areas related to peace and security. The Resolution spelled out roles and obligations of key actors, including UN Member-States, parties to armed conflict, and all UN entities and bodies, particularly those involved in peace and security work.[2]

A Cross-cutting Report[3] brought out by the Security Council before the 2010 October Ministerial-Level Open Debate, however, points to the fact that the implementation of the Resolution has been inconsistent and uneven at all levels. The Report demonstrates that during the past decade, the Security Council has attempted to address the Resolution in a cross-cutting way the issues facing women in conflict in its consideration of country specific situations. But its approach has not been systematic. The Council, says the Report, appears to have been considerably more successful in addressing the protection rather than the participation aspects of the Resolution. It also points that Council has lacked consistent, high-level leadership on this issue.[4] Notwithstanding this, significant steps have been taken by the Security Council and other stakeholders, the UN Entities, the Member-States and civil society organizations to change this Resolution from written words to reality by developing policies, action plans, guidelines and indicators: increasing access to gender expertise; providing training; promoting consultation with and participation of women; increasing attention to human rights, and supporting the initiatives of women's groups. These are discussed in the following pages.

A. IMPLEMENTATION BY THE UNITED NATIONS

The Security Council Resolution 1325 mandates all the United Nations bodies to take steps to ensure gender parity in all aspects of peace-keeping and post-conflict situations. As of date, however, no mechanism has been developed within the UN system which is responsible for overseeing its implementation. Nonetheless, different organs of the UN and its entities have from time to time taken a number of steps and initiatives on this Resolution. The actions of these organs and entities to implement this Resolution are as follows:

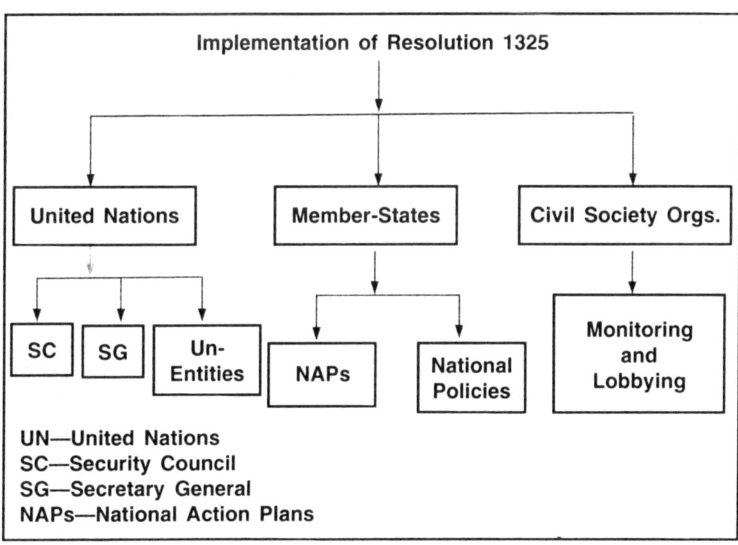

I. Implementation by the Security Council

The UN Charter gives the Security Council primary responsibility for the maintenance of international peace and security.[5] With its powers under the UN Charter, the Council plays an influential role by determining what items are placed on its agenda, what constitutes a threat to international peace and security, and how those issues are to be addressed by the UN Member-States and the UN entities. The Security Council's intervention with regard to women's rights during armed conflict helps to strengthen international humanitarian law and to promote women as stakeholders in the peace process. Since the adoption of the Resolution 1325, the Security Council has become more engaged in women and peace issues. During the last decade, the Council has established a wide normative framework under the theme of women, peace and security through its Resolutions and Presidential Statements. This framework engages the Member-States, entities of the United Nations system, civil society and other relevant actors to develop clear strategies and action plans on the thematic issue of women, peace and security.

The Security Council has incorporated gender issues in its *mandated field missions.* The Council-mandated missions include peace-keeping operations, special political missions and peace-building support missions. At present there are fourteen peace-keeping operations,[6] and one special political mission in Afghanistan.[7] The Department of Peace Keeping Operations (DPKO) administers and directs peace-keeping operations while the United Nations Department of Political Affairs (DPA) administers political missions. The increase in references to women, peace and security in the Council mandates seems to reflect the commitment of the Council to the issue. With one exception,[8] all the mission mandates established by the Council since the adoption of 1325 have included a reference to women, peace and security issues.

(a) Security Council Resolutions

An increasing number of Security Council Resolutions include direct reference to Resolution 1325 or to women, including peace-keeping mandates and situation-specific resolutions. On December 20, 2005, both the Security Council and General Assembly adopted concurrent Resolutions (S/RES/1645) and (A/RES/60/180) to establish the UN Peacebuilding Commission[9] to assist the countries in the period between the end of formal hostilities and the onset of post-conflict reconstruction and long-term peace-building.[10] The Peace-building Commission serves as a subsidiary organ of the General Assembly and the Security Council.

The Council has also adopted 19 relevant thematic resolutions since the adoption of the Resolution 1325. Three of these are specifically on women, peace and security (Resolutions 1820, 1888 and 1889). The obligations in the resolutions extend from the international to the local level, as well as from inter-governmental bodies, such as the United Nations, to national level governments. A brief reference to these Resolutions, that is, Resolutions 1820, 1888 and 1889 that are complementary to 1325 may be in order.

(i) United Nations Security Council Resolution 1820 (2008)

Resolution 1820[11] builds on Resolution 1325, but uses more forceful language in its condemnation of sexual violence against civilians in conflict and post-conflict situations. The Resolution considerably expands upon the legal dimensions addressed by Resolution 1325 in several ways. It lists the possible measures parties could take to protect women and children from sexual violence and reinforces measures ending impunity. This Resolution lays down that rape and other forms of sexual violence can constitute a war crime, a crime against humanity or a constitutive act with respect to genocide. It also reinforces the capacity components of Resolution 1325, in particular the need to develop and deliver training for peace-keeping and humanitarian personnel deployed by the UN to better prevent, recognise and respond to sexual violence and other forms of violence against civilians. While Resolution 1820 includes some mention of women's involvement in peace processes but it is more in the context of addressing sexual violence that occurred during the conflict in question.

Likewise, women's involvement in post-conflict peacebuilding efforts is addressed in the context of protection of women in the camps for internally displaced persons (IDPs), throughout demobilisation and reintegration programmes and in justice and security sector reform and addressing the long-term consequences of sexual violence in rebuilding society.

The Resolution :

- Stresses that sexual violence when used as a deliberate tactic of war or as part of a general campaign to attack civilian populations can exacerbate armed conflict and impede the restoration of peace;

- Expresses the Council's readiness to take steps to address widespread sexual violence when considering situations on its agenda;
- Demands the immediate cessation by all parties to armed conflict of all acts of sexual violence and demands that they also take immediate steps to protect women and girls from sexual violence. Measures include appropriate military discipline and command responsibility, training for troops, and vetting of security forces to take into account past conduct;
- Calls upon member-states to end impunity and comply with their obligations to prosecute persons responsible for sexual violence and human rights abuses;
- Calls upon member-states to ensure equal access for women and girls to justice;
- Requests the Secretary-General to develop and implement appropriate training programs for peace-keeping and humanitarian personnel deployed by the UN;
- Requests the Secretary-General to continue to strengthen the UN's zero tolerance policy with respect to sexual exploitation connected to UN peace-keeping missions;
- Encourages troop and police contributing countries to consider steps to heighten the awareness and responsiveness of their personnel participating in UN operations to include security that takes into account the day-to-day realities of the lives of women and girls, including through the possible deployment of a higher percentage of women as part of these missions; and
- Urges member-states, UN agencies and financial institutions to support the strengthening of the capacities of national institutions for justice and health and local civil society networks, in order to provide sustainable assistance to victims.

Resolution 1820 therefore condemns explicitly sexual violence and exploitation committed during and in the period following armed conflict. The roles of multiple actors are addressed and each is given responsibilities for its implementation.

(ii) United Nations Security Council Resolution 1888 (2009)

Another significant Resolution was passed by the Security Council in 2009, that is, SCR 1888. [12] It builds on Resolution 1820, but includes more strong and specific monitoring, reporting and accountability requirements. These include :

- Appointment of a Special Representative of Secretary General on sexual violence in armed conflicts by Secretary-General
- Deployment of a team of experts to situations of particular concern with respect to sexual violence in armed conflict
- Inclusion of specific provisions in peace-keeping mandates, as appropriate, for the protection of women and children from rape and other sexual violence, including the identification of women's protection advisers among the gender adviser and human rights protection units in peace-keeping missions.

Resolution 1888 also provided that the Council would review the mandates of the Special Representative and the team of experts within two years, that is 2011.

Other new elements included: urging states to undertake comprehensive legal and judicial reforms with a view to bringing perpetrators of sexual violence in conflict to justice and ensuring appropriate treatment of survivors of sexual violence; urging parties to a conflict to ensure that all reports of sexual violence committed by civilians or by military personnel are thoroughly investigated and civilian superiors and military commanders use their authority and power to prevent sexual violence; encouraging states to increase access to the necessary support services for victims of sexual violence; encouraging local and national leaders, including traditional and religious leaders, to play a more active role in sensitising communities on sexual violence to avoid marginalisation and stigmatisation of victims; urging Special Representative and the Emergency Relief Coordinator of the Secretary-General to work with member states to develop joint government-UN comprehensive strategies to combat sexual violence; and encouraging increased briefings and documentation on sexual violence in armed conflict to the Council.

Resolution 1888 also ordains the Secretary-General to devise urgently and preferably within three months, specific proposals on ways to ensure monitoring and reporting in a more effective and efficient way within the existing UN system on the protection of women and children from rape and other sexual violence in armed conflict and post-conflict situations.

Commenting on the Resolution, Ban Ki-Moon, the Secretary General of the United Nations, said that "with its resolution today, the Security Council is sending an unequivocal message—a call to action". On November 24, 2010, the Secretary General submitted a report[13] on the implementation of these Resolutions. He, however, regretted sexual violence continues to be committed and that "perpetrators generally operate with impunity".[14]

(iii) Security Council Resolution 1889 (2009)

A third Resolution was passed in row by the Security Council-Resolution 1889 to further strengthen the implementation and monitoring of SCR 1325.[15] It focused on the question of how to implement a key provision of Resolution 1325, i.e. the increased participation of women in negotiating and implementing peace processes and in other aspects of post-conflict peacebuilding, by identifying obstacles to their full participation and seeking to address those obstacles.

The bulk of Resolution 1889 reinforced key elements and language of Resolution 1325. The Resolution for the first time urged the Member-States, UN bodies, donors and civil society:

- to ensure women's empowerment is taken into account during postconflict needs assessment and planning, and factored into subsequent funding disbursements and programme activities;
- to take all feasible measures to ensure women and girls' equal access to education, given the vital role of education in the promotion of women's participation in post-conflict decision-making; and
- requested the Secretary-General to ensure full cooperation and coordination between the Special Representative for Children and Armed Conflict and the Special Representative for Sexual Violence in Conflict.

In particular, this Resolution calls for the establishment of global indicators to track the implementation of Resolution 1325; reiterates its mandate for increasing women's participation; reinforces call for mainstreaming gender perspectives in all decision-making processes, especially in early stages of post-conflict peacebuilding; and ending impunity by prosecuting those responsible for perpetrating Crimes of Sexual violence.

(b) United Nations Security Council's Open Debates

The Security Council's annual Open Debates on the issue of women, peace and security are another monitoring mechanism to assess the progress and gaps of Resolution 1325. In the Open Debates all the fifteen members of the Security Council along with the Member-States, representatives from the UN entities, Inter-governmental agencies and nongovernmental organization participate.

Representatives of other intergovernmental organisations such as the Inter-Parliamentary Union and the Commonwealth Secretariat have also addressed the Council during these debates. The thematic debates have also afforded non-governmental organizations a rare opportunity to address the Council in a formal meeting. This started in 2004, when Agathe Rwankuba a lawyer at the Bukavu Court of Appeals in South Kivu, DRC, and a member of the organisation Women's Network for the Protection of Human Rights and Peace *(Réseau des femmes pour la défense des droits et la paix)* was invited under the UK presidency to address the Council. The Council has also invited representatives of women's NGOs from Afghanistan, West Africa, Burundi and Timor-Leste to speak at debates in 2005 and 2006. The representatives of the NGO Working Group on Women, Peace and Security have been also invited to speak on three occasions, starting in 2007.

Apart from the gains, gaps and challenges to the implementation of Resolution 1325, future strategies and actions needed for the full implementation of the Resolution are discussed in the Open Debates. These debates address a broad range of issues including gender mainstreaming in peace-keeping operations, increasing the number of women at the highest levels of decision-making and ending impunity for those committing sexual and gender-based violence women, reconstruction & peace-building, UN system reform, role of civil society (CSO), conflict prevention, disarmament and DDR, displacement, human Rights & international humanitarian laws, implementation by Member-States, implementation by the Security Council, implementation by the UN System, and the security sector reforms.

The Secretary General's Reports on the implementation of the Resolution are presented and discussed in these debates. Till date, the Secretary-General has submitted eight *reports*[16] to the Security Council on the thematic topic of women, peace and security which include two UN System-wide Action Plans (2005-07 and 2008-09) developed on the implementation of Resolution 1325 and the 2010

Report recommending a global set of indicators in four key areas: women's participation in conflict prevention and peace-making; prevention of violence against women; protection of women's rights during and after conflict; and women's needs in relief and recovery. The use of these indicators would be a clear step forward for improving accountability and implementation of the Resolution, serving to assess where women are experiencing exclusion and threats to their security.

The Council has held *eleven debates* so far and these debates have over the years provided opportunities for a large number of countries and other stakeholders to address the Council. Unfortunately, however, the Resolution 1325 has never been taken seriously by the Member-States and the UN entities. These debates have become more of a ritual. The Open Debates are open to all the Security Council members, non members and representatives of the UN entities but it is disappointing to note that since its adoption only Australia and Liechtenstein, have participated in all the debates and the Office for the Coordination of Humanitarian Affairs (OCHA) has never addressed the Security Council specifically under this agenda item.

The South Asian countries do not seem to be taking the debates seriously. A perusal of the Open Debates (OD) reveals that they have not been participating in the debates regularly. Bangladesh is the only country which has attended the debates ten times followed by India which has attended seven times. Afghanistan and Pakistan have participated four times, Nepal three times and Sri Lanka has participated just once. It clearly establishes that these countries do not attach much importance to the Resolution. Their speeches have mostly focused on the impact of armed conflict situations on women and children and appraising the Resolution. However, a suggestion made by Bangladesh and supported by India is worth mentioning. In 2008, Open Debate the formation of a working group on women, peace and security in the Security Council was suggested to monitor the progress, gaps and challenges to the Resolution.[17]

Presidential Statements (PRSTs) of the Open Debates

Every open debate is followed by a Presidential Statement.[18] Since the adoption of the Resolution, there have been so far Ten Presidential Statements[19] and one Press Release on Women, Peace and Security. The Presidential Statements are important in the sense that these highlight specific accomplishments, while also recognizing the areas that still need improvement. They are also in the nature of reminders to the Member-States, the United Nations system and the civil society to take actions for the full implementation of the Resolution, including through the development of strategies and action plans with goals and timetables, the establishment of monitoring and accountability mechanisms at the international and national levels and ensuring full and equal participation of women in all peace processes.

II. UN Secretary-General

The UN Secretary-General, as the head of the UN Secretariat, has several responsibilities under the SCR 1325. For example, he is specifically required to appoint more women as special representatives and envoys; to implement his strategic plan to increase the participation of women at decision-making levels related to conflict resolution; to expand the role and contribution of women in the UN field-based operations; ensure, where appropriate, that UN operations include a gender component; and, provide member-states with training guidelines on the protection, rights and particular needs of women in situations of armed conflict.

Till date, the Secretary-General has submitted eight reports to the Security Council on the thematic topic of Women, Peace and Security Resolution 1325, and one on Resolution 1820.[20] Apart from Reports (eight) to the Security Council on 1325, the Secretary General had developed two *UN System Wide Action Plans (2005-07 and 2008-09)* developed on the implementation of Resolution 1325.

(a) Secretary-General's System Wide Action Plan (2005-07) and Updated Action Plan (2008-09)

The Secretary General's System Wide Action Plan (SWAP) is an instrument to assess the progress made at the UN System level. The SWAP *(2005-07)* and *Updated Action Plan (2008-09)* provide a holistic and coherent framework for the implementation of the Resolution at the UN level.

The attempt to create a System-wide Action Plan has proven to be very challenging due the lack of leadership and coordination within the UN, and also because of the scale of the UN system. Before the formulation of SWAP, an Inter-Agency Action Plan served as an international document to map the current and future activities of each UN entity in regard to their progress made towards the implementation of Resolution 1325. But it was not updated regularly and did not include any ongoing assessment of effectiveness of the activities underway and completed. The UN SWAP is a first attempt to develop an integrated and coherent approach to promote the issues of women, peace and security and mainstream a gender perspective into the UN programmes and policies dealing with women, peace and security at the highest level.

It was in 2004 that the Secretary-General was asked to submit an action plan for the UN System and in October 2005, the Secretary General presented the UN System-wide Action Plan (SWAP) to the Council in his Report (S/2005/636). The Action Plan was formulated by Inter-Agency Task Force on Women, Peace and Security, under the leadership of Office of the Special Adviser Gender Issues and Advancement of Women (OSAGI). The Plan was formulated in consultations with the UN bodies, Member-States as well as the civil society.[21]

The Plan covered all the major areas of concerns reflected in the mandates of Resolution 1325, all the relevant Presidential Statements[22] on the Resolution 1325, the report of the High-level Panel on Threats, Challenges and Change (A/59/565) and the report of the Secretary-General, "In larger freedom: towards development, security and human rights for all" (A/59/2005) and commitments made by the world leaders in the 2005 World Summit Outcome (GA.R.60/I) to the implementation of the Resolution 1325 effectively.

The main purpose of the System Wide Action Plan (2005-07) was to provide a framework for United Nations entities to:

(a) Formulate concrete strategies, actions and programmes, in a consistent and effective manner, to advance the role of women in peace and security areas;
(b) Ensure more efficient support to Member-States and other actors in national and regional level implementation of Resolution 1325;
(c) Strengthen the commitment and accountability of the United Nations system at the highest levels; and
(d) Enhance inter-agency cooperation.[23]

The SWAP covered all the areas related to the full implementation of the Resolution 1325. And it directed the UN entities to identify those objectives that fall within their respective mandates and proposed strategies and actions for their fulfillment under each are of action of the SWAP. It also indicated the expected outcomes related to the SWAP within the specific time. The action plan also tried to avoid the overlapping of actions and strategies running in the UN entities for women, peace and security issues.

The Plan had been divided into 12 areas of actions, each area further divided into sub-area of actions. The 12 areas of actions were : Conflict prevention and early warning, peace-making and peace-building; Peace-keeping operations, humanitarian response; Post-conflict reconstruction and rehabilitation; Disarmament, demobilization and reintegration; Preventing and responding to gender-based violence in armed conflict; Preventing and responding to sexual exploitation and abuse by United Nations staff, related personnel and United Nations partners; Gender balance, coordination and partnership, monitoring and reporting, financial resources.

The Action Plan (2005-07) was a time bound plan. To assess the progress and institutional gaps, the Security Council requested the Secretary-General to review the SWAP. The review period was divided into two phases. The first implementation review covered the period from November 1, 2005 to June 30, 2006 and the second phase covered the period from July 1, 2006 to July 1, 2007.

The reviews were conducted by the OSAGI and the main focus was on:

- Achievements in the implementation of the Action Plan under the major operational areas of action, including examples of good practices
- Gaps and challenges in an institutional and organizational capacity to implement the Action Plan, including lessons learned
- Recommendations for future action to address the challenges identified and accelerate the implementation of Resolution 1325.[24]

The same methodology was applied in both the reviews. A questionnaire was developed that was sent to all 39 UN[25] entities. In the first review only 29 UN entities responded and in the second review 30 entities responded. Both the reviews of the Action Plan revealed that the gender perspective had been incorporated by the UN entities in their mandates and work. A number of entities developed gender action plan, organized consultations and capacity-building programmes on women and peace issues for their staff, military personnel and civil society organizations working in conflict areas. Even then the reviews revealed a number of challenges for effective implementation of the Resolution. These challenges include issues like incoherence, inadequate funding of gender-related projects, fragmentation and insufficient institutional capacity for oversight and accountability for system performance as well as low capacity for gender mainstreaming and unavailability of sex disaggregated data. Lack of political will to give priority to women's issues was another major obstacle in the way of implementation of the Resolution.

National Governments have the primary responsibility for implementing the Resolution. The national mechanisms and machineries for the advancement of women need to be strengthened to ensure women's active participation in public policy formulation on matters of war and peace Furthermore, the active support and involvement of a broad and diverse civil society is essential for the implementation and monitoring of the Resolution. The absence of effective links between the Action Plan and national implementation efforts remains a serious challenge.

The major weakness of the Action Plan, however, was that it did not establish any tool for monitoring, evaluation and accountability. Furthermore, there was no system-wide strategy. The review reflected just a compilation of ongoing activities by the United Nations entities or in those areas of action where expertise and resources were available. In addition, it did not provide a link between the actions reported and their impact on the lives of women in conflict and post- conflict situations.

Keeping in view all these weaknesses and challenges, the Security Council asked the Secretary-General to update, monitor and review the implementation and integration of the Action Plan on an annual basis and report it to the Council. The updated System-wide Action Plan for 2008-09 based on the Resolution and all subsequent Presidential Statements on women, peace and security[26] was developed in a results-based framework and was consolidated into only five thematic areas rather than 12 areas of actions contained in the 2005-07 Action Plan. The five thematic areas are: prevention; participation; protection; relief and recovery; and normative.

The goals of the updated Action Plan in the five thematic areas are as follows:

(a) *Prevention*: Mainstream a gender perspective into all conflict prevention activities and strategies, develop effective gender-sensitive early warning mechanisms and institutions, and strengthen efforts to prevent violence against women, including various forms of gender-based violence;

(b) *Participation*: Promote and support women's active and meaningful participation in all peace processes as well as their representation in formal and informal decision-making at all levels; improve partnership and networking with local and international women's rights groups and organizations; recruit and appoint women to senior positions in the United Nations, including Special Representatives of the Secretary-General, and in peace-keeping forces, including military, police and civilian personnel;

(c) *Protection*: Strengthen and amplify efforts to secure the safety, physical or mental health, well-being, economic security and/or dignity of women and girls; promote and safeguard human rights of women and mainstream a gender perspective into the legal and institutional reforms;

(d) *Relief and recovery*: Promote women's equal access to aid distribution mechanisms and services, including those dealing with the specific needs of women and girls in all relief recovery efforts; and

(e) *Normative*: Develop policy frameworks, ensure effective coordination and awareness-raising to advance the implementation of Resolution 1325.[27]

In response to the Security Council Resolution 1889 (2009), the UN Secretary-General Ban Ki-moon submitted on 22 April 2010 to the Council a set of *26 indicators*[28] for use at the global level to track implementation of 1325. The indicators were developed by 14 UN entities under the leadership of the Office of the Special Adviser on Gender Issues in close consultation with the Member States and women's groups. The UN Women are assigned the technical lead role. These *26 indicators* are classified into 4 key areas : Prevention, Participation, Protection, and Relief and Recovery. These areas reflect the 2008-09 UN System-wide Action Plan.

1. *Prevention*: Reduction in conflict and all forms of structural and physical violence against women, particularly sexual and gender-based violence;
2. *Participation*: Inclusion of women and women's interests in decision-making processes related to the prevention, management and resolution of conflicts;

3. *Protection*: Women's safety, physical and mental health and economic security are assured and their human rights respected; and
4. *Relief and Recovery*: Women's specific needs are met in conflict and post-conflict situations.

The goal of this process is to see action taken and positive results for women in conflict. The United Nations has described Indicators as "signposts of change along the path to development" that can help to understand the actual implementation. They indicate trends and allow tracking of progresses towards intended results or targets.

(b) UNiTE to End Violence against Women Campaign

Initiated in 2008, Secretary-General Ban Ki-Moon's *UNiTE to End Violence against Women campaign* brings together a host of UN agencies and offices to galvanize action across the UN system to prevent and punish violence against women.[29] The campaign is covering the period from 2008 to 2015. The campaign is also actively involve men and boys, recognizing the fundamental role they play in preventing and eradicating violence against women and girls.

The campaign focuses on three main aspects to coordinate action:

(a) *Global advocacy*, with all the United Nations agencies and the Trust Funds working together with the high-level authorities, political leaders, civil society groups and public opinion leaders.

(b) *United Nations leadership by its institutional example*, and strengthening the role of the United Nations System in active commitment to promote prevention and elimination of violence against women and girls at the national, regional and world level. The promotion of coexistence values, responsiveness and mobilization of resources to implement policies in developing countries, the promotion of laws and programmes, will also focus on encouraging greater emphasis on prevention.

(c) *Strengthening effective actions and alliances nationally, regionally and internationally*, including spearheading regional components of the campaign linked to national and local initiatives.

The campaign focuses action on achieving *five overall outcomes*:

(1) National laws are in place and enforced to address and punish all forms of violence against women and girls in line with international human rights standards.
(2) National plans of action are adopted that are multi-sectoral and adequately resourced, with implementation underway.
(3) Data collection and analysis systems are institutionalized and periodic surveys are undertaken on prevalence of various forms of violence against women and girls.
(4) National and/or local campaigns are launched and social mobilization engages a diverse range of civil society actors in preventing violence and supporting abused women and girls.
(5) Sexual violence in conflict situations is systematically addressed in all peace and security policy and funding frameworks and mechanisms for protection and prevention of systematic rape are implemented.[30]

The Secretary-General appointed Ms. Margot Wallstrom (Sweden) as his first ever Special Representative on Sexual Violence in Conflict in 2010 and *Special Representative of the Secretary-General for Children and Armed Conflict in 2006.* There is also a Security Council working group on children and armed conflict that reviews reports generated by the monitoring and reporting mechanism.

(c) Zero Tolerance Policy on Sexual Exploitation and Abuse (SEA) by the personnel in United Nations Peace-keeping Missions

Ironically, a large number of cases of sexual exploitation and abuse by the peace-keeping personnel during Peace-keeping Missions have been reported. Earlier the Conduct and Discipline Teams (CDT) were established in all peace-keeping missions to deal with such cases of sexual exploitation and abuse (SEA) by the UN and related personnel reported in the late 1990s and early 2000s. However, the Zero Tolerance Policy on Sexual Exploitation and Abuse framed by the Secretary-General in 2003 [31] set the standards of behavior for all UN personnel during the United Nations Peace-keeping Missions.

The number of allegations of SEA against DPKO/DFS personnel, as reported to OIOS, increased to 112 in 2009, compared with 83 in 2008.[32] Most of this increase is attributed to MONUC in DRC with 59 allegations in 2009 compared to 40 in 2008; this increase may be partly due to better reporting as a result of three CDT sub-offices being opened in eastern Congo, and by an increase in troop numbers.

According to the UN statistics, the UN Stabilization Mission in Haiti (MINUSTAH) and the UN Mission in the Sudan (UNMIS) also reported increased number of allegations of SEA in 2009 as compared to 2008 while the UN Mission in Liberia (UNMIL) reported an overall increase in the allegations but a decrease in the number involving non-consensual sex. The UN Operation in Côte d'Ivoire (UNOCI) reported a decrease; few allegations (1-3 in each country) were reported in 2009 by the BINUB in Burundi, the UN Mission in Chad (MINURCAT), the UN Mission in Darfur (UNAMID) the UN Mission in Timor Leste (UNMIT) and the UN Mission in Lebanon (UNIFIL) reported none.[33] The UN Mission in Sierra Leone (UNIPSIL) also reported that there are currently few allegations of SEA by peace-keepers. An issue of great concern is that 46 per cent of the allegations of SEA by peace-keepers in 2009 involved minors.

III. Implementation by UN Entities

(a) Department of Political Affairs (DPA)

Within the UN Secretariat, the Department of Political Affairs (DPA) is responsible for some of the provisions underlined in Resolution 1325. The mandate of the Department of Political Affairs covers four areas of peace and security work such as conflict prevention and early warning, peace-making, peace-building, and governance. The Department works in the Secretariat to produce reports, and offer political advice to the Secretary-General and the Security Council on thematic and country-specific situations.

The Department of Political Affairs is responsible in the context of peace-keeping to:

- Increase the number of women appointed as Special Representatives, Representatives and Envoys and other senior-level positions in UN field operations,
- Provide training guidelines on women's rights and women's involvement in peace-building processes to Member-States
- Increase the number of women in decision-making at all levels,
- Integrate a gender perspective and women's rights approach into all Security Council missions to the field, and

- Exclude amnesty provisions for sexual and other violent crimes against women and girls from peace agreements and national legislation

The Department supports national efforts, the United Nations entities, within their respective mandates to achieve the goals set in Resolution 1325. The Department in its operational support to the peace processes, developed a guidance note for mediator teams on the role and participation of women in peace processes and peace agreements. It is included in the United Nations Peace-maker Databank.[34] The DPA does not have a Senior gender adviser at the headquarter because of budgetary constraints and formalities.[35]

(b) Department of Peace-keeping Operations (DPKO)

The DPKO is the primary UN body responsible for peace-keeping operations. It plays an important role in ensuring that the UN personnel and those from contributing states act appropriately in conflict zones, and also provides training and research in relation to conflict issues.[36] This Department was created in 1992. Till date, the peace-keeping missions were operated by the United Nations Office of Special Political Affairs. The training of military and civilian police personnel deployed as part of the UN Missions is a key element of Resolution 1325. Gender mainstreaming became an integral part of DPKO in 2000 when the DPKO's Lessons Learned Unit held a seminar on the topic of "Mainstreaming a Gender Perspective in Multidimensional Peace Support Operations" in Windhoek, Namibia.[37] The seminar adopted the Windhoek Declaration and accompanying Namibia Plan of Action. The Namibia Plan of Action, discusses at length areas of the peace-keeping process in which gender mainstreaming is needed and provides guidance on how to accomplish this mainstreaming.

The Windhoek Declaration and Namibia Action Plan as discussed earlier are the major precursor in the adoption of SCR 1325. It is clear that the Namibia Plan of Action is closely aligned with the goals of Resolution 1325 that seeks the UN to ensure that a gender perspective is mainstreamed into all peace-keeping operations. This includes specialized training for all peace-keeping personnel on the protection, special needs and human rights of women and girls in conflict situations and the establishment of effective institutional arrangements to guarantee their protection, especially against gender-based violence. This responsibility also includes ensuring full and effective participation of women in peace negotiations and agreements, as well as increased representation of women at all decision-making levels. SCR 1325 also specifically calls for the expanded role and contribution of women in the United Nations field-based operations, especially among military observers.[38]

The real work to include gender perspective in peace-keeping mandates started after submission of the Report of the Secretary-General on Women and Peace and Security (S/2002/1154) and (S/2004/814) on the Resolution 1325.[39] The first report outlined the way women were affected by conflict and post conflict situations, but did it not discuss how the UN was reacting to these effects. The second Report of the Secretary General on Women, Peace, and Security in October of 2004 specified clearly how the Resolution 1325 had been and should be implemented in peace-keeping operations and also developed a system by which the UN and others could evaluate peace-keeping operations. The report classifies peace-keeping missions into eleven areas of operation:

1. Conflict Prevention and Early-warning,
2. Peace Process and Negotiations,
3. Peace-keeping Operations,
4. Humanitarian Response,
5. Post-Conflict Reconstruction,
6. Disarmament, Demobilization, and Reintegration,
7. Preventing and Responding to Gender-based Violence in Armed Conflict,
8. Gender Balance in Recruitment,
9. Preventing and Responding to Sexual Violence by UN Personnel,
10. Coordination, and
11. Monitoring and Reporting.[40]

The DPKO has made some positive strides towards the incorporation of gender perspectives in peace-keeping operations. In 2003, it developed gender awareness training material for use in pre-deployment and induction training for military and civilian police personnel. In the same year, the DPKO issued directives for disciplinary matters for uniformed and civilian personnel serving in United Nations peace-keeping operations that cover several forms of misconduct, such as sexual exploitation and sexual abuse and sexual harassment. A "Gender Resource Package for Peace-keeping Operations," on gender issues was produced by the DPKO in 2004 which provides guidance on gender issues in various functional areas covered by multidimensional peace-keeping operations to the peace-keeping personnel. In June 2004, the DPKO and the UNAIDS undertook a joint mission in Haiti to establish an HIV/AIDS programme before the arrival of the main peace-keeping contingents, setting an important precedent for future operations.

The DPKO Policy Directive: Gender Equality in UN Peace-keeping Operations *was formally adopted by DPKO in 2006.41 Furthermore, in December 2006, the Department of Peace-keeping Operations launched the Gender Community of Practice, which seeks to facilitate sharing good practices and lessons learned in peacekeeping.*

In 2009, the Department of Peace-keeping Operations undertook monitoring visits to Timor-Leste, Darfur (the Sudan), Chad, and the Democratic Republic of the Congo to assess the implementation of its Policy Directive on Gender Equality in the United Nations Peace-keeping Operations and to support the development of mission wide action plan for implementation of Resolution 1325.

There are currently five female heads[42] and four female Deputy Special Representatives of peace keeping missions.[43] including integrated missions. They provide technical guidance to the heads of mission on gender mainstreaming to increase women's participation in the implementation of the mandate of the operation. Five traditional missions have a gender focal point, a staff member who has the gender portfolio in addition to other tasks.[44] The Department of Peace-keeping Operations has also developed guidelines to ensure that gender advisers are serving as effective catalysts for gender mainstreaming. In addition, there are two all-female formed police units in the UN Peace-keeping operations. It had all-female police contingent in Liberia (from India) and Haiti (from Bangladesh). In 2007, the first all-female UN Peace-keeping force was deployed by the Indian Government. They sent 103 women police officers to Liberia.[45] According to early assessments, their presence helped to get Liberian women to register complaints and more women came to see the police as a potential source for employment.

The Secretary-General has noted in his reporting on Liberia that this deployment has positively contributed to a three-fold increase in the number of applications from women to join the Liberian National Police.[46]

The UN Department of Field Support works with member-states, relevant UN offices, the Integrated Mission Training Centres and deployed trainers to ensure that UN military and civilian personnel have the knowledge and skills to meet the evolving challenges of Peace-keeping operations in accordance with the UN principles and guidelines.[47] The Department of Peace-keeping Operations established conduct and discipline teams in the Department headquarters and in eight peace operations. Furthermore, the Department of Peace-keeping Operations launched the Gender Community of Practice under the Best Practices Section of DPKO, which seeks to facilitate sharing good practices and lessons learned in peace-keeping.[48]

The Special Committee on Peace-keeping Operations has increasingly paid attention to women peace and security issues, called for the full implementation of Resolution 1325, underlined the gravity of all acts of sexual violence, and stressed the importance of addressing the needs of all victims of such acts.[49] The United Nations Mine Action Service (UNMAS)[50] of the Department of Peace-keeping Operations has also developed gender guidelines for mine action programmes in 2004 and reviewed and updated them in 2010.[51]

The United Nations has in recent years strengthened its commitment to increasing the deployment of women peace-keepers and the mainstreaming of gender perspectives in all areas of UN peace-keeping operations, as exemplified and prescribed in the four UN Security Council Resolutions on women, peace and security. The challenge to make peace-keeping more gender balanced is formidable. As of July 2008, 82 out of 2,227 U.N. military observers were women. Further, out of 70,525 deployed troops, 1982 were women. In 2010, women comprised 3.2 per cent of total military personnel deployed to peace-keeping.[52] According to the Department of Peace-keeping Operations, the total number of United Nations field mission international civilian staff at the Professional level is 2,939, out of which 29.5 per cent are women.[53]

(c) The Commission on the Status of Women (CSW)

The United Nations Commission on the Status of Women (CSW) was set-up in 1946 but issue like impact of conflict on women and role of women in peace process was never on its agenda as a priority issue. It was only in 1998 when the Commission addressed this issue at the Forty Second Session followed by Forty Eight Session (2004) and the Twenty Third UN Special Session of the General Assembly in 2000.

(d) Office of the United Nations High Commissioner for Refugees (UNHCR) and Office of the High Commissioner for Human Rights (OHCHR)

The Office of the UNHCR was established in December 1950

by the General Assembly. The office is mandated to lead and co-ordinate international action to protect refugees and resolve refugee problems worldwide.

The UNHCR estimates that women and children make up between 75 and 80 per cent of war refugees and displaced persons. The challenge is not only to protect these civilians, but also to take into consideration the specific protection needs of women and children. The UNHCR has conducted gender training in the context of the implementation gender and diversity mainstreaming strategy in more than 100 countries.[54] In 2006, the OHCHR Women's Human Rights and Gender Unit (WRGU) was established, with the priority to develop a gender sensitive administration of justice.[55] The OHCHR supports the implementation of SCR 1325 both within the UN system and nationally. The OHCHR continues to provide training to military and police personnel deployed or to be deployed to peace-keeping operations on gender issues, women's rights and trafficking.[56]

(e) The United Nations Entity for Gender Equality and the Empowerment of Women (UN Women)

While all the UN entities are responsible for integrating the provisions of SCR 1325 in their activities, the United Nations Entity for Gender Equality and the Empowerment of Women (UN Women)[57] is playing a lead role in the implementation of the Resolution. The UN Women has been created to consolidate the important work of four previously distinct parts of the UN system: United Nations Development Fund for Women (UNIFEM); the Office of the Special Adviser on Gender Issues (OSAGI); the Division of the Advancement of Women (DAW); and the United Nations International Research and Training Institute for the Advancement of Women (INSTRAW).[58]

This entity is intended to accelerate women's rights, their empowerment and gender equality internationally. The entity's broad mandate is contained in the resolution adopted by the General Assembly. The entity will be guided by the Beijing Platform for Action, adopted at the Fourth World Conference on Women in 1995, the Outcome Document of the 23rd special session of the General Assembly and other applicable United Nations instruments, standards and resolutions.[59]

The core paragraph establishing the agency's normative and operational mandates is as follows:

"Based on the principle of universality, the Entity shall provide, through its normative support functions and operational activities, guidance and technical support to all Member-States, across all levels of development and in all regions, at their request, on gender equality, the empowerment and rights of women and gender mainstreaming."[60]

To support and spread knowledge about the women, peace and security agenda, especially SCR-1325 as a tool for enhancing women's participation and decision-making in conflict prevention and post-conflict situations is one of the goals of the UN Women. It is thus a key actor in promoting the role of women in peace-making, peace-keeping and peacebuilding efforts, as well as advocating for the active participation of women at all levels of decision-making.

The UN Women works with other UN entities and relevant actors to ensure that all parties to negotiations understand why and how the integration of gender perspectives in peace processes can contribute to sustainable peace. Some examples of the UN Women's contributions include:

(1) supporting women's involvement in peace negotiations, such as recently in mediation efforts to end conflicts in *Uganda*, *Sudan*, and the *Democratic Republic of Congo*;
(2) supporting initiatives aimed at strengthening the presence and capacity of female officers in peace operations, such as in *Afghanistan*;
(3) strengthening the development of gender-sensitive early warning strategies to prevent the outbreak of conflict in *Colombia* and the *Solomon Islands*; and
(4) advocating for women's inclusion in the design, implementation and conduct of post-conflict elections in *Burundi*.

Before the four entities were merged to form UN Women, each one of them in their own way addressed the agenda of women and peace. Hereunder are some of their efforts and initiatives.

(i) Office of the Special Adviser on Gender Issues and Advancement of Women (OSAGI)

Established in 1997, the OSAGI's (now UN Women) main objective was to promote and strengthen the effective implementation of the UN Millennium Declaration and the Beijing Platform for Action and its subsequent outcome documents.[61] As part of its mandate, the OSAGI also worked on implementation of UNSC Resolution 1325 in the UN system.

OSAGI had played a key role in monitoring activities of the United Nations system on women, peace and security issues. The Office of the Special Adviser was the secretariat of the Inter-Agency Network on Women and Gender Equality and had played a critical role in liaising with the Member-States, civil society and other actors. It chaired as mentioned earlier the Inter-Agency Task Force on Women and Peace and Security, preparing the annual report of the Secretary-General to the Security Council on the basis of inputs provided by the United Nations entities, and provided advice to the United Nations senior managers on issues related to women and peace and security. On the whole, the Special Adviser to the Secretary-General was a strong advocate for the implementation SCR 1325 both within the United Nations system and in the national and international forums.

(ii) United Nations Division for the Advancement of Women (DAW)

As part of the Department of Economic and Social Affairs, the DAW[62] worked closely with the Governments, its partners in the United Nations system and civil society in supporting gender mainstreaming in peace and security. The Division provided substantive services to the Commission on the Status of Women (CSW) and to the Committee on the Elimination of Discrimination against Women (CEDAW) in the area of peace and security .This work focused on research and analysis, the publication of materials, and providing substantive support for inter-governmental conferences and review conferences related to gender equality at the UN, including the world conferences on women and the UN Commission on the Status of Women.

The DAW and OSAGI prepared an updated version of the Inventory of the United Nations Resources on Women, Peace and Security.

(iii) United Nations Development Fund for Women (UNIFEM)

UNIFEM[63] now a part of the UN Women has been most active among other organizations on SCR 1325. In 2002 UNIFEM commissioned a study by independent experts: "Women, War, Peace, The Independent Expert's Assessment on the Impact of Armed Conflict on Women and Women's Role in Peace-building." To increase access to information specifically on women, peace and security, UNIFEM had created a web portal[64] which acts as a centralized repository of information from a wide variety of sources, with links to reports and data from the United Nations system, and also from experts, academics, NGOs and media sources. The aim of portal was to track progress on the implementation of Security Council Resolution 1325, and to encourage researchers, policy-makers, analysts and NGOs to routinely include, seek and contribute more information and analysis on women, war and peace.[65]

Active in the field, the UNIFEM provided a Gender Advisor to the office of the Special Envoy of the UN Secretary-General for the peace talks in northern Uganda, in order to raise awareness about women's issues and ensure that they were effectively addressed during the peace process. In Darfur, UNIFEM supported a Gender Expert and Support Team (GEST) to participate in the Abuja Inter-Sudanese Peace Talks in 2006. As a result, a substantial portion of women's priorities were integrated into the Darfur Peace Agreement, including provisions on wealth-sharing and land rights, physical security, women's participation in the DDR process, and a gender-responsive reconciliation commission.[66]

UNIFEM collaborated with DPKO and on behalf of the UN Action against Sexual Violence in Conflict developed an analytical inventory of best practices by peace-keepers to prevent and respond to conflict-related sexual and gender-based violence. This inventory compiled innovative solutions by the UN missions, including firewood patrols, community liaison initiatives, and joint protection teams.

UNIFEM had also hosted conferences and other discussions among stakeholders, to help strengthen the understanding of the appropriate role of peace-keepers in the protection of women from sexual violence, and to develop good practices. It hosted a three-day conference in 2008 titled Women Targeted or Affected by Armed Conflict: What Role for Military Peace-keepers? which focused on current peace-keeping practices in the prevention of widespread and systematic sexual violence in conflict and post-conflict contexts. It did a review of 832 early warning indicators compiled by the Center for Strategic and International Studies in 2008 that revealed that only 11 made a reference to gender, and that only one indicator monitored women's human rights violations.[67]

(iv) International Research and Training Institute for the Advancement of Women (INSTRAW)

The INSTRAW was established in 1976 with the objective to

promote gender equality and women's advancement worldwide through research, training and the collection and dissemination of information. INSTRAW has produced a conceptual and policy implications paper on gender in conflict and conflict prevention which describes a framework for analysis of gender perspectives in peace and security issues. It also developed and posted on its website a special collection of information resources on gender aspects of conflict and peace.[68]

The INSTRAW released "A Guide to Policy and Planning on Women, Peace and Security" in 2007 that provides helpful information for the development of action plans.[69] It also organized two virtual dialogues entitled "Filling the gaps: a virtual discussion on gender, peace and security research on women and peace and security" and "Planning for action: good practices on implementing Resolution 1325 at the national level" in 2008 to assess current debates in gender, peace and security research, exchange information, identify research gaps and build a platform for further collaboration. The dialogues highlighted existing efforts to implement Resolution 1325 and strengthened awareness about the good practices in the preparation of national action plans. In addition, The Gender and Security Sector Reform Toolkit, developed by INSTRAW, helped to multiple stakeholders. INSTRAW established a web section on security sector reform and coordinated a global virtual network for practitioners, academia and the United Nations agencies with over 150 members worldwide

Furthermore, in August 2008, INSTRAW and the Office of the Gender Adviser of the United Nations Mission in Liberia, with the support of UNFPA and UNDP country offices, established an inter-agency team to support the Ministry of Gender and Development during preparation of the national action plan in Liberia.

IV. Others

(a) Peace-building Commission (PBC)

With the end of the cold war, the United Nations shifted its focus from peace-keeping and monitoring ceasefires to the development of means for sustainable peace. Since then the United Nations has been engaged in reconstructing societies, political affairs, humanitarian relief, human rights, and legal and judicial affairs in the war trodden societies through the Peace-building Commission (PBC). The PBC is an inter-governmental advisory body that was created out of the 2005 UN World Summit Outcome Document (60/1) and by concurrent Resolutions of the Security Council (S/RES/1645) and the General Assembly (A/RES/60/180). The Commission is envisioned as a dedicated institutional mechanism to assist countries in the period between the end of formal hostilities and the onset of post-conflict reconstruction and long term peacebuilding.[70]

For effective functioning of PBC, a Peacebuilding Support Office (PBSO) and a Peacebuilding Fund (PBF) have been established as components of the Commission's institutional infrastructure. Though the Commission is not established only to implement the SCR 1325, the provisions of Resolution 1325 have been well integrated into the country-specific work of the Commission, particularly in the strategic peacebuilding frameworks for Burundi and Sierra Leone.[71]

(b) Inter-Agency Task Force on Women, Peace and Security (IANWGE)

A Task Force on Women, Peace and Security was set up in 2001 under the Inter-Agency Network on Women and Gender Equality[72] to follow up on the implementation of SCR1325. The Task Force has been serving as a focal point for Inter- Agency consultations and coordinating Members States, inter- governmental bodies and non-governmental organizations on the implementation of the Resolution. The Task Force also works on the Critical Area of Concern of the Beijing Platform for Action- Women and Armed Conflict and other relevant UN mandates on women, peace and security.[73] It comprises of 22 UN entities and eight observers[74].The Task Force was headed by the Special Adviser on Gender Issues and Advancement of Women (OSAGI) till the time it was not merged into the new gender entity, that is UN Women. The Task Force, however, is the only consultative technical body with no decision-making authority.

(c) International Criminal Court (ICC)

In the decade under review, an historic achievement has been in the creation of the *International Criminal Court (ICC)*. The Rome Statute of the ICC provides rape, sexual slavery, enforced prostitution, forced pregnancy, enforced sterilization, or any other form of sexual violence of comparable gravity as war crimes and crimes against humanity. When domestic legal systems of a country are incapable or otherwise unlikely to prosecute the crimes, the Security Council refers the cases to the International Criminal Court.

There are currently cases of seven countries before the ICC: the Democratic Republic of the Congo; Uganda; Darfur, Sudan; the Republic of Kenya; the Libyan Arab Jamahiriya and the Republic of Côte d'Ivoire.[75] The leaders of the Lord's Resistance Army (LRA) (Joseph Kony, Vincent Otti, Okot Odhiambo and Dominic Ongwen) and militia leaders of Democratic Republic of the Congo (DRC) (Germain Katanga and Mathieu Ngudjolo Chui) are charged with the allegation of sexual enslavement, attempted sexual enslavement, rape and inducing of rape constituting war crimes and crimes against humanity.[76]

(d) UN Action on Sexual Violence in Conflict-"Stop Rape Now"

To address the problem of sexual and gender based violence in conflict, the *UN Action on Sexual Violence in Conflict (UN Action)-"Stop Rape Now"*—a program was launched in March 2007. The UN Action unites the work of 13 UN entities[77] with the goal of ending sexual violence during and in the wake of conflict. It is a concerted effort by the UN to improve coordination and accountability, amplify programming and advocacy, and support national efforts to prevent sexual violence and respond effectively to the needs of survivors.[78]

UN Action has three main pillars:

1. *Country Level Action*: strategic support to UN action at country level, including efforts to build capacity, and targeted support for joint UN programming. For example, UN Action supported development of the first-ever Comprehensive Strategy on Combating Sexual Violence in the DRC.
2. *Advocating for Action:* action to raise public awareness and generate political will to address sexual violence as part of a broader campaign to Stop Rape Now.
3. *Learning by Doing:* creation of a knowledge hub on sexual violence in conflict, including data collection methodologies, international jurisprudence and effective responses.[79]

According to the UN Action Against Sexual Violence in Conflict statistics, as many as 50,000 women were raped in the Rwandan Genocide, 64;000 in the Sierra Leone conflict, 40,000 in the Bosnia and Herzegovina War, 4,500 in a single province in the Democratic Republic of the Congo in merely six months, and hundreds of women are raped every single day in the Darfur region of Sudan.[80]

(e) *Gender Mainstreaming in the Monitoring, Evaluation and Reporting Systems*

Resolution 1325 calls on the Secretary-General to include in his reporting to the Council progress on gender mainstreaming and other aspects relating to women and to appoint more women to pursue good offices on his behalf, particularly as Special Representatives and Special Envoys (S/PRST/2008/39).

An analysis of 313 reports of the Secretary-General to the Security Council dating from January 2004 to July 2008, including 286 country-specific and 27 thematic reports, revealed that 61 per cent of the reports made no mention of gender equality; 23 per cent contained negligible gender references; and only 16 per cent made multiple references to gender equality. Compared to the period from October 2000 to December 2003, some progress has been made, resulting in an increase of 6 per cent of reports with no mention of gender equality and an increase of 8 per cent in reports with minimal gender references. There was no noticeable change in the percentage of reports with multiple references to gender equality.[81]

The analysis also revealed that reporting on sexual violence, especially rape, is on the rise—from 23 per cent in 2000-03 to 32 per cent in 2004-08, but not all peace operations' related mandates. The problem of impunity was covered in 4 per cent of reports in 2000-03 and there was no information about it in reports in 2004-08. Gender mainstreaming was also increased from 2 per cent in 2000-03 to 4 per cent of reports in 2004-08.[82] Since the passing of Resolution 1325 on 31 October 2000, till 3 November 2009, 125 out of 336, i.e., 37 per cent of country-specific Security Council resolutions contained specific language on women or gender.[83]

The Security Council has consistently called upon the Secretary-General to appoint more women to pursue good offices on his behalf, particularly as Special Representatives and Special Envoys. As of December 2009, three missions were led by female Special Representatives[84] and eight peace-keeping and special political missions have had women as Deputy Special Representatives.[85] In addition, three women have been nominated as Special Envoys, and five others are Special Representatives of the Secretary-General. In March 2010, the Secretary-General appointed a female police officer from Sweden as the top United Nations police official. The Department of Peace-keeping Operations and the Department of

Political Affairs have deployed gender advisers to 13 of the 34 peace-keeping and special political missions in 2009. Six peace-keeping missions have a gender focal point who covers the gender portfolio in addition to other tasks. These advisers have been instrumental in ensuring that gender perspectives are incorporated into the work of the missions.

The gender equality, as a matter of fact, seems to be a distant goal itself within the UN System. There are only 38.3 per cent women of all staff in the professional and higher Categories; 27.3 per cent of all staff at the D-1 level and above; and 39.3 per cent of all staff at the P level are women. Gender balance has only been achieved at the P-1(50%) and P-2 levels (51.5%).[86] The challenge to make peace-keeping more gender balanced is formidable. As of July 2008, only 82 out of 2,227 U.N. military observers were women. Further, out of 70,525 deployed troops, only 1982 were women. In 2010, women comprised 3.2 per cent of total military personnel deployed to peace-keeping.[87] According to the Department of Peace-keeping Operations, the total number of United Nations field mission international civilian staff at the Professional level is 2,939, out of which 29.5 per cent are women.[88] The United Nations Volunteers programme (UNV) has increased the number of gender specialists from 3 in 2004 to19 in 2008.

The areas of peace and conflict resolutions are still male dominated. UNIFEM research shows that in the 11 years since the SCR 1325 was passed, there is no woman appointed as Chief or Lead peace mediator in the UN-sponsored peace talks and women's participation in peace negotiations remains *ad hoc*, not systematic—it averages 7.6 per cent of the *11* peace processes for which such information is available. Only *2.4* per cent of signatories to peace agreements are women.[89] To date, out of 30 peace operations (peace-keeping, political and peace building missions) there are currently three women appointed as *Special Representatives of the Secretary-General (SRSG),* one woman in the position of *Deputy Special Representatives of the Secretary-General (DSRSG)*[90] and still there is no woman appointed as Special Envoy of the Secretary General. In 60 years of the United Nations peace-keeping—from 1948 to 2008—only seven women have ever held the post of Special Representative of the Secretary-General especially in the context of peace-keeping missions.[91] Out of 191 permanent representatives to the UN in New York, as of September 2010, 24 or 12.5 per cent are women. In the 65 years history of the General Assembly, there has been only three female Presidents of the General Assembly.[92]

B. IMPLEMENTATION OF THE RESOLUTION 1325 BY THE MEMBER-STATES

The major responsibility to implement Resolution 1325 is on the Member-States.[93] They can play a critical role in promoting gender equality and the empowerment of women in the areas of peace and development and in that context national implementation of SCR 1325 and related Resolutions (SCR 1820, SCR 1888 and SCR 1889). The Security Council has repeatedly advised the Member-States to implement the Resolution by developing national action plans or other national level strategies.

Resolution 1325 envisages the Member-States to take action at the national level in the following key areas:

- Increased women's participation in decision-making and peace processes.
- The protection of women and girls in armed conflict situations and to put an end to impunity and to prosecute those responsible for genocide, crimes against humanity, war crimes including those relating to sexual violence against women and girls, and in this regard, stresses the need to exclude these crimes, where feasible from amnesty provisions;
- Gender training in the national training programmes for military and civilian police personnel in preparation for deployment.

National governments are the central actors in the implementation of the Resolution because of their role in conflict resolution, peace-building and reconstruction. There are a number of ways in which the States can put Resolution 1325 into practice. Some States have developed national action plans while others incorporate elements of Resolution 1325 (2000) into their national legislation so that the gender perspective is mainstreamed into different aspects of their peace and conflict policies.

I. National Action Plan on Women, Peace and Security

A National Action Plan is a document that details the actions that a Government is currently taking, and those initiatives that it will undertake within a given time-frame as per mandate of the Resolution. An Action Plan can increase the visibility and accountability of national efforts to implement gender, peace and security policies, and can help "tie together the different policy and operational areas within a government's diverse institutions and programs".[94] To date 41 countries worldwide have developed National Action plans. A brief outline of the NAPs is given below.

Denmark

Denmark was the first Country which adopted National Action Plan on the implementation of Security Council Resolution 1325 in June 2005. The main objective of the Plan is to achieve greater active participation of women in peace-building at the international and local levels.

The Action Plan includes *three* prioritized focus areas :

1. increase gender balance in recruitment of staff members of Danish defense forces and in their role in international operations,
2. protection of women's and girl's rights in areas where Danish troops are deployed, and
3. and increased participation and representation of women in peace-building and reconstruction processes in areas where Danish troops are deployed.

The Plan was *updated in 2008* to cover the period 2008-13 and includes achievements and lessons learned during the 2005-07 period.[95]

Norway

The *Norwegian Government's Action Plan for the Implementation of UN Security Council Resolution 1325 on Women, Peace and Security*[96] was launched on March 8, 2006. The Action Plan includes 89 specific actions, which are divided between national measures, and actions to be taken in relation with a variety of international, regional, and civil society organizations. The thematic headings of the Action Plan are:

1. international efforts and peace operations;
2. conflict prevention, mediation, peace-building;
3. to strengthen the efforts on human rights protection in conflict and post-conflict situations; and
4. and follow up, revision and cooperation.

United Kingdom

The United Kingdom High Level National Action Plan was

released on 8 March 2006.[97] The Plan was viewed as an internal working document and thus has not been publicly released. It includes twelve commitments listed under five headings: UK Support to the United Nations; training and policy within the government; gender justice including gender-based violence; disarmament, demobilization and reintegration; and working with non-government organizations. The Plan addresses all the provisions by providing concrete actions and strategies for its implementation within a time frame. The Plan was revised in 2012.

Sweden

The Swedish Government adopted its Action Plan in October 2006[98] which categorically states that the implementation of Resolution 1325 is the only way to achieve sustainable peace.

The Action Plan outlines four priority areas:

1. increase the participation of women in conflict prevention and peace support operations and support women's peace initiatives in conflict areas;
2. ensure the participation of women in institutions and in decision-making in post-conflict situations and in transition processes from conflict to peace;
3. strengthen the protection of the human rights and special needs of women and girls in connection with war and conflict; and
4. incorporate a gender perspective in peace support, security-building and humanitarian operations.

The Plan initially covered the period of three years and it was *updated in 2009* and now the Swedish Government also works on the Resolution 1820 (2008) so as to achieve the full implementation of Resolution 1325.

Cote D'Ivoire

The Cote D'Ivoire's National Action Plan for Resolution 1325/ 2000 of the Security Council of the UN[99] was launched in January 2007. It was the first African country to formulate Action Plan and was supported in this effort by the United Nations Development Programme (UNDP), UNIFEM and the Government of Norway The Action Plan covers the period from 2008-12. This plan sets an example for other African countries where armed conflicts are causing a disproportionate and devastating impact on women.

The Action Plan identifies four major areas:

1. protecting women and girls against sexual violence and female circumcision;
2. inclusion of gender issues in development policies and programs;
3. participation of women and men in National Reconstruction and Reinsertion Process; and
4. and strengthening participation of women in decision-making processes.

The plan identifies specific results for each priority area, and indicators to monitor progress against these results.

Switzerland

The Swiss *National Action Plan for the implementation of the UN Security Council Resolution 1325 on Women, Peace and Security* was launched in February 2007 and covers the period from 2007 to 2009.[100] The aim of the NAP 1325 is to ensure that gender aspects are taken into consideration in all areas of peace policy and in all concrete peace-building measures. The Action Plan focused on three concrete objectives:

1. greater involvement of women in peace-building;
2. prevention of gender-based violence and protection of the rights and needs of women and girls during and after armed conflicts; and
3. and a gender-sensitive approach to all peace-building projects and programs.

The first implementation phase of UNSCR 1325 Plan in Switzerland came to an end in 2009. Based on the findings detailed in the progress reports and in the light of the follow-up of the UNSC Resolutions 1820, 1888, 1889, the Plan was revised in October 2010. The main goals of the Plan are:

1. Greater participation of women in peace-building;
2. Prevention of gender-based violence, and protection of the needs and rights of women and girls during and after violent conflicts; and
3. A gender-sensitive approach to all peace-building.

The revised Plan covers the period from 2010-12.

Austria

On August 8, 2007, the *Austrian Action Plan on the implementing UN Security Council Resolution 1325*[101] was released. The main objectives of the Austrian Action Plan are:

1. increasing the participation of women in the promotion of peace and the resolution of conflicts, in particular by supporting local peace initiatives of women
2. preventing gender-based violence and protecting the needs and rights of women and girls within the scope of peace missions, humanitarian operations, as well as in refugee and IDP camps
3. Increasing representation of Austrian women in international peace operations as well as in decision-making positions in international and European organizations.

Spain

The Spanish Action Plan of the Government of Spain for the Application of the Resolution 1325 of the United Nations Security Council (2000), about Women, Peace and Security" was formulated in November 2007. The Plan identifies six main objectives:

1. to strengthen participation by women in peace missions and in peace missions' decision-making bodies;
2. to promote the inclusion of the gender perspective in all peace-building activities;
3. to ensure specific training for personnel participating in peace operations;
4. to protect the human rights of women and girls in conflict and post-conflict areas and to foster women's empowerment and participation in the processes where peace accords are negotiated and applied;
5. to incorporate the principle of equal treatment and opportunities for women and men in the planning and execution of activities for Disarmament, Demobilization and Reintegration; and
6. to foster Spanish civil society's participation in connection with Resolution 1325.

Netherlands

The *Dutch National Action Plan on Resolution 1325* was released in December 2007.[102] This Action Plan is unique as it was drafted with the consultation of a number of partners, including the civil society organizations and various ministries, and is signed by 18 partners.[103] The objective of the Plan is to gain systematic recognition and support for women's role in conflict and post-conflict situations, and to identify different stakeholders' responsibility in the process.

The Action Plan focused on five areas: the international legal framework; prevention, mediation and reconstruction; international cooperation; peace missions; and harmonization and coordination. It is significant to note that the Plan explicitly provides that civil society organizations produce *shadow reports*. Evaluating the Dutch National Action Plan on UNSC Resolution 1325 after one year of implementation, a *Shadow Report* was prepared by the Working Group 1325 on Women, Peace and Security.

Iceland

The Icelandic government launched its Action Plan on *Women, Peace and Security: Iceland's Plan of Action for the Implementation of United Nations Security Council Resolution 1325* on 8 March 2008. It includes 10 action items divided into what the Plan identifies as the three main focuses of the Resolution: increased women's participation in decision-making and peace processes; protection of women and girls in conflict zones; and integration of gender perspectives and gender education into peace-keeping. The Plan of Action was due to revised and updated three years after its release, that is, 2011. But it is yet to be revised.

Finland

Finland launched its *National Action Plan for the period 2008-11*[104] on 19 September 2008. The objective is to mainstream the gender perspective in all conflict prevention policies. The Action Plan includes nine action areas and divided the responsibilities of national, international and local actors. The categories are: conflict prevention, peace negotiations and peace-building; crisis management; and strengthening, protecting and safeguarding the human rights of women and girls. The Action Plan covers the years from 2008 through 2011.

Uganda

The *Uganda Action Plan on UN Security Council Resolutions 1325 & 1820 and the Goma Declaration*[105] was released in December 2008.[106] The Action Plan defines a systematic framework for national actions and monitoring system to assess progress and impact of interventions at all levels.

The Action Plan identifies five areas:

1. legal and policy framework;
2. improved access to health facilities, medical treatment and psychosocial services for gender-based violence victims;
3. women in leadership and decision-making;
4. prevention of gender-based violence in society; and
5. budgetary allocations for implementation of Resolutions 1325 and 1820 and the Goma Declaration.

The Ugandan Action Plan is unique because it is based on the Security Council Resolutions 1325 and 1820 and the Goma Declaration which emphasises on the eradication of sexual violence and ending impunity.

Liberia

The Liberia National Action Plan *was adopted on 8 March 2009.*[107] Liberia was the first country in a post-war situation to adopt a National Action Plan. The Plan was fully supported by the UN System including the Office of the Gender Adviser of the United Nations Mission in Liberia and the United Nations Institute for Research and Training on the Advancement of Women. It covers the period from 2009-13. It mainly focused on four areas:

1. Protection;
2. Prevention;
3. Participation; and
4. Empowerment and Promotion.

Each area is further divided into strategic issues and priority areas.

Belgium

The *Belgian National Action Plan* was launched on 8 May 2009.[108] The aim of this Action Plan is to achieve a better gender equality in its policy and in the implementation of its policy, both nationally and internationally. The National Action plan includes 95 guidelines and action items under five thematic headings: normative framework; violence against women; conflict prevention and peace-building; development cooperation; and peace-keeping.

Chile

The Chilean National Action Plan on the 1325 was launched on 3 August 2009.[109] It identifies four areas with specific actions for coordinating ministries. These areas are: gender, human rights, participation, and coordination. The Chilean National is unique because it focuses almost exclusively on the participation of the armed forces, putting particular emphasis on the participation of Chilean troops in peace support operations.

Portugal

The *Portuguese National Action Plan (2009-13)* was released in August 2009.[110] It focuses on five strategic objectives and 30 specific goals. Activities and indicators that measure the Plan's implementation process are identified. The objectives are: to increase representation and participation of women in peace and security operations, and in decision-making process at the national and international levels; to train and educate individuals involved in peace operations on gender equality, and Resolutions 1325 and 1820; to promote and protect the rights of women and girls in conflict zones; to broaden public and decision-making bodies' understanding on women, peace and security; and to promote the participation of civil society in the implementation of Resolution 1325.

Sierra Leone

The Sierra Leone National Action Plan for the Full Implementation of United Nations Security Council Resolutions 1325 and 1820 was released in March 2010.[111] The Plan has five pillars with corresponding indicators. The five pillars are: Prevention of conflict including violence against women and children (SGBV); protection, empowerment of victims and vulnerable persons especially women/girls; prosecute, punish perpetrators effectively and safeguard women and girls' human rights to protection during and post-conflict as well as rehabilitate victims/survivors of SGBV and perpetrators; participation and representation of women; promote coordination of the implementation process including resource mobilization, monitoring and evaluation of and reporting on the National Action Plan.

Philippines

Philippines adopted its National Action Plan for UN Security Council Resolutions 1325 and 1820 in March 2010 to strengthen and protect the rights of women and to protect women during armed conflict.[112] With this, the Philippines became the *first Asian country* to come up with an Action Plan on the said two SCRs.

The Plan focuses on four areas with corresponding outcomes and indicators. These are: Protection and Prevention—to ensure the protection of women's human rights and prevention of these rights in armed conflict and post-conflict situations; Empowerment and Participation—to empower women and ensure their active and meaningful participation in areas of peace-building, peace-keeping, conflict prevention, conflict resolution and post-conflict reconstruction; Promotion and Mainstreaming—to promote and mainstream gender perspective in all aspects of conflict prevention, conflict resolution and peace-building; Capacity Development and Monitoring and Reporting—to institutionalize a system to monitor, evaluate and report on the implementation of the NAP in order to enhance accountability for successful implementation and the achievement of its goals.

Rwanda

The Rwandan National Action Plan (2009-12) was launched on May 18, 2010.[113] The National Action Plan (NAP) includes five priorities: prevention of gender-based violence; protection and rehabilitation of survivors' dignity; participation and representation; women and gender promotion; and coordination, follow-up and evaluation of activities.

Bosnian-Herzegovinian

The Bosnian-Herzegovinian *Action Plan for 2010-13 was launched in July, 2011.*[114] The Plan has outlines *eight* areas of action which further divide into several activities. The eight areas of actions are:

1. Increased participation of women in decision-making position at all levels of government in Bosnia and Herzegovina
2. Increased number of women in military and police forces and promotion of women as holders of leadership positions in military and police structures
3. Increased participation of women in peace-keeping operations and introducing the gender perspective in the training of personnel training for peace-keeping missions
4. Fighting human trafficking

5. Reduced risk of mine contaminated areas in Bosnia and Herzegovina
6. Improving support and assistance networks to women and girls victims during the war conflict
7. Increased knowledge and capacity of state services to apply UNSCR 1325
8. Improving cooperation with non-governmental and international organizations to implement UN R. 1325 in BiH

Canada

Canada's Action Plan for the Implementation of United Nations Security Council Resolutions on Women, Peace and Security was launched on 5 October 2010.[115] This Action Plan is intended to guide the Government of Canada in the implementation of the group of United Nations Security Council Resolutions on Women, Peace and Security which recognize and address the experiences of women and girls in conflict and post-conflict situations, and to improve Canada's capacity to safeguard and support affected populations during all phases of peace operations (peace-keeping, peace-building, peace-making, peace-enforcement, conflict prevention, mediation, and stabilization and reconstruction), and in fragile states and conflict-affected situations.

Estonia

The *Estonian's National Action Plan* (2010-14) was launched in October 2010.[116] The objective of this Action Plan is to systematize and enhance Estonia's efforts to implement the Security Council Resolution 1325 and its follow-up Resolutions. The Plan incorporates Estonia's activities related to women, peace and security in the field of foreign policy, human rights, development cooperation and humanitarian assistance as well as international military and civil missions. Involvement of a number of Ministries like the Ministry of Foreign Affairs, Ministry of Defense, Ministry of the Interior, Ministry of Social Affairs, Ministry of Justice, Ministry of Education and Research, their agencies and civil society organizations is envisaged in the implementation of the Action Plan.

Nepal

The Nepalese *National Action Plan for the Implementation of UNSCR* was launched in October 2010.[117] Nepal is the first country in South Asia to draft and adopt a National Action Plan (NAP) on women, peace and security and is the second country in Asia, after the Philippines. The Nepal Government has developed Action Plan for the implementation of UNSCR 1325 and 1820 in the next five years—(2011-17). The main goal of the Action Plan is to achieve sustainable peace and just society with the objective to ensure proportional and meaningful participation of women at all levels of conflict transformation and peace processes; and protection of women and girls'rights.

France

France launched its National Action Plan in November 2010.[118] The action plan is structured in four parts:

1. Protecting women against violence and working to ensure respect for their fundamental rights
2. Participation of women in managing conflict and post-conflict situations
3. Raising awareness of respect for women's rights in training programmes
4. Developing political and diplomatic action

The Plan covers a three-year period and it stipulates regular monitoring.

Italy

Italy launched its *National Action Plan on Women, Peace and Security (2010-13)* on 23 December 2010.[119] The Plan focuses on the following six main areas:

1. Increasing the number of women in the national police and armed forces, and strengthening the inclusion of women in peace operations and the decision-making bodies of peace operations.
2. Promoting the inclusion of a gender perspective in all Peace-keeping Operations
3. Providing special training for personnel on peace missions, with a focus on resolution 1325
4. Protecting the human rights of women, children and other vulnerable groups either fleeing armed conflicts or living in conflict and postconflict areas (including in refugee camps) and strengthening women's participation in peace processes. Civil Society's commitment to the implementation of resolution 1325

6. Monitoring and Follow-up Activities

Croatia

The *Croatian National Action Plan for the Implementation of UNSCR 1325 (2011 to 2014)* was adopted in 2011.[120] The Action Plan is divided into four measures (Prevention, Participation, Protection and Post-Conflict Recovery and Implementation and Monitoring) and each measure has listed objectives are as under:

Measures and Objectives

1. Prevention

Objective 1: Strengthening gender perspective through documents and participation in international activities for the implementation of resolution 1325 and related resolutions.

Objective 2: Integration of gender perspective in the education programs for the implementation of resolution 1325 and related resolutions.

2. Participation

Objective 1: Introduce gender balance in the activities of the security system.

Objective 2: Increasing the representation of women in decision-making activities and processes concerning security and peace building.

Objective 3: Implementation of the program of international development assistance for education about gender equality and the role of women in the protection of their rights and in the post-conflict recovery.

3. Protection and Post-Conflict Recovery

Objective 1: Promotion of the protection of the rights of women and girls—victims of gender-based violence in the areas of armed conflicts and after conflicts abroad.

Objective 2: Implementation of the protection of the rights of women and girls—war victims in the Republic of Croatia with a view to their post-conflict recovery.

4. Implementation and Monitoring

Objective 1: Improvement of cooperation in the implementation of resolution 1325 and related resolutions.

Objective 2: Supporting the implementation of resolution 1325 and related resolutions.

NAP includes the four year period between 2011 and 2014, following which it will be revised in accordance with its performance.

Slovenia

The *Slovenian National Action Plan for the Implementation of UNSCR 1325 and 1820 (2010-15)* was released in July 2011.[121] The main objectives of the Action Plan are:

1. Gender mainstreaming into policies for conflict prevention and resolution and into decision-making and implementation processes, and strengthening of the role of local women in conflict prevention and post-conflict reconstruction;
2. Increased participation of women in international peace operations and missions and in peace-building; and
3. Prevention of sexual violence against girls and women and their protection during and after armed conflicts.

Georgia

The *Georgian National Action Plan is a composite Plan as it covers UN Security Council Resolutions 1325, 1820, 1888, 1889 and 1960 on Women, Peace and Security (2012-15)*. It was adopted in December 2011.[122] The Plan is divided into five priority areas with several activities and indicators under these areas. The priority areas are:

1. *Participation*: Participation of women at decision-making level in conflict elimination, prevention and management processes.
2 *Prevention*: Consideration of women's needs in conflict prevention and elimination of all forms of violence against women.
3 *Prevention*: Consideration of women's needs in conflict prevention and eliminating all forms of violence against women, especially sexual and gender-based violence.
4 *Protection*: Protecting conflict affected women's human rights; ensuring their physical, social, economic and political security.
5 *Relief and Recovery*: Addressing special needs of women in war/conflict and post-conflict situations.

United States of America

The *United States* launched its *National Action Plan on Women,*

Peace and Security was launched in December 2011.[123] The Plan is targeted at the following five high-level objectives:

1. *National Integration and Institutionalization:* Through interagency coordination, policy development, enhanced professional training and education, and evaluation, the United States Government will institutionalize a gender-responsive approach to its diplomatic, development, and defense-related work in conflict-affected environments.
2. *Participation in Peace Processes and Decision-making:* The United States Government will improve the prospects for inclusive, just, and sustainable peace by promoting and strengthening women's rights and effective leadership and substantive participation in peace processes, conflict prevention, peace-building, transitional processes, and decision-making institutions in conflict-affected environments.
3. *Protection from Violence:* The United States Government will strengthen its efforts to prevent—and protect women and children from—harm, exploitation, discrimination, and abuse, including sexual and gender-based violence and trafficking in persons, and to hold perpetrators accountable in conflict-affected environments.
4. *Conflict Prevention:* The United States Government will promote women's roles in conflict prevention, improve conflict early-warning and response systems through the integration of gender perspectives, and invest in women and girls' health, education, and economic opportunity to create conditions for stable societies and lasting peace.
5. *Access to Relief and Recovery:* The United States Government will respond to the distinct needs of women and children in conflict-affected disasters and crises, including by providing safe, equitable access to humanitarian assistance.

In order to achieve the above objectives a number of actions have been set-up under each objective.

Senegal, Guinea and Guinea—Bissau are other countries that also adopted NAPs in 2011.

And in June 2010, the Democratic Republic of Congo also launched its National Action Plan for the implementation of the UNSCR 1325.[124]

Australia

Austrailia is the latest country to adopt NAP. On International Women's Day, 8 March 2012, launched the *Australian National Action Plan on Women, Peace and Security 2012-18.*[125] The Action plan is based on the five key thematic area (prevention, participation, protection, relief and recovery and normative) which have been identified by the United Nations on women, peace and security agenda.[126] These five thematic areas reflect the content of UNSCR 1325 and the related resolutions, as well as the UN 2008-09 System-wide Action Plan.

The strategies that the Australian Government will undertake to progress the Women, Peace and Security agenda are:

1. Integrate a gender perspective into Australia's policies on peace and security.
2. Embed the Women, Peace and Security agenda in the Australian Government's approach to human resource management of Defence, Australian Federal Police and deployed personnel.
3. Support civil society organisations to promote equality and increase women's participation in conflict prevention, peace-building, conflict resolution, and relief and recovery.
4. Promote Women, Peace and Security implementation internationally.
5. Take a co-ordinated and holistic approach domestically and internationally to Women, Peace and Security.

There are a number of detailed actions outlined under each strategy to implement this plan.

The above analysis shows that majority of the countries that have formulated the Action Plans are European, a few from Africa and just two from Asia. The USA, Australia and Kyrgyzstan have joined lately this club of nations with Action Plans and Kyrgyzstan is the latest. How effectively are the Action Plans being implemented is another matter but these countries have at least taken the initiative. Majority of the countries still have to take action in this regard. None of the South Asian countries except Nepal has taken step in this direction. Its speaks of indifference of the States in the region to this Resolution.

II. Incorporating SCR 1325 into Existing National Framework by the Member-States

There are some countries which have integrated strategies and actions on women, peace and security into their existing national policies and strategies on the effective implementation of Resolution 1325 at national level. For example, The Ministry of Foreign Affairs of *Colombia*, in collaboration with the Presidential Advisory Office on Gender Equality, set-up a working group on women and peace and security to support the participation of women related to the promotion of peace in the country.[127] Likewise in *Azerbaijan* a national "Coalition 1325", comprising women parliamentarians, non-governmental organizations (NGOs) and media representatives, was established to raise awareness of Resolution 1325 and the role of women in decision-making processes, including in conflict resolution and peace-building.[128]

A few other examples that can be cited are those of Germany, Argentina and New Zealand. In *Germany* women in armed conflict and their role in conflict management is one of the key issues covered in the Gender Action Plan, 2009-12 of the Federal Ministry for Economic Cooperation and Development. It comprises measures to support women's groups and networks that promote peace and non-violent conflict resolution, the inclusion of women in peace negotiations and the deployment of female gender advisors and human rights observers in peace missions.[129] In *Argentina* the Ministry of Defence created a working group for the diagnosis and analysis of measures and actions for the effective implementation of the gender perspective in the field of defence and in the context of International Peace-keeping Operations.[130] In *New Zealand* a number of concrete steps have been taken to reinforce its support for Resolution 1325. Up to 30 per cent of all our police peace-keeping deployments are female.[131]

There are some countries that have NAPs but have also incorporated changes in their existing policies. For example, *Sweden's* "Genderforce" brings together government agencies and NGOs to develop common approaches on how to implement resolution 1325 focusing on issues such as training and planning for international missions.[132]

In 2001, *Canada* created a committee on women and peace and security which comprised of parliamentarians, representatives of civil society and government officials with the objective to focus on advocacy, capacity-building and training on SCR 1325.

In 2003, the Ministries of Defence, Foreign Affairs and the Interior and Kingdom Affairs of the Netherlands established a task force on women in conflict situations and peace-keeping that was charged with implementing Resolution 1325.[133]

In *Norway*, a forum comprising representatives from relevant ministries and members of civil society was established to follow-up the implementation of resolution 1325 (2000).

C. THE CIVIL SOCIETY AND THE SECURITY COUNCIL RESOLUTION

It may not be out of place to mention here that there is a strong partnership between the civil society organizations and the UN. The Security Council as discussed in the preceding pages closely works with the civil society through Arria Formula[134] meetings addressing thematic issues. The meetings provide valuable inputs and opportunity to the Security Council to dialogue with non-governmental organizations. Another forum for the interaction with these organizations is *'Friends of 1325'* a group led by Canada.

The most significant lobby group that works on the implementation of SCR is the New York based *NGO Working Group on Women, Peace and Security.*[135] It was formed in 2000. It meets regularly with the most relevant member-states and is, routinely invited as an observer to all meetings of the ' Friends of 1325'. It has also built strong links to the UN entities such as OSAGI (now UN Women), and has observer status at meetings of the UN Inter-Agency Task Force on Women, Peace and Security.[136]

Women's International League for Peace and Freedom *(WILPF)* that played a central role in the adoption of the SCR 1325, continues to be a strong advocate for the implementation of the Resolution. Through its *Peace Women Project*, it promotes not only the role of women in preventing conflict, and the equal and full participation of women in all efforts to create and maintain international peace and security, it monitors the implementation of the Resolution by the Security Council and the UN System. Another initiative of this Project is the translation of the Resolution with the aim of addressing the language barrier in creating awareness of the Resolution. This initiative aims to promote local ownership and women's participation in conflict prevention and peace-building. PeaceWomen has successfully compiled over 100 translations of SCR 1325.

On the *whole*, it may be said that SCR 1325 is an important milestone in setting right "the dimensions of contemporary security politics by accepting women's equality agenda". The Resolution recognized the gendered nature of war and peace process and was further strengthened by follow-up Resolutions 1820, 1888 and 1889. However, its historic and operational value, observes *Anwarul K. Chowdhury*, the main advocate of this Resolution, has been undercut by the disappointing record of its implementation. The Security Council, the Secretary General, the UN entities and the Member States as discussed above have taken notable steps to implement the Resolution but much remains to be done to truly realise the spirit of the Resolution.

The Open Debates organized reflect a ritual exercise repeated every year where the Member-States make customary speeches in recognizing how conflicts impact women and that women's participation is essential for peace but at the national level, no serious steps are taken to implement it. There is an increased attention to women's participation in decision-making and peace processes which has created more opportunities for women and women's organizations to contribute to the prevention of conflict and to participate in conflict resolution, peace-building and peace negotiations. But it is more on the notional side than a widely practiced reality.

An increasing number of countries are developing Action Plans to implement this Resolution. As of date, 43 countries have developed the Action Plans, latest to join this group are the United States of America and Australia. However, it is mostly the European countries who have been active on this front. In a couple of African countries that have formulated the Plans, it is because of the presence of the UN Missions in those countries. Even in Nepal, the only South Asian country to have NAP, it has been possible because of the donor assistance and facilitation (Norway). Its actual implementation remains to be seen.

All the UN entities are expected to mainstream and incorporate 1325 in their activities but as it is, only the UN Women and DPKO are mainly working on this Resolution. The appointment of a Gender Advisor in the Department of Political Affairs is still awaited. Although a System Wide Action Plan has been developed to bring greater coherence to the work of the United Nations on Women, Peace and Security, the performance of the System Wide Action Plan has fallen short of expectations.

Women and their perspectives are still neglected in the peace process as much as the areas of peace and conflict remain male dominated. Overall under representation of women at all levels of decision-making shows the lack of political will of the Member-States and the United Nations itself. The UN with all its commitments is yet to attain gender equality in its own system. It is observed that in more than 60 years, the UN has never had a female Secretary General. To this day, only a few Special Representatives of the Secretary General (SRSGs) have been women. So far, very few peace-keeping missions have been led by women. According to Stephen Lewis, former UN special envoy for HIV/AIDS in Africa agues that "yet, if the promotion of women in the UN continues at its present rate, the goal of 50% women at the UN in Geneva will be achieved in the year 2072 and at the Department of Peace-keeping Operations in New York in 2100."[137]

The Security Council has not developed any coordinating mechanism to oversee the implementation of the Resolution. As a matter of fact, the Security Council, rightly opines *Anwarul K. Chowdhury*, "has yet to internalize gender consideration into the operational behaviour of its actions". Commenting on the role of the Secretary-General and the UN Secretariat, he says, it " leaves much to be desired to say the least. Undoubtly there is a clear need for his genuinely active and dedicated engagement in using the moral authority of the United Nations and the high office he occupies for the effective implementation of 1325."[138]

How effectively is the Resolution implemented in South Asia in terms of its key elements is discussed in the next chapter.

Notes and References

1. Ana Miruna Bucurescu (2011), *Security Council Resolution 1325 on Women, Peace and Security Effective Ways to Implement it at a National level, National Action Plans or Gender Mainstreaming Approach? A comparative Case Study on Swedish and German Implementation Designs*, Norway, Uppsala University, p. 1.
2. Christy Fujio (2008), *From Soft to Hard Law: Moving Resolution 1325 on Women, Peace and Security Across the Spectrum*, Georgetown Journal of Gender and the Law, Vol. 9, No. 1, pp. 215-36, p. 215.
3. United Nations Security Council (2010), *Security Council Cross-Cutting Report on Women, Peace and Security*, New York, United Nations.
4. *Ibid.*
5. United Nations Charter (1945), Security Council, Chapter V, Article 27.
6. The Department of Peace Keeping Operations (DPKO) administers and directs peace-keeping operations while the United Nations Department of Political Affairs (DPA).

   Peace Keeping Operations : Africa, UN Organization Stabilization Mission in the Democratic Republic of the Congo (MONUSCO), African Union-UN Hybrid Operation in Darfur (UNAMID), UN Mission in the Sudan (UNMIS), UN Operation in Côte d'Ivoire

(UNOCI), UN Mission in Liberia (UNMIL), UN Mission for the Referendum in Western Sahara (MINURSO) (Americas), UN Stabilization Mission in Haiti (MINUSTAH), Asia and the Pacific, UN Integrated Mission in Timor-Leste (UNMIT), UN Military Observer Group in India and Pakistan (UNMOGIP), Europe, UN Peace-keeping Force in Cyprus (UNFICYP), UN Interim Administration Mission in Kosovo (UNMIK), Middle East, UN Disengagement Observer Force (UNDOF), United Nations Interim Force in Lebanon (UNIFIL), UN Truce Supervision Organization (UNTSO).

7. Political Affairs Operation : UN Assistance Mission in Afghanistan (UNAMA).
8. UNAMA's first mandate established in 2002 through Resolution 1401 which included no reference at all to Resolution 1325 or women.
9. United Nations General Assembly (2005), *In larger Freedom: Towards Development, Security and Human Rights for All*, World Summit Outcome, Resolution (A/RES/60/1), New York, United Nations
10. Provisions of Resolution 1325 have also been well integrated into the country-specific work of the Peacebuilding Commission, particularly in the strategic peacebuilding frameworks for Burundi and Sierra Leone
11. UN Security Council Resolution 1820 (2008) adopted by the Security Council at its 5916th meeting on 19 June 2008,(S/RES/1820), New York, United Nations.
12. UN Security Council Resolution 1888 (2009) adopted by the Security Council at its 6195th meeting on 30 September 2009, (S/RES/1888), New York, United Nations.
13. United Nations Security Council (2009), Report of the Secretary-General pursuant to Security Council Resolution 1820 and 1888, (A/65/592 and S/2010/604), New York, United Nations.
14. *Ibid.*
15. UN Security Council Resolution 1889 (2009) adopted by the Security Council at its 6196th meeting on 5 October 2009, (S/RES/1889), New York, United Nations.
16. United Nations Secretary General Reports on Women, Peace and Security, (S/2002/1154), (S/2004/814), (S/2005/636), (S/2006/770), (S/2007/567), (S/2008/622), (S/2009/465), (S/2010/173), (S/2010/498).
17. Statement made by Bangladesh in the 2008 Security Council Open Debate. India also supported this suggestion.
18. Presidential statements (known as PRSTs) are similar to declarations in content, tone and format, but they are not legally binding. The adoption of a Presidential statement requires consensus amongst members of the Security Council, although members may also choose to abstain. They are usually adopted when there are significant developments on the ground in a country on the Council's agenda, or to reinforce important points following open debates or the release of key UN documents. They are also adopted when the Council cannot reach consensus or when the Council is prevented from passing a resolution due to a permanent member's veto, or threat thereof.
19. Women, Peace, Security Presidential Statements (PRSTs) as of January 2011 [S/PRST/2001/31, S/PRST/2002/32, S/PRST/2004/40, S/PRST/

2005/52, S/PRST/2006/42,S/PRST/2007/5, S/PRST/2007/40, S/PRST/2008/39), S/PRST/2010/8 & (S/PRST/2010/22)].

20. United Nations Secretary General Reports on Women, Peace and Security, (S/2002/1154), (S/2004/814), (S/2005/636), (S/2006/770), (S/2007/567), (S/2008/622), (S/2009/465),(S/2010/173) and (S/2010/498).
21. The members of the Task Force are: Office of the Special Adviser on Gender Issues and Advancement of Women (Chair), Division for the Advancement of Women, Department of Economic and Social Affairs, Department for Disarmament Affairs, Department of Political Affairs, Department of Public Information, Department of Peace-keeping Operations, Office for the Coordination of Humanitarian Affairs, Economic and Social Commission for Western Asia, Office of the United Nations High Commissioner for Human Rights, Office of Human Resources Management, Special Representative of the Secretary-General for Children and Armed Conflict, International Labour Organization, United Nations International Research and Training Institute for the Advancement of Women, United Nations Development Programme, United Nations Children's Fund, United Nations Development Fund for Women, United Nations Population Fund, United Nations Human Settlements Programme, Office of the United Nations High Commissioner for Refugees, World Food Programme, United Nations University, United Nations Permanent Forum on Indigenous Issues.
    The observers are: International Organization for Migration, Commonwealth secretariat and the NGO Working Group on Women and Peace and Security, comprising Femmes Africa Solidarité, Hague Appeal for Peace, International Alert, International Women's Tribune Centre, Women's Action for New Directions, Women's Commission for Refugee Women and Children, Women's Division of the General Board of Global Ministries, United Methodist Church and Women's International League for Peace and Freedom. Affiliate members include Amnesty International and the Women's Environmental and Development Organization.
22. *Presidential Statements on women, peace and Security,* (S/PRST/2001/31, S/PRST/2002/32 and S/PRST/2004/40).
23. United Nations Security Council (2005), *Report of the Secretary-General on Women, Peace and Security (S/2005/636)*, New York, United Nations, p. 2.
24. United Nations Security Council, (2007), *Report of the Secretary-General on Women, Peace and Security (S/2006/770)*, New York, United Nations, p. 2.
25. Department of Economic and Social Affairs; Department of Political Affairs; Department of Public Information; Department of Peace-keeping Operations; Economic Commission for Africa (ECA); Economic and Social Commission for Asia and the Pacific (ESCAP); Economic and Social Commission for Western Asia (ESCWA); Food and Agriculture Organization of the United Nations (FAO); International Criminal Tribunal for Rwanda; International Research and Training Institute for the Advancement of Women (INSTRAW); Office for the Coordination of Humanitarian Affairs; Office for Disarmament Affairs; Office of the

United Nations High Commissioner for Human Rights (OHCHR); Office of the Special Adviser on Gender Issues and Advancement of Women; Office of the Special Representative of the Secretary-General for Children and Armed Conflict; United Nations Development Programme (UNDP); United Nations Environment Programme (UNEP); United Nations Educational, Scientific and Cultural Organization (UNESCO); United Nations Population Fund (UNFPA); Office of the United Nations High Commissioner for Refugees (UNHCR); United Nations Children's Fund (UNICEF); United Nations Interregional Crime and Justice Research Institute (UNICRI); United Nations Development Fund for Women (UNIFEM); United Nations Institute for Training and Research (UNITAR); United Nations Office for Project Services (UNOPS); United Nations Relief and Works Agency for Palestine Refugees in the Near East (UNRWA); United National System Staff College; World Bank; World Food Programme (WFP); and World Health Organization (WHO).

26. The Presidential Statements on Women, Peace and Security,(S/PRST/ 2001/31, S/PRST/2002/32, S/PRST/2004/40, S/PRST/2005/52, S/ PRST/2006/42 and S/PRST/2007/5).
27. United Nations Security Council (2007), *Report of the Secretary-General on Women, Peace and Security, (S/2007/567),* New York, United Nations, p. 13.
28. *Indicators :*
    - 1a. Prevalence of Sexual Violence.
    - 1b. Patterns of sexual violence in conflict and post-conflict situations Text of recommendations section to report on: Types of measures (proposed *vs.* implemented), Types of violations, Type of perpetrator, Specific groups affected (ethnicity, geographical location, age).
    - 2. Extent to which United Nations Peace-keeping and Special Political Missions include information on violations of women and girls' human rights in their periodic reporting to the Security Council.
    - 3a. Extent to which violations of women's and girls' human rights are reported, referred and investigated by human rights bodies Report on: Number and types of cases reported, referred and investigated, Account of actions taken/recommended to address violations.
    - 3b. Number and percentage share of women in governance bodies of National Human Right Bodies (NHRB).
    - 4. Percentage of reported cases of sexual exploitation and abuse allegedly perpetrated by uniformed, civilian peace-keepers and/or humanitarian workers that are acted upon out of the total number of referred cases
    - 5a. Extent to which measures to protect women's and girls' human rights are included in Peace-keeper Heads of Military Components and Heads of Police Components Directives.
    - 5b. Extent to which measures to protect women's and girls' human rights are included in national security policy frameworks. Existing and new gender-specific language to report on: Type of document, Context analysis of security threats to women and girls, Types of measures.

6. Number and type of actions taken by the Security Council related to resolution 1325 (2000) Report on: Count of actions, Types of an international tribunal, refer a situation to ICC, Type of document (i.e. resolution, PRST).
7. Number and percentage share of women in the Executive leadership of relevant regional and sub-regional organizations involved in preventing conflict Regional and sub-regional organizations will include those identified in A/RES/55/285.
8. Percentage of peace agreements with specific provisions to improve the security and status of women and girls.
9. Women's share of senior UN positions in field missions.
10. Percentage of field missions with senior level gender experts.

11a. Representation of women among mediators, negotiators and technical experts in formal peace negotiations.

11b. Women's participation in an official observer status at the beginning and the end of formal peace negotiations.

12a. Women's political participation in parliaments and ministerial positions. Report on women's share of: Seats in parliament, Ministerial positions.

12b. Women's political participation as voters and candidates. Report on women's share of: Persons registered to vote, Persons who actually vote, Parliamentary candidates.

13. Extent to which Security Council missions address specific issues affecting women and girls in the Terms of Reference and Mission Reports.
14. Index of women's and girls' physical security. Survey-based indicator to measure three dimensions:
    Perceptions of physical security of women and girls (by location, time of day), Proxy variables measuring how women's and girls' ability to participate in public life has been affected, Proxy variables measuring how women's and girls' regular activities have been affected.
15. Extent to which national laws to protect women's and girls' human rights are in line with international standards.
16. Level of women's participation in the justice and security sector.
17. Existence of national mechanisms for control of illicit Small Arms and Light Weapons (SA/LW). This indicator reports on: Existence of a national coordination agency on SA/LW or National Focal Point (paragraphs 4 and 5 of Section II of the POA), Record-keeping on holdings and transfers of SA/LW (para 9 in section II of the POA).
18. Percentage of (monetary equivalent, estimate) benefits from temporary employment in the context of early economic recovery programmes received by women and girls.
19. Percentage of referred cases of sexual and gender-based violence against women and girls that are reported, investigated and sentenced.
20. Hours of training per capita of decision-making personnel in security and justice sector institutions to address SGBV cases.

21a. Maternal mortality rate.

21b. Net Primary and secondary education enrolment rates, by sex.

22a. Proportion of budget related to indicators that address gender equality issues in strategic planning frameworks.

22b. Proportion of budget related to targets that address gender equality issues in strategic planning framework.
23a. Proportion of total disbursed funding to Civil Society organizations that is allocated to address gender equality issues.
23b. Proportion of total disbursed funding to support gender equality issues that isallocated to Civil Society organizations.
24a. Proportion of disbursed Multi Donor Trust Funds (MDTFs) used to address gender equality issues.
24b. Proportion of total spending of UN system used to support gender equality issues.
25. Extent to which Truth and Reconciliation Commissions include provisions to address the rights and participation of women and girls
26a. Percentage of (monetary equivalent, estimate) benefits from DDR programmes received by women and girls.
26b. Percentage of (monetary equivalent, estimate) benefits from DDR programmes received by women and girls.

29. http://www.un.org/en/women/endviolence/
30. *Ibid.*
31. United Nations Secretary-General's Bulletin (2003), *Special Measures for Protection from Sexual Exploitation and Sexual Abuse*, (UN DocST/SGB/2003/13), New York, United Nations, para 3.2(c).
32. United Nations Department of Peace-keeping Operations and Department of Field Support (2010), *Ten-year Impact Study on Implementation of UN Security Council Resolution 1325 on Women, Peace and Security in Peace-keeping* , New York, United Nations, p. 39.
33. *Ibid.*, p. 39.
34. http://www.· :.org/Depts/dpa/intro.html
35. *Ibid.*
36. http://www.un.org/en/peacekeeping/about/dpko/
37. United Nations Department of Peace-keeping Operations (2000), *Windhoek Declaration and Namibia Plan of Action on Mainstreaming a Gender Perspective in Multidimensional Peace Support Operations,* (A/55/138-S/2000/693), New York, United Nations.
38. United Nations Security Council (2000), *United Nations Security Council Resolution 1325 on Women, Peace and Security (S/RES/1325),* New York, United Nations, paras 4, 5 and 6.
39. *Ibid.*, para 16.
40. United Nations Security Council, (2004), *Report of the Secretary-General on Women, Peace and Security, (S/2004/814*), New York, United Nations, United Nations, p. 4.
41. This Policy Directive defines and describes requirements for ensuring the equal participation of women, men, girls and boys in all peace-keeping activities. It embraces gender mainstreaming as a strategy to advance the goal of gender equality in post-conflict societies.
42. BINUCA (CAR), UNMIL (Liberia), UNMIT (Timor-Leste), UNMIN (Nepal) and UNFICYP (Cyprus).
43. MINURCAT (Chad/CAR), MONUSCO (DRC), UNMIL (Liberia) and UNAMI (Iraq).

44. United Nations Mission for the Referendum in Western Sahara, United Nations Observer Mission in Georgia, United Nations Truce Supervision Organization, United Nations Peace-keeping Force in Cyprus, United Nations Interim Force in Lebanon.
45. United Nations, Security Council Security Council Open Debate on Women, Peace and Security, October 2007. http://www.un.org/womenwatch/feature/wps/
46. United Nations Security Council, (2009), *Nineteenth Progress report of the Secretary-General on the United Nations Mission in Liberia, (S/2009/411)*, New York, United Nations, p. 14.
47. http://www.un.org/en/peacekeeping/its.shtml.
48. *Ibid.*
49. Official Records of the General Assembly, Sixty-second Session, Supplement No. 19 (A/62/19).
50. *The United Nations Mine Action Service* (UNMAS) is a section of the Department of Peace-keeping Operations and was formed in October 1997 to serve as the United Nations focal point for mine action and to support the UN vision of a "world free of the threat of *landmines* and *unexploded ordnance*".
51. http://www.un.org/en/peacekeeping/its.shtml.
52. Department of Peace-keeping Operations, Gender Statistics by Mission for the month of August 2010.
53. *Ibid.*
54. United Nations Security Council, (2008), *Report of the Secretary-General on Women, Peace and Security, (S/2008/622)*, New York, United Nations, p. 12.
55. http://www2.ohchr.org/english/issues/women/index.htm
56. http://daccess-dds-ny.un.org/doc/UNDOC/GEN/G09/151/33/PDF/G0915133.pdf?OpenElement
57. UN Women has been operationalised from 1 January 2011. One of the critical first steps from both a practical and symbolic perspective was the Secretary-General's appointment of the first head of UN Women, who will hold the rank of Under-Secretary-General and will report to the Secretary-General. Michelle Bachelet, the former President of Chile, has been appointed as the Executive Director. Ms. Bachelet will in turn be supported by an Executive Board, composed of 41 member states. The Executive Board will act as the governing body of the Entity to provide intergovernmental support to and supervision of its operational activities. The Executive Board will report annually to the UN General Assembly through the Economic and Social Council. Decisions on other important details needed to round out the full picture of UN Women, such as the budget, remain to be finalized and will be closely watched by observers.
58. United Nations General Assembly, (2010), *General Assembly Adopts Consensus Text on System-wide Coherence, Establishing Composite Entity—UN Women—To Accelerate Gender Equality, Empowerment, (GA/10959)*, New York, United Nations http://www.un.org/News/Press/docs/2010/ga10959.doc.htm.
59. United Nations General Assembly Resolution, (2010), *System-wide Coherence*, (A/RES/64/289, 64th Session, New York, United Nations.

60. *Ibid.*, para 51 (b).
61. http://www.un.org/womenwatch/osagi/aboutosagi.htm.
62. The Division for the Advancement of Women (DAW) was established in 1946 as the *Section on the Status of Women, Human Rights Division, Department of Social Affairs.* In 1972, the section was upgraded as the *Branch for the Promotion of Equality for Men and Women.* Again in 1978, the branch was renamed as the Branch for the Advancement of Women. And finally, in August 1993, the unit was renamed as the Division for the Advancement of Women became part of the Department of Economic and Social Affairs (DESA) in 1996.
63. Established in 1976 as an autonomous entity to the UNDP, UNIFEM aimed to advance women's issues and achieve gender equality.
64. www.womenwarpeace.org
65. *Ibid.*
66. http://www.unifem.org/gender_issues/women_war_peace/prevention_early_warning.php
67. http://www.unifem.org/gender_issues/women_war_peace/prevention_early_warning.php
68. www.un-instraw.org
69. United Nations International Research and Training Institute for the Advancement of Women (UN-INSTRAW), (2006), *Securing Equality, Engendering Peace: A Guide to Policy and Planning on Women, Peace and Security*, Costa Rica, United Nations. http://www.un-instraw.org/en/docs/1325/1325-Guide-ENG.pdf
70. http://www.un.org/peace/peacebuilding/
71. The UN Peacebuilding Commission (PBC) began its formal country-specific meetings in October 2006 by considering the situations in Sierra Leone and Burundi.
72. The Inter-Agency Network on Women and Gender Equality (IANWGE) is a network 25 entities of the United Nations system, i.e. offices and departments of the United Nations Secretariat, regional commissions, funds and programmes, specialized agencies, and the Bretton Woods institutions. It is chaired by *UN Women*. The Network has played a central role in promoting gender equality throughout the United Nations system and in follow-up to the Fourth World Conference on Women in Beijing in 1995 and the twenty-third special session of the General Assembly (Beijing +5) in 2000.
73. http://www.un.org/womenwatch/ianwge/taskforces/wps/national_level_impl.html
74. *The members of the Task Force are*: Office of the Special Adviser on Gender Issues and Advancement of Women (Chair), Division for the Advancement of Women, Department of Economic and Social Affairs, Department for Disarmament Affairs, Department of Political Affairs, Department of Public Information, Department of Peace-keeping Operations, Office for the Coordination of Humanitarian Affairs, Economic and Social Commission for Western Asia, Office of the United Nations High Commissioner for Human Rights, Office of Human Resources Management, Special Representative of the Secretary-General

for Children and Armed Conflict, International Labour Organization, United Nations International Research and Training Institute for the Advancement of Women, United Nations Development Programme, United Nations Children's Fund, United Nations Development Fund for Women, United Nations Population Fund, United Nations Human Settlements Programme, Office of the United Nations High Commissioner for Refugees, World Food Programme, United Nations University, United Nations Permanent Forum on Indigenous Issues. *The observers are*: International Organization for Migration, Commonwealth secretariat and the NGO Working Group on Women and Peace and Security, comprising Femmes Africa Solidarité, Hague Appeal for Peace, International Alert, International Women's Tribune Centre, Women's Action for New Directions, Women's Commission for Refugee Women and Children, Women's Division of the General Board of Global Ministries, United Methodist Church and Women's International League for Peace and Freedom. Affiliate members include Amnesty International and the Women's Environmental and Development Organization.

75. http://www.icc-cpi.int/Menus/ICC/Situations+and+Cases/
76. *Ibid.*
77. The Department of Political Affairs, the Department of Peace-keeping Operations, the Office for the Coordination of Humanitarian Affairs, the Office of the United Nations High Commissioner for Human Rights, UNAIDS, UNDP, UNFPA, the Office of the United Nations High Commissioner for Refugees, UNICEF, UNIFEM, WFP, WHO and the United Nations Peacebuilding Support Office.
78. United Nations, (2007), *UN Action Against Sexual Violence in Conflict, "Stop Rape Now—About"*, New York, United Nations. http://www.stoprapenow.org/about/
79. *Ibid.*
80. http://stoprapenow.org/about.html
81. United Nations Security Council, (2008), *Report of the Secretary-General on Women, Peace and Security, (S/2008/622)*, New York, United Nations, p. 18.
82. *Ibid.*
83. www.peacewomen.org
84. BINUCA, UNMIL and the United Nations Mission in Nepal.
85. United Nations Integrated Office in Burundi, United Nations Mission in the Central African Republic and Chad, United Nations Organization Stabilization Mission in the Democratic Republic of the Congo (MONUSCO), MINUSTAH, United Nations Assistance Mission for Iraq, United Nations Special Coordinator for Lebanon, UNMIL and the United Nations Mission in the Sudan.
86. United Nations, Office of the Special Adviser on Gender Issues and Advancement of Women: *The Status of Women in the United Nations System and in the Secretariat* (from 1 July 2007 to 30 June 2009).
87. Department of Peace-keeping Operations, Gender Statistics by Mission for the month of August 2010.
88. *Ibid.*

89. UNIFEM research based on the UN Peace-maker Peace Agreement database; United States Institute for Peace's Peace Agreements digital collection (Papua New Guinea, Cote d'Ivoire).
90. www.Peacewomen.org
91. United Nations Security Council (2010), *Security Council Cross-Cutting Report on Women, Peace and Security*, New York, United Nations, p. 35.
92. The three women were : Vijay Lakshmi Pandit of India (in 8th Session), Angie Elizabeth Brooks of Liberia (in 24th Session) and Sheikha Haya Rashed Al Khalifa of Bahrain (in 61st Session).
93. Article 25 of the UN Charter states that "The Members of the United Nations agree to accept and carry out the decisions of the Security Council in accordance with the present Charter". The member states obligations flow from the authority they confer on the Council under Article 24(1) to act on behalf of member-states while the Council exercise its responsibility for the maintenance of international peace and security.
94. Sherriff, Andrew and Barnes, Karen (2008), *Enhancing the EU Response to Woman and Armed Conflict With Particular Reference to Development Policy: Study for the Slovenian EU Presidency*, United Kingdom, International Alert http://www.international-alert.org/pdf/Sherriff_WAC%20study_DP84_April08.pdf
95. http://www.peacewomen.org/assets/file/NationalActionPlans/denmark_nationaactionplan_june2005.pdf http://www.peacewomen.org/assets/file/NationalActionPlans/nap_danish1325actionplan2008-2013_2010.pdf
96. http://www.peacewomen.org/assets/file/NationalActionPlans/norway-nationalactionplan_march2006.pdf
97. http://www.peacewomen.org/assets/file/NationalActionPlans/uk_nationalactionplan_november2010.pdf
98. http://www.peacewomen.org/assets/file/NationalActionPlans/swedish_nationalactionplan_october2006.pdf
99. Côte d'Ivoire *"National Action Plan for Resolution 1325/2000 of the Security Council of the UN"*, January 2007, http://www.peacewomen.org/assets/file/NationalActionPlans/cotedivoire_nationalactionplan_january2007.pdf
100. The Swiss *National Action Plan for the implementation of UNSCR 1325* was launched in February 2007, and *revised* in October 2010. http://www.peacewomen.org/assets/file/NationalActionPlans/switzerland_nationalactionplan_february2007.pdf http://www.peacewomen.org/assets/file/NationalActionPlans/switzerland_nationalactionplanrevised_october2010en.pdf
101. The Austrian *National Action Plan on Implementing UNSCR 1325* was released on 8 August 2007. http://www.peacewomen.org/assets/file/NationalActionPlans/austria_nationalactionplan_august2007.pdf
102. http://www.peacewomen.org/assets/file/NationalActionPlans/dutch_nationalactionplan_december2007.pdf

103. Amnesty International Netherlands, Centre for Conflict Studies, University of Utrecht, Platform for Women and Sustainable Peace (member organizations), Cordaid, Department of Social Sciences, Wageningen University, Gender Concerns International, ICCO and Kerk in Actie (Church in Action), Ministry of Defence, Ministry of Foreign Affairs, Ministry of the Interior and Kingdom Relations Netherlands Organization for Scientific Research, Oxfam Novib, People Building Peace Netherlands (Steering Committee), SNV Netherlands Development Organization, Women's Global Network for Reproductive Rights, Women's International League for Peace and Freedom, Women Peacemakers Programme/International Fellowship of Reconciliation, WOMEN/Dutch Gender Platform.
104. Finland launched its *National Action Plan for the Implementation of UNSCR 1325* on 19 September 2008. http://www.peacewomen.org/assets/file/NationalActionPlans/finland_nationalactionplan_september 2008.pdf
105. In 2008 Uganda endorsed the Goma Declaration on Eradicating Sexual Violence and Ending Impunity in the Great Lakes Region.
106. http://www.peacewomen.org/assets/file/NationalActionPlans/uganda_nationalactionplan_december2008.pdf
107. http://www.peacewomen.org/assets/file/NationalActionPlans/liberia_nationalactionplanmarch2009.pdf
108. http://www.peacewomen.org/assets/file/belgium_nap_2009.pdf
109. http://www.peacewomen.org/assets/file/NationalActionPlans/chile_nationalactionplan_august2009.pdf
110. http://www.peacewomen.org/assets/file/NationalActionPlans/portugal_nationalactionplan_august_2009.pdf
111. http://www.peacewomen.org/assets/file/NationalActionPlans/sierra_leone_nap.pdf
112. http://www.peacewomen.org/assets/file/NationalActionPlans/philippine_nap.pdf
113. *The Rwandan* National Action Plan for the implementation of the UNSCR 1325 *was launched in May 2010. http://www.peacewomen.org/assets/file/NationalActionPlans/rwandan_national_action_plan_1325.pdf*
114. http://www.peacewomen.org/assets/file/bosniaherzegovina_nationalactionplan_2010.pdf
115. http://www.peacewomen.org/assets/file/Resources/Government/canada_nationalactionplan_october2010.pdf
116. http://www.peacewomen.org/assets/file/NationalActionPlans/estonia_nationalactionplan_november2010.pdf
117. http://www.peacewomen.org/assets/file/nepal_-_nap.pdf
118. France *National Action Plan on UNSCR 1325 Women,Peace & Security* was launched in November 2010. http://www.peacewomen.org/assets/file/NationalActionPlans/france_nationalactionplan_2010.pdf
119. http://www.peacewomen.org/assets/file/NationalActionPlans/italy_nationaactionplan_2010.pdf
120. http://www.peacewomen.org/assets/file/NationalActionPlans/croatia_nationalactionplan_2011.pdf

121. http://www.mzz.gov.si/fileadmin/pageuploads/Zunanja_politika/CP/NAP_1325_Slovenia_eng.pdf
122. http://www.nsc.gov.ge/files/files/NAP%201325_Georgia_Adopted%20Dec%2027_2011_%20Eng.pdf
123. http://www.peacewomen.org/assets/file/NationalActionPlans/us_nationalactionplan_2011.pdf
124. http://www.peacewomen.org/pages/about-1325/national-action-plans-naps
125. http://www.fahcsia.gov.au/sa/women/pubs/govtint/action_plan_women_peace/Documents/Aus_NAP_on_Women_2012_2018.pdf
126. United Nations Security Council, 2010, Women Peace and Security: Report of the UN Secretary-General, (S/2010/173), New York, United Nations.
127. http://www.peacewomen.org/commitments/?adhocpage=6560.
128. *Ibid.*
129. *Ibid.*
130. *Ibid.*
131. *Ibid.*
132. *Ibid.*
133. *Ibid.*
134. The term Arria formula refers to informal meetings outside Security Council chambers, where members of the Security Council are able to listen to the views of outsiders (usually NGOs) on a particular topic or conflict. The meeting format is named after Diego Arria, the Venezuelan ambassador to the UN who initiated the first meeting through inviting members to gather over coffee in the Delegates Lounge to hear the views of a Bosnian priest in 1993 an informal exchange between Council members and NGOs. The Arria Formula has been used more regularly since 1999 to provide expertise and testimony on thematic issues taken up by the Council, in particular on humanitarian issues, the Protection of Civilians in Armed Conflict, Children and Armed Conflict and more recently on Women, Peace and Security.
135. The NGO Working Group membership consists of the following organizations:

     Amnesty International, Consortium on Gender, Security and Human Rights, Femmes Africa Solidarité, Global Action to Prevent War, Global Justice Center, Human Rights Watch, International Action Network on Small Arms, International Alert, International Rescue Committee Open Society Institute, Refugees International, The Institute for Inclusive Security, Women's Action for New Directions, Women's Division, General Board of Global Ministries of the United Methodist Church, Women's International League for Peace and Freedom, Women's Refugee Commission.
136. www.womenpeacesecurity.org
137. http://www.1000peacewomen.org/media/Broschueren/PWAG_1325_overview%20posters_en.pdf
138. Anwarul Chowdhury (2011), *The Intrinsic Role of Women in Peace and Security—Genesis and Follow-up of UNSCR 1325*, Palestine-Israel Journal, Vol. 17, No. 3, p. 2. http://www.pij.org/details.php?id=1365.

4

Women, Peace and Security in South Asia—Perspectives and Implementation of Resolution 1325

South Asia, comprising seven States,[1] though culturally rich and diverse, is the most conflict ridden region in the world. Low in the ranking of Human Development Index (HDI)[2] and Gender Inequality Index (GII),[3] the region is home to one-fifth of world's population, accountable for fifty per cent world's illiterate and forty per cent of the world's poor.[4]

The most malnourished region ironically is the most militarized region. The extent of human deprivation in the region contrasts with the large armies, modern weapons and increasing defense budgets, arms race, and nuclear power struggle, which keeps the region with growing unrest. Low on Global Peace Index (GPI),[5] the region is high on military spending. A database on Military Budgets of Stockholm International Peace Research Institute (SIPRI) 2010, shows that India with ninth rank in the world is one of the highest military spending country. While Pakistan is on the 30th position, other South Asian Countries, Sri Lanka, Nepal, Bangladesh are on 66th, 70th and 106th position respectively in the world.[6]

Table 4.1 presents the trends in military spending and expenditure on social sectors in South Asia from 1995 to 2005. Over

TABLE 4.1

Trends in Military Spending and Expenditure on Social Sectors in South Asia (1995-2005)

Countries	*Ranking of the Spending on the military and defense*	*Defense Expenditure (US$ million)*			*Defense expenditure as % of education and health expenditure US $ millions*		
		1995	*2005*	*Annual Growth (1995-2005)*	*1995*	*2005*	*Annual Growth (1995-2005)*
(1)	*(2)*	*(3)*	*(4)*	*(5)*	*(6)*	*(7)*	*(8)*
Afghanistan	n/a	n/a	n/a	n/a	n/a	n/a	n/a
Bangladesh	70	536	669	2.2	40	38	-0.6
India	10	9753	22268	8.6	72	55	-2.7
Nepal	106	40	175	16.0	20	40	7.1
Pakistan	30	3544	4537	2.5	162	178	0.9
Sri Lanka	66	686	612	-1.1	120	68	-5.5
South Asia		145559	28260	6.9	79	66	-1.7

Sources : SIPRI 2010 and World Bank Report, 2007.

the decade (1995-2005), the growth in defense expenditure is 6.9 per cent in the region, while the expenditure on social sectors has decreased by 1.7 per cent. India's annual growth on defense budget increased by nearly 8.6 per cent, while Pakistan increased it by nearly 2.5 per cent. Similarly, Nepal increased it by 16 per cent and Bangladesh increased by 2.2 per cent. Only Sri Lanka's annual growth was reduced by -1.1 per cent. However, the defense expenditure as percentage of education and health expenditure has gone down in India, Bangladesh and Sri Lanka. In Pakistan and Nepal, this ratio has gone up. The higher defense expenditure of South Asian countries continues to be an area of concern.[7]

South Asia, with the exception of Bhutan and Maldives continues to be one of the most volatile regions of the world with both external and internal conflicts. The post-colonial history has witnessed two partitions,[8] five inter-state wars,[9] armed struggle for self-determination, a struggle for democracy, a long time militancy and low intensity of armed conflict. Accordingly the Global Peace Index (GPI) reports do not palace the region as a peaceful region. The 2011 GPI Report in fact shows that the South Asian countries have fallen sharply in maintaining peace. Table 4.2 reflects the ranking of the South Asian Countries in the Global Peace Index (2007-11) that covers 153 countries. Afghanistan and Pakistan are the most unpeaceful countries in the region followed by India. Afghanistan has been ranked at 150th position, as against its 137th rank in 2008, 143rd in 2009 and 147th in 2010.

Pakistan is ranked as the world's eighth most unstable country, better than only Afghanistan, Iraq, Somalia, Congo, DPR Korea, Russian Federation and Sudan. It is at 146th position, 29 ranks lower than its 2007 position.

India's position also continues to be adverse as it is ranked at 135th position, 7 and 26 points lower than its position in 2010 and 2007 respectively. Sri Lanka though has improved its position by 7 ranks, still it is at 126th position. Nepal has plunged in GPI ranking of peaceful nations from 77th rank in 2009, 82nd rank in 2010 to 95th position in 2011.

Bangladesh and Bhutan continue to improve as Bangladesh has moved from 90th position in 2009 to 87th in 2010 and 83rd position in 2011. Bhutan has the distinction of being the most peaceful country in the region and has moved up from its 36th rank in 2010 to 34th in 2011.

TABLE 4.2
Ranking of South Asian Countries in Global Peace Index, 2009-11

Countries	*2011*	*2010*	*2009*	*2008*	*2007*
Afghanistan	150	147	143	137	—
Bangladesh	83	87	90	86	86
Bhutan	34	36	40	26	19
India	135	128	122	107	109
Nepal	95	82	–	–	–
Pakistan	146	145	137	127	115
Sri Lanka	126	133	125	125	111

Source : The Institute for Economics and Peace (IEP).

Most of the region being unpeaceful and conflict ridden, the implementation of SCR 1325 assumes added significance. More so, as stated earlier, the focus of most of the studies has been on Africa and Middle East. There are many faces of women in conflicts in South Asia, to quote Rita Manchanda. How does Resolution 1325 impact the women in terms of prevention and protection of women and girls, their contribution to conflict resolution and sustainable peace needs a critical analysis. The Member-States have onerous obligations as envisaged in the Resolution 1325. How far the South Asian Governments have been active and serious in giving effect to the provisions of the Resolution is examined in the following pages.

Before the implementation of SCR 1325 is analyzed, it may be in the fitness of things that conflict situations and their impact on women in their different facets are discussed in South Asia country-wise.

Afghanistan

Conflict has been a feature of life in *Afghanistan* since 1973. The Soviet Union invaded the country in 1979 in an attempt to help the Communist movement in Afghanistan. After ten years of fighting against the religious *mujahideen*, the Soviet army withdrew in 1989, leaving behind a big reserve of arms and ammunition. Civil war continued among a number of ethnic militias for several years until the emergence of the Taliban, a group of young fighters belonging to the *Pashtun* ethnic group and espousing an extreme interpretation of Islam. The Taliban managed to win several military victories, and by

1997, were in control of most of the country. They were initially welcomed for their role in establishing law and order, but grew unpopular over time for their brutal code of justice, and for enforcing extremely strict rules on the population.[10]

After the attack of September 11, 2001, the United States and its NATO allies invaded Afghanistan and toppled the Taliban regime within a few weeks. However, the top leaders of Taliban managed to escape. They then regrouped in the eastern provinces of Afghanistan, with the help of the Pashtun population in tne border areas of Pakistan. Taliban activities continue to harm and threaten civilians, as does the government's lack of resolve on protecting civilians from criminals and human rights violators. The situation is one of on-going conflict. Talibans, other insurgent groups (like Hekmatyar group), criminal cartels, drug rings, warlords, local militias and former majahideen commanders continue to destabilize communities and the country and perpetuate a violent system that denies rights to both men and women.[11]

In the 30 years of war, women and girls have suffered immensely. The Afghan Women's Network in their *Report on UNSCR 1325—Implementation in Afghanistan* authored by Zarin Hamid records that "during the armed phase of each violent conflict in Afghanistan, women have faced not only the dangerous conditions violent conflict brings to life, limb, and property, they have also withstood negative cultural practices that existed long before any war erupted in the country, rape, physical insecurity due to gender, forced and early marriage, customary practices of *bad* and *badal kardan* 14, denial of the right to education, access to justice and health care, the right to work, the right to be involved in the public and social affairs of their communities, and the right to self-determination. These denials and abuses existed before violent conflict erupted and mutated over the past 30 years, but the war environment further exacerbated the denials and abuses faced by women and girls all over Afghanistan".[12]

The Report further points out that even former mujahideen and communist governments were equally responsible for violence and sexual violence affecting women and girls. Rape, sexual violence, assault and harassment are not topics that are openly discussed in Afghanistan, says the Report. "From informal discussions with women who have lived through all phases of the conflict", affirms the Report, "it is clear that rape and sexual violence or the threat of either have been a part of the experience of war for Afghan women. Women's survival during the conflict often included the fear of and tactic to fend of possibilities of rape or kidnapping by militia soldiers or even members of a community. During conflict, rapists and other violators acted with impunity".[13]

Bangladesh

Bangladesh emerged as a nation state in 1971. On the partition of India in 1947, East Bengal being predominantly populated by Muslims, became part of Pakistan and came to be known as East Pakistan. The region always felt discriminated and exploited. Linguistic, cultural and ethnic differences further heightened the estrangement between the two wings of Pakistan. Denial of political space to political leadership from East Pakistan, an indefinite postponement of National Assembly elections by President Yahya Khan in 1971 and finally military crackdown in East Pakistan led to the liberation war and declaration of Independence. There was massive exodus of Bengali population to India. The army committed horrible repression and sought to stop secession. Fighting grew between Pakistan Army and Bengali Mukti Bahini. Anthony Mascarenhas in *Bangladesh: A Legacy of Blood* estimates that during the entire nine-month liberation struggle more than 1 million Bengalis may have died from the hands of the Pakistan Army.[14] India extended its support to Mukti Bahini and that escalated into a full war between India and Pakistan. Pakistan army surrendered in East Pakistan on December 16, 1971, a new nation was born and it changed its name to Bangladesh on January 11, 1972.

Bangladesh though a relatively peaceful country has had its own history of internal conflicts with religious extremism and fundamentalism affecting the polity on one side, military coups and insurgency in Chiittagong Hill Tracts (CHT) interspersing its history on the other.

The *Chittagong Hill Tracts Conflict* was a political conflict and an armed struggle between the Government of Bangladesh and the Parbatya Chattagram Jana Sanghati Samiti (PCJSS)—(United People's Party of the Chittagong Hill Tracts) and its armed wing, the Shanti Bahini over the issue of autonomy and the rights of the indigenous peoples and tribes of the Chittagong Hill Tracts.The Shanti Bahini launched an insurgency against the government forces in 1977, and the conflict continued for twenty years until the government and the PCJSS signed the Chittagong Hill Tracts Peace Accord in 1997.[15]

Both the *liberation war* and the conflict in *Chittagong Hill Tracts* have affected women in Bangladesh. During the liberation war against Pakistan and the nine months of turmoil, numerous women were tortured, raped and killed at the hands of Pakistani soldiers. Exact figures not being available, Susan Brownmiller in her ground-breaking work, *Against Our Will: Men, Women and Rape* writes "200,000, 300,000 or possibly 400,000 women were raped. Eighty percent of the raped women were Moslems, reflecting the population of Bangladesh, but Hindu and Christian women were not exempt." Hit-and-run rape of large number of Bengali women was brutally simple in terms of logistics as the Pakistani regulars swept through and occupied the tiny, populous land."[16]

The Sheikh Mujibar Rahman had proclaimed all raped women as "heroines" of the war of independence but the reality is that these women were not accepted by the traditional society, they were ostracized and lived a life of ignonimity.

Brownmiller gives horrific accounts of several individual women who suffered sexual violence citing different sources. "Rape in Bangladesh had hardly been restricted to beauty," writes Brownmiller.[17] "Girls of eight and grandmothers of seventy-five had been sexually assaulted ... Pakistani soldiers had not only violated Bengali women on the spot; they abducted tens of hundreds and held them by force in their military barracks for nightly use."[18] Some women may have been raped as many as eighty times in a night".[19] Pakistan army kept numerous Bengali women as sex slaves inside the Dhaka Cantonments. Thousands of war babies were born. Bangladesh sources cite a figure of 2,00,000 such raped women giving birth to their war babies.[20]

In the CHT conflict which claimed hundreds of lives, the indigenous women were targeted for their ethnicity and gender, which centred on their central role as the transmitters of their culture to future generations. There are countless reports of rape, forced marriages and abductions of indigenous Jumma women. Many women were gang raped by the soldiers of the Bangladesh Army, often in front of their children. The Bangladesh military systematically used rape as a deliberate tactic to destroy or damage the Jumma nation. According to the Hill Women's Federation (HWF), there have been 47 reported cases of rapes between January 1991 and June 1992, five in 1993, four in 1994 and twelve in 1995.[21]

Although the Peace Accord of 1997 has paved the way for a return to normalcy in the Hill Tracts, with the military maintaining a constant and continuous presence in the region, indigenous women do not feel secure, and there are continuing reports of rape and sexual violence, committed by the armed forces, and/or the settlers.[22]

India

India is the largest democracy in the world. It emerged as a sovereign independent State with partition of the country in 1947. It has a unique history of facing wars both at its borders with China and Pakistan, a long drawn proxy war in Jammu and Kashmir and ongoing conflicts in the form of separatist movements in the North-East.

The partition of the country into India and Pakistan took a massive toll in the two countries in terms of violence and mass movement of people both within and across borders as displaced persons and refugees. In 1962, it fought a war with China, followed by successive wars with Pakistan in 1965 and 1971 and another limited war with Pakistan in 1999. Although India does not declare officially any of its zones of violence as conflict zones, it is fighting armed groups for decades in many of its States. This is especially true of Kashmir, the North-Eastern States.

Kashmir continues to be a bone of contention between India and Pakistan since 1948. But the valley has been hit hard by militancy since 1989 with the cry for 'Azadi'. The Kashmir Valley is highly militarized because of the open support of Pakistan to the militants in the valley and proxy war which has caused a number of deaths and displacement of people. Commenting upon the situation, Rita Manchanda writes :

> "In the Kashmir Valley and the hill districts girdling it, 1989-90 saw a popular upsurge for self-determination which brought women, men, and children out on the streets raising the cry for azadi. Within the mass popular protest was the undertow of a fledgling armed militancy. The Indian state retaliated with severe repression and military force. In the ensuing armed conflict, an estimated seventy thousand people have been killed, more than two thousand have 'disappeared' or are in illegal detention. There are fifteen thousand widows and thousands of half widows of the disappeared. A generation has grown up which has known nothing other than armed conflict. The social capital of Kashmir has been destroyed as multiple armed agencies are at large with little or no accountability. More than half a million people have been displaced."[23]

The confrontation between India and Pakistan became especially dangerous after 1998, when both the countries conducted a series of nuclear tests and showed the world their ability to build nuclear weapons. During his visit to the region in March 2000, the then President Bill Clinton of USA declared Kashmir to be "the most dangerous place on earth". His assessment was based not on an evaluation of day-to-day security threats faced by the civilians in Kashmir, but on the concern that the territory might become the cause of a nuclear exchange that would have far-reaching effects.[24] The strife-torn region witnessed a period of relative calm in the last decade, but 2010 saw the resurgence of protests in response to 'Quit Jammu Kashmir Movement' and call for 'Azadi' by Hurriyat Conference led by Syed Ali Shah Geelani and Mirwaiz Umar Farooq. It is a grim reminder of the tension in Kashmir.[25] Complete demilitarization of Jammu and Kashmir is demanded along with withdrawal of the Armed Force (Special Power) Act (AFSPA).

The North-East consisting of seven States[26] is a region strife with insurgency and violence with strong inter-ethnic rivalries and secessionist movements. Insurgency in Assam began in 1979, with the formation of the United Liberation Front of Assam (ULFA) aimed at establishing a "sovereign, socialist Assam". Since 2005, ULFA has been in a process of indirect negotiations with the government via a People's Consultative Group. However, they continue their campaign of violence, and did not respond to a unilateral ceasefire announced by the government in 2006. The government was more successful in dealing with another insurgency in Assam, which began in the late 1980s with the goal of autonomy and greater recognition for the Bodo tribe. A series of peace accords with various Bodo groups culminated in the formation of a Bodoland Territorial Council for the Bodo-dominated areas in 2003, and the inclusion of the Bodo language in the Constitution of India.[27]

The insurgency in Manipur is also a long standing one, beginning with the formation of the United National Liberation Front (UNLF) in 1964, which has independence for Manipur as its goal. Since then, numerous other violent groups have espoused the same cause.[28] Nagaland also faced a strong secessionist movement. However, the level of violence has come down quite substantially in the most recent years with the negotiations between the government and the militant groups. A ceasefire has been in place between the government and the National Socialist Council of Nagaland—Isak-Muivah (NSCN-IM) since 1997, and with the NSCN-Khaplang since

2004; both these groups aim at establishing a "greater Nagaland". However, these groups continue to have clashes with each other and with other militant groups in Nagaland and in Manipur.The off and on disputes between Nagaland and Manipur leading at times to economic blockade of Manipur.

The entire North-East belt because of insurgency and security reasons has heavy deployment of armed forces. Similarly, the "Naxalite" movement in India which is especially active in the States of Bihar, Chhattisgarh, Jharkhand, Orissa and West Bengal, and Andhra Pradesh is also contributing to armed conflict situation in the country. This has been identified by Prime Minister Manmohan Singh as "the single biggest security challenge to the Indian State."[29]

A number of studies have appeared lately that reveal how women have been impacted by the conflict situations in India. The partition of the country that resulted into communal violence affected women on both sides of the borders. Women faced brutal sexual violence. To save their 'honour' women in large number jumped into the wells or were poisoned to death by their parents. A study by Urvashi Butalia on *The Other Side of Silence: Voices from the Partition of India* provides statistical evidence to the gruesome violence during partition. The study reveals that around 2 million people died in violence and an estimated 75,000-1,00,000 women were abducted and raped."[30]

Likewise women have been the major sufferers of conflict in Kashmir. According to Urvashi Bhutalia, in situations of conflict and particularly those involving religious identities, women are targeted in specific ways. "In times of conflict, particularly religious conflict" she writes, "it is women who carry the honor of the community on their backs and bodies and defiling their bodies usually through rape is a way of hitting back at the other community".[31] While the militants have used rape as a common way to humiliate members of the "other community", Indian security forces have used rape primarily as an instrument to punish those who were in any way connected to militants. During the height of militancy and as part of the counter-insurgency operations, one of the most frightful incidents of human rights violations by Indian security forces were the 1993 Shopian and Kunan Pushpora incidents. In the Shopian case, two young women were gang raped while in the Kunan Pushpora incidents, approximately 53 women were gang raped by Indian army personnel. The victims were old women as well as young girls.[32] A 1994 study carried out by the Kashmiri Women's Initiative for Peace and

Disarmament (KWIPD) found that most of them were unmarried and carried the stigma of the incident.[33]

They suffer at the hands of hard core militants as well. These militants seek to enforce an 'Islamic' code of behavior and resort to violent attacks on women. Intriguing is role of the women's militant organization Dukhtaran-e-Millat (Daughters of the Nation) who often joins hands with these extremists to threaten women and issue warnings to women not to come outside without *burqas.*[34] On May 13, 1993 when such a 'dictat' was issued, the militants reportedly sprayed paint on the women who defied the order, such that four students were hospitalized with dye injuries from the point.[35] It is estimated that over 9,000 women have been raped and molested, 22,000 women widowed and around 10,600 children orphaned in Kashmir conflict from January 1989 to June 30, 2010.[36] Based on her interviews of displaced Kashmiri women, Asha Hans records the narratives of massacre of women and children, of abductions of whole families and mass suicides by women wanting to escape sexual abuse.[37]

One of the repercussions of the conflict has been the increasing number of widows and half widows[38]. Meera Khanna writing on the problems of Kashmiri widows observes : "The stress of responsibility, widowhood, the trauma of losing the loved ones have left many women suffering from mental disorders, insomnia, poor physical health. Widowhood has brought a drastic change in nutrition levels since the former is often accompanied by poverty. Many of the women affected by conflict complain of poor menstrual cycles thus impacting their reproductive life. Problems are acute as medical help is absent particularly in the inaccessible regions. Many women are maimed when caught in cross firing between militants and security forces or due to mine fields. Finally, there are a large number of young women and widows with very little hope of a marital relationship since there is a paucity of eligible males. A generation has been wiped out by the armed conflict."[39]

According to the Association of Parents of Disappeared Persons (APDP) in Kashmir more than 10,000 people have been subject to enforced disappearance by state agencies.[40] The conflict has left "half-widows" in the valley. Exact number of such widows is not known. According to media reports and local sources, their number ranges between 1000 and 1500.[41] Saeed ur Rehman Siddiqui records that "the Indian government does not provide any relief to half-widows before the expiry of seven years from the date of disappearance. And even after the completion of seven years from the date of disappearance, they get either a one-time grant ranging from US$ 1,000 and US$ 2,000 or a monthly pension of US$ 10. Further, a half-widow cannot remarry until the expiration of seven years from the date of disappearance of her husband whose whereabouts must not be known in these seven years. In the meantime, the right to her husband's property are often threatened. Some widows, who intend to remarry, largely do not find men who are willing to marry them."[42]

Similarly, the Dardpora, a border village in Kashmir is referred to as the 'village of widows'. The village has about 300 orphans and 122 widows.[43] These women are frequently left without land, homes, inheritance, social assistance and pensions. They are equally vulnerable to harassment from men.

The insurgency in Kashmir has led since 1989 to the internal displacement of 90 per cent of Hindu Kashmiri Pandits, an estimated 250,000-350,000 people.[44] They fled for two reasons, fear or economic uncertainty and the fear of sexual assault of women by the militants and security personnel. Displaced women face not only a continual threat of rape, but also other forms of gender-based violence including prostitution, sexual humiliation, trafficking and domestic violence.[45]

Likewise the North-East region has been suffering from gross violations of civil and political rights directly impacting upon women's rights. The militarization of the region, the presence of the military forces and armed militant groups has intensified the violence faced by women which takes the form of sexual, mental and physical abuse. A study done by the Centre on North-East Studies and Policy Research "Bearing Witness—the Impact of Conflict on Women in Nagaland and Assam (2009-10)" documents how women have suffered in the two States since the first conflict between the Naga insurgents and the Indian security forces.

Another study done by the North-East Network (NEN) on "Violence Against Women in North-East" that focuses on Assam and Manipur discuses at length with the support of field case studies the gendered impact of conflict on the lives of women. Trafficking, forced migration, vulnerability to HIV/AIDS, increased number of female headed households and above all the resurgence of patriarchal values and norms, which have brought with them new restrictions on the movement of women, the dress they wear and more overtly physical violence such as rape which is systematically used as tactic against a particular community, points out the study.[46]

The security forces enjoy immunity under the Armed Force (Special Powers) Act. One of the human rights defender Irom Sharmila has been fasting for the last 10 years against this Act.

Nepal

Politically, *Nepal* was a monarchy till 1990, when widespread protests led to the establishment of a multi-party democracy. The first parliamentary elections were held in 1991, followed by the general elections conducted in 1994 and 1999. Insurgency broke out in 1996 when the Communist Party of Nepal-Maoist (CPN-M) launched a violent "People's War" in the western districts of Rolpa and Rukum. Structural inequality, exclusion and discrimination, concentration and abuse of power and poverty were key factors behind the insurgency. The main objectives of the insurgents were to abolish the monarchy, establish a people's republic and elect a Constituent Assembly to draft a new Constitution for the country.

Started from two districts in 1996, the Maoist movement in Nepal spread all over the country within a decade. The ten-year long insurgency in Nepal ended when the Government of Nepal and the Maoists signed a Comprehensive Peace Accord (CPA) in 2006 with abolition of monarchy. The damage to life, and infrastructure was unparalleled, with more than 13,000 men, women and children estimated to have died.[47] It is estimated that more than 200,000 people, of whom more than 80 per cent were women and children, were internally displaced during the conflict period (1995-2006).[48]

Even after the 2006 ceasefire, about 100,000 people remain displaced. Insurgency impacted the lives of women and girls in many ways. The supporters of armed groups were equally subjected to torture, rape, etc. According to the Watchlist on Children and Armed Conflict Report, in 2004 approximately 1040-1200 women suffered violations related to rape, abductions, injuries and some were even killed by both Maoists and government forces.[49] Girls were also raped and subjected to other forms of sexual violence by Maoists and government forces. Survivors of gender-based violence often remain silent due to lack of protection for them.

Trafficking of women and girls was a problem even before the armed conflict but it was exacerbated by the insurgency. Approximately 5,000 to 12,000 Nepalese girls are trafficked into forced prostitution each year.[50] In addition, children who are orphaned or separated from their parents and families due to the armed conflict are at a higher risk of ending up on the streets, in unsafe labour conditions, including commercial sex work, and in other vulnerable situations.[51]

Women were disproportionately affected by the decade-long conflict and its aftermath: Sexual violence was prevalent during rebel attacks, war widows were subjected to violence and discrimination, and national insecurity led to an increase in trafficked women. Displaced women who are not widows, sexual violence victims or former combatants also doubt their potential to resume their pre-conflict lives. About 19,000 of these former female fighters are demobilized in cantonment camps.[52]

Pakistan

Since independence from British India in 1947, *Pakistan* has experienced multiple inter-state and intra-state conflicts including wars with India. Pakistan is currently embroiled in a number of conflicts on several fronts. The continuous terrorist attacks, clashes between the security forces and the militants, military operations, political violence, inter-tribe sectarian clashes and border clashes are the biggest threat to the state and citizens of Pakistan. The regions of the Federally Administered Tribal Areas (FATA) and the North-West Frontier Province (NWFP), which share a border with Afghanistan and are the conflict prone areas due to the resurgence of the Taliban in 2005. Balochistan is another disturbed area of Pakistan where sepratist movement is very strong. An armed insurgency was active in 1974-77 led by the Balochistan People's Liberation Front. A negotiated settlement in 1977 ended the conflict leading to the withdrawal of government troops and release of militant leaders. The conflict resumed in 2004 when new Baloch groups again challenged the government, but after the assaination of the leading separatist leader (Nawab Akbar Bugti) by the military in 2006, the separatist movement was weakened. Subsequently, groups such as the Balochistan Liberation Army, Balochistan Republican Army, and Baloch Ittihad have been up in arms against the government in 2009.[53]

Another group that is active for autonomy in Pakistan is that of Muttahidda [Mothaidda] Quami Movement (MQM), formerly known as the Mohajir Quami Movement. It is a political group which represents the Urdu-speaking immigrant urban Mohajir population which migrated from India at the time of creation of Pakistan in 1947 and has been demanding more autonomy and recognition as a constituent ethnic group of Pakistan. The Mohajir Quami Movement came into being on March 18, 1984,[54] became active in 1999 and again in 1995 and 1996. In 2007, fighting resumed between the government and the MQM group. The Group promoted the replacement of the Pakistani system of government with an Islamic caliphate.[55]

Pakistan faces massive displacement of its population due to armed conflicts. Over the past seven years five million have been displaced. In December, 2011 almost one million remained internally displaced by armed conflict in North-West. According to the Human Rights Commission of Pakistan after the Afghan refugee crisis that began in 1979, large scale involuntary displacement has been caused by military operations against militants in Malakand region of Khyber Pakhtunkhwa province in 2009 with an exodus of 2.3 million people and again military offensive against Taliban militant in Federally Administered Tribal Area (FATA) bordering Afghanistan caused displacement of 2.7 million persons.[56] Though it goes without saying that women suffer more and are vulnerable in such situations but there is no gender disaggregated data. Najam U Din, the author of the Commission Report cites the United Nations Population Fund (UNFPA) to say that in June 2009, 69,000 pregnant women were among the population displaced and living in camps at increased risk as a result of massive offensive against the militants in Swat and other areas. He further concedes that it is established that women face specific risks and violation of their rights.

The Talibans had effectively banished women from the public sphere, even barring them from leaving homes, access to education had been effected as most of the educational institutions were bombed by the militants and girls were barred by the families from attending schools. "Even a cursory analysis of the enforced displacement crises in Pakistan demonstrates", writes Najam U Din, "that displaced women have had unequal access to assistance and protection... The situation has been particularly difficult for displaced families headed by women... Female headed families and women even in camps were not approached separately through female staff."[57] It is recommended that "Humanitarian action in Pakistan in general needs to be more firmly grounded in the principle of gender equality and women need to be equally consulted and engaged in decision-making process. It is also important to ensure an enabling environment in camps so that women are able to raise protection and assistance concerns."[58]

Sri Lanka

The *Sri Lankan Civil War* between the Liberation Tigers of

Tamil Eelam (LTTE) and the Government of Sri Lanka dates back to 1983. The LTTE had been fighting for an independent Tamil state—Tamil Eelam in the north and the east of the Island. The civil war caused significant hardships for the population, environment and the economy of the country, with an estimated 80,000-100,000 people killed during conflict.[59] After nearly two decades of continuing violence, the government signed a cease fire agreement with the LTTE in 2002, resulting in a declining trend in violence through 2004. Violence erupted again and it is only in May 2009, the Sri Lankan military defeated the Tamil Tigers.

The armed conflict in *Sri Lanka* which began in 1983 between government forces and Liberation Tigers of Tamil Elam (LTTE) have resulted over 281,000 people internally displaced[60]. In Jaffna, Sri Lanka, there were 19,000 registered widows and 2100 children living in the government welfare centers.[61] Women have experienced gender-based violence but it is greatly underreported, particularly in conflict situations.

From the above discussion clearly establishes that with the exception of Bhutan, the whole South Asia has been conflict zone and the conflicts have directly/indirectly affected the lives of civilians. Women have suffered disproportionally. They have been dehumanized, their bodies used as a battlefield and sexual violence used systematically as a weapon of war. Their rights have been violated, they have been excluded, stigmatized and traumatized, deprived of their livelihoods and of access to health care and education—as evidenced by the increased female illiteracy rate, and increased infant and maternal mortality rate. To date, there is no accountability for the thousands of crimes of sexual gender-based violence (SGBV) and other human rights abuses committed during the conflict and insurgent situations, which continues in localized areas.

IMPLEMENTATION OF THE SECURITY COUNCIL RESOLUTION 1325 IN SOUTH ASIA

The premise of SCR 1325 is gender equality. The implementation of the Resolution therefore directly correlates it. While gender inequality is a worldwide phenomenon faced by all the regions of the developed and developing world, in South Asia almost all the countries are rather low on the Gender Development Index (GDI), now called as Gender Inequality Index (GII) of the Human

Development Report. Patriarchy is still a strong social norm in the region. Illiteracy and gender-based violence further limit women's participation in public and private sphere of life.[62]

TABLE 4.3

Gender Inequality Index (GII), 2010

Countries	*Gender Inequality Index (GII)*
Afghanistan	134
Bangladesh	116
India	122
Nepal	110
Pakistan	112
Sri Lanka	72

Table 4.3 represents the *Gender Inequality Index (GII)* ranking of South Asian countries. All the South Asian Countries are at the bottom of the index. Only Sri Lanka occupies 72nd rank in the GII. While India's rank is 122, Pakistan's rank is 114 and that of Nepal is 110. Afghanistan has the worst ranking in GII; it is at the bottom of all the countries of South Asia with 134th rank.

The low level of gender equality in South Asia, as would be seen in the following pages, reflects the state of implementation of SCR in the region. Resolution 1325 is an action document. It is a framework for bringing change to the lives of women and girls affected by war. The Resolution puts women at the centre, articulating the unique ways in which war affects women and the measures needed to integrate women's voices into peace processes and reconstruction.

The Security Council Resolution 1325 as seen in the provisions chapter focuses on *THREE* broad themes which are :

A. *Participation* of Women in Decision-making and Peace Processes.
B. *Protection* and *Prevention* of Gender-based Violence Against Women and Girls through the *Promotion* of Women's Rights, Accountability and Law Enforcement..
C. *Gender Mainstreaming* in Peace Keeping Operations.

The implementation of the Resolution in South Asia and several initiatives undertaken at the regional and at the national levels are discussed under the above three broad themes.

A. Participation of Women in Decision-making and Peace Processes

The participation of women is one of the crucial factors for sustainable peace-building. Paragraph 1 of SCR 1325 obligates the Member States to ensure increased representation of women at all decision-making levels in national, regional and international institutions and mechanisms for the prevention, management, and resolution of conflict. The Resolution is not about the inclusion of women for the sake of political correctness. It is rooted in the premise that women's inclusion—their presence and participation in the processes, their perspectives and contribution to the substance of talks, will improve the chances of attaining viable and sustainable peace. It is also rooted in the knowledge that gender equality itself is a source of sustainable peace.

As far as women's participation in the decision-making bodies is concerned, the scenario is not a very happy one. Women constitute half of the world's population. Yet their participation in the world's formal political structures and processes remains insignificant. With clear-cut public and private dichotomy, women earlier were not considered fit for public domain of politics. The ancient democracies failed to recognize women as citizens. Political thinker, Aristotle, equated women with slaves and children and denied them the right to participate as citizens in the political life in his book *Politics.* He said "the slave has no deliberative faculty at all; the woman has, but it is without authority"[63] Therefore, he concludes that the male is by nature superior, and the female inferior; and the one rules, and the other is ruled.[64] Indeed, he declares, women are incapable of rationality; hence must be excluded from the noblest pursuit, that is art of politics. Similarly, other political thinkers and philosophers such as Hegal, Kant, Lock and Rousseau legitimised the exclusion of women from the public sphere. They believed that the subordination of woman was due to her biological origin, which made her inferior to man. These arguments ascribed 'socio-cultural construct' to legitimise domination of man in politics. This situation has not changed and politics continue to be the considered as masculine activity.

It is only towards the end of the Eighteenth Century and the beginning of the Nineteenth Century, that voices began to be raised for women's equality and liberty. Mary Wollstonecraft, Margarate Fuller, Elizabeth Stanton, the Grimke sister need special mention who took up the cause of women's rights. So did J.S. Mill in his *The Subjection of Women* and Federick Engels in his *Family, Private Property and State.* The suffrage movement for women gained momentum almost the same time and New Zealand became the first country to grant right to vote to women towards the end of the Nineteenth Century (1893), followed later by other countries.[65]

Over the decades, women's movements, International Conventions and national policies are working to ensure a more adequate representation of women in decision-making mechanisms. There has been a growing recognition of the importance to society of full participation of women in power and decision-making at all levels and in all forums. However, it is hard to claim even in this present era that gender equality has been achieved in this arena. The Convention on the Elimination of All Forms of Discrimination against Women stresses the importance of equal participation of women with men in government. Under Article 21 of the Universal Declaration of Human Rights, "everyone has the right to take part in the government of his country ... Everyone has the right to equal access to public service in his country."[66] Under Article 13 of the International Covenant on Civil and Political Rights, "every citizen shall have the right and the opportunity ... to take part in the conduct of public affairs .. to have access, on general terms of equality, to public service in his country."[67]

Special mention may be made here to the Nairobi Forward Looking Strategies (NFLS) adopted at the Nairobi Conference (1985), the Beijing Platform for Action (1995) and the Outcome Document for Further Initiatives adopted at the UN GASS in 2000. The NFLS states categorically that " women by virtue of their gender, experience discrimination in terms of denial of equal access to the power structure that controls society and determines development issues and peace initiatives".[68] It recommended that efforts must be made to remove obstacles that inhibit women from joining this male exclusive domain and that alternate electoral systems be resorted to, such as quota to enhance women's representation.

The Beijing Platform for Action lists this issue as one of the twelve critical areas of concern for action. It states "*Women's empowerment and their full participation on the basis of equality in all spheres of society, in changing participation in the decision-making process and access to power, are fundamental for the advancement of equality, development and peace*"[69]

The BPFA categorically affirms that women should have at least thirty per cent share in decision-making positions. However, the Beijing +5 Review revealed that much headway had not been made in this direction. It is conceded in the Outcome Document adopted at the Special Session of the General Assembly in 2000 that "*the goals set and commitments made in the Platform for Action have not been fully achieved and implemented, and have agreed upon further actions and initiatives at the local, national, regional and international levels to accelerate the implementation of the Platform for Action and to ensure that commitments for gender equality, development and peace are fully realized.*[70]

It continues further to add that: "*despite general acceptance of the need for a gender balance in decision-making bodies at all levels, a gap between de jure and de facto equality has persisted. Notwithstanding substantial improvement of de jure equality between women and men, the actual participation of women at the highest levels of national and international decision-making has not significantly changed since the time of the Fourth World Conference on Women in 1995, and gross under representation of women in decision-making bodies in all areas, including politics, conflict prevention and resolution mechanisms, the economy, the environment and the media, hinders the inclusion of a gender perspective in these critical spheres of influence. Women continue to be underrepresented at the legislative, ministerial and sub-ministerial levels...*"[71]

TABLE 4.4

Women in World Parliaments as on 31 March, 2011

Women in World Parliaments	*Men*	*Women*	*Total*	*Percentage of Women (%)*
Single House or Lower House	29,865	7,156	37,021	19.3
Upper House	5,581	1,250	6,861	18.3
Both Houses Combined	35,446	8,406	43,852	19.2

Table 4.4 clearly presents the position of women in world Parliaments. As of March 31, 2011, there are 43,852 members of Parliament. Out of these, women make up 19.3 per cent in the lower parliamentary houses and 18.3 per cent in the upper parliamentary houses.[72]

Table 4.5 represents the Regional Averages of Women in Parliament. According to the Inter-Parliamentary Union (IPU), the Nordic countries have distinctly led the way in having 41.6 per cent seats occupied by women in the Lower House[73] followed by Americas with 22.4 per cent, Europe—OSCE with 21.9 per cent, Sub-Sahara with 19.0 per cent, Asia with 18.3 per cent, Pacific with 12.4 per cent and the Arab States being at the bottom with only 11.4 per cent women in the Lower Houses.

TABLE 4.5

Regional Averages of Women in Parliaments as on 31 March, 2011

Regions	*Single House or Lower House (%)*	*Upper House or Senate (%)*	*Both Houses combined (%)*
Nordic countries	41.6	—	—
Americas	22.4	23.5	22.6
Europe—OSCE member-countries including Nordic countries	21.9	19.7	21.5
Europe—OSCE member-countries excluding Nordic countries	20.0	19.7	20.0
Sub-Saharan Africa	19.0	19.7	19.1
Asia	18.3	15.3	18.0
Pacific	12.4	32.6	14.7
Arab States	11.4	7.3	10.7

As of January 1, 2010, only 35 women leaders preside over one of the Houses of the existing 262 Chambers of Parliaments. Of these 187 Parliaments, 75 are bicameral legislatures.[74] Only 9 women out of 151 are the Head of the State.[75]

(i) Women's Representation in Governance in South Asia

The region of South Asia is unique in respect of having the largest number of women leaders who have been either the head of the State or the government in their respective countries. (Srimavo Bandaranaike, Indira Gandhi, Benazir Bhutto, Sheikh Hasina, Khalida Jia and Chandrika Kumaratunga). The first female head of any State in the world, was from South Asia. Srimavo Bandaranaike of Sri Lanka had that distinction of becoming the First Head of the State in the world in 1960, followed by Indira Gandhi who became the first Head of the Government (Prime Minister) of the largest democracy in the world in 1964. But this lead is not translated or reflected in women's representation in the legislative bodies of the countries in the region.

Since the Beijing Conference, the number of women in all the South Asian Parliaments[76] has increased considerably as shown in the Table 4.6 but this has primarily been possible because of the *quota system*.

In *Afghanistan* after the collapse of the Taliban regime, as a result of international pressure and lobbying by the human rights groups, two women out of 30 got a space in the Interim Government.[77] Later to enhance their participation in decision-making and leadership roles, quota system was introduced. It provides for 27 per cent seats for women in Wolesi Jirga (Lower House) and 17 per cent in the Meshrano (Upper House). Women currently occupy 27.2 per cent seats in the Lower House and 27.5 per cent in the Upper House. It is a major gain for women and those who dared to contest elections faced many challenges.

In *Bangladesh* likewise, there is a substantial increase in representation with the introduction of quota system. It has improved from 2 per cent in 2001[78] to 18.6 per cent. Under the quota system 13 per cent seats are reserved for women in the National Parliament (Jatiya Sangsad)[79] and one-third seats are reserved for women at the local level.

It is interesting to note that in the Alternate Report for *Bhutan* for the Committee on CEDAW (2009) though it is pointed out that "women are currently under-represented in Parliament as well as in the top bureaucratic positions. There is no female minister, ambassador, or anyone in the cabinet rank as of today", the NGOs felt that there "was no urgent need to try and have 50% representation on all fronts. It was felt that it would serve women better to have targeted strategic representation to begin with rather than to settle for quota bases parity representation."[80] In its Concluding Comments the CEDAW Committee has recommended that "special measures must be taken to increase the number of women at the national and local decision-making levels in government, governmental bodies and public administration."[81] In *Bhutan,* there are 8.5 per cent women in the Lower House and 24.0 per cent women in the Upper House.[82]

Maldives has only 6.5 per cent seats occupied by women in the Lower House.[83] In Maldives, too there is no quotas or reservations at either local or national level. In Maldives women are allowed to vote, but are barred from holding the office of President and Prime Minister.[84]

In *India*, the percentage has increased from 7.2 per cent in 1997 to 10.8 per cent in 2009 in Lok Sabha (Lower House) an all time high

TABLE 4.6

Women in National Parliaments in South Asia as on 31 March, 2011

Country		Single House or Lower House					Upper House or Senate			
		% of Women (1997)	*Seats*	*Men*	*Women*	*% W*	*Seats*	*Men*	*Women*	*% W*
(1)	*(2)*	*(3)*	*(4)*	*(5)*	*(6)*	*(7)*	*(8)*	*(9)*	*(10)*	*(11)*
1.	Afghanistan	—	249	180	69	27.7%	102	74	28	27.5%
2.	Bangladesh	9.1	345	271	64	18.6%	—		—	—
3.	Bhutan	—	47	43	4	8.5	25	19	6	24.0%
4.	India	7.2	543	484	59	10.8%	242	217	25	10.3%
5.	Maldives	—	77	72	5	6.5%	—	—	—	
6.	Nepal	3.4	594	397	197	33.2%	—		—	—
7.	Pakistan	2.3	342	266	76	22.2%	100	83	17	17.0%
8.	Sri Lanka	5.3	225	213	12	5.3%	—		—	—
	Total		2422	1936	486	20.06				

figure. It is 10.3 per cent in the Upper House, that is, Rajya Sabha.It must, however, be stated here that while India took a revolutionary step in the region by reserving 33 per cent seats for women in urban and rural local bodies, electing there by over one million women to the local bodies, there continues to be a strong opposition to reservation of seats for women in Parliament and State Assemblies. The Reservation Bill has been passed by the Rajya Sabha but is pending in Lok Sabha for its approval. For fear of strong opposition from certain parties and leaders, the government is dithering on the bill in the name of consensus. There is, however, a move to enhance local level representation from 30 per cent to 50 per cent, some States have already done it but in Parliament and State Assemblies without reservation, the representation is dismal. It is less than that of Afghanistan, Bangladesh, Nepal and Pakistan.

Nepal is the first and the only State which has 33 per cent women in the Constituent Assembly. However, women had never comprised more than 5.8 per cent of *Nepal*'s Parliament till 1999.[85] In the election of 2008 of Constituent Assembly, 197 women leaders (33.2%) were elected out of 575 seats.[86] The Interim Constitution of *Nepal* has made 33 per cent quota for women in Lower House. In the Local Self-Government Act, 1999, especial provision has been made to increase the participation of women at local level with 40 per cent quota for women in the local bodies.[87] (See Table 4.7)

The most remarkable increase, however, is seen in *Pakistan*, where the number of women in the lower house of the National Assembly has increased from 2.3 per cent in 1997 to 22.2 per cent in 2010. In Pakistan, the system of reserved seats for women in legislative assemblies has existed in one form or the other since its creation. The 1956 Constitution provided for 10 reserved seats for women in the National Assembly. The present Constitution provides for 17 per cent reservation for women in the National Assembly and 4 per cent in the Upper House. 76 women are elected to the National Assembly, 60 are elected against the reserved seats and 16 on general seats. (See Table 4.7)

Sri Lanka, which is high on other indicators of the development as compared to other South Asian States, has very poor representation of women in the Parliament in the absence of quota system. There are only 12 women in the Parliament out of 225 members (5.3%)[88] and the number remains the same as was in 1997. Women's organizations have been protesting and demanding 25-30% quota both at the national and local levels. This demand, however, has not been conceded so far. The policy makers have agreed only to a 25 per cent quota of nominations for women.[89] It does not necessarily ensure adequate representation of women in the Parliament or the local bodies.

TABLE 4.7
Quota for Women in South Asia

Countries	*Quotas for Women at the Local Level*	*Quotas for Women at the National Level*
1. Afghanistan	25 per cent in Provincial Councils	27 per cent—*Wolesi Jirga (Lower House)* 17 per cent—*Meshrano Jirga (Upper House)*
2. Bangladesh	33 per cent	13 per cent—National Parliament (Jatiya Sangsad)
3. Bhutan	No Quota	No Quota
4. India	33 per cent	A Bill for 1/3rd Reservation for women in Parliament and State Legislatures passed by Rajya Sabha, pending in Lok Sabha
5. Maldives	No quota	No quota
6. Nepal	40 per cent	33 per cent—Lower House
7. Pakistan	33 per cent	17 per cent in the National Assembley and Four out of the 100 seats in the Upper House
8. Sri Lanka	No quota	No quota

Even if there has been significant increase in the percentage of women Parliamentarians, they still are under-represented in the ministerial positions. Table 4.8 clearly shows that only 9.4 per cent (20/211) women hold ministerial positions in the region.

The Ministers in Nepal, Bangladesh and Pakistan are occupying important portfolios like that of defence and foreign (external) affairs; in other countries they are holding charge of 'soft ministries'. Assigned *gender-stereotyped portfolios* is an additional challenge for women in politics. Sri Lanka has one woman Minister, Nepal and Afghanistan have two woman Ministers each, Pakistan has three Ministers and Bangladesh has four. India has largest number of women Ministers that is eight. Out of these eight, two are Cabinet Ministers, two are with Independent Charge and four are Ministers of State. The Minister for Women and Child Development is the Minister of State with Independent Charge and does not enjoy Cabinet rank.

TABLE 4.8
Women in Ministerial Positions in South Asia, 2010

	Countries			Percentage (%)
1.	Afghanistan			7.4 (2/27)
2.	Bangladesh			16.0 (4/25)
3.	Bhutan			Nil
4.	India	Cabinet Ministers	5.8 (2/33)	10.1 (8/78)
		Ministers of State with Independent Charge	25.0 (2/7)	
		Ministers of State	10.8 (4/37)	
5.	Maldives			N/A
6.	Nepal			7.7 (2/23)
7.	Pakistan			7.5 (3/40)
8.	Sri Lanka			5.9 (1/17)
	South Asia			9.4 (20/211)

(ii) Women in Peace Processes in South Asia

While it is established that women face gender-based violence in the conflict situations, it is equally true that their role in peace negotiations, peace agreements and mediation is very nominal. Even when women participate or are included in the formal peace negotiations, their role can be limited to a formal presence without having the capacity, or mandate to contribute to setting or shaping the agenda of such negotiations. As Elisabeth Porter says, "Despite the significance of Resolution 1325 on Women, Peace and Security, women remain absent or are marginalised from negotiating tables, political decision-making opportunities and senior advisory positions. Inclusion matters. Without plural inclusivity, there is no peace with justice and equality..."[90]

According to a UNIFEM factsheet since 1992, women represented, on average, fewer than 10 per cent of official negotiating delegations in peace talks, and only 2.1 percent of signatories to peace agreements.[91] Studies proved that women's participation enriches the process, since women "are likely to make a different contribution to the peace process. When compared to men, women are more likely to put gender issues on the agenda, introduce other conflict experiences, and set different priorities for peace-building and rehabilitation, and they may bridge political divides better"[92].

A report of UNIFEM published in 2002 entitled "Women, War and Peace: The Independent Experts' Assessment on the Impact of Armed Conflict on Women and Women's Role in Peace-Building" which analyzes the disproportionate impact of armed conflict and violence on women and children explores the ways and procedures for involving women in the peace process. One of the main messages of this report is that peace agreements work better when women are involved in the peace process. Based on the extensive reviews and documentation, it highlights that a critical mass of women, in negotiations and peace talks not only improves the quality of agreements reached but also equally or even more importantly increase chances of implementing the peace accords.[93]

One of the essentials of the SCR 1325 is that women must be at the peace table. In South Asia, as anywhere else the participation of women in peace processes, peace negotiations and mediation is negligible. One key reason cited for the low number of women involved in peace negotiation teams is the corresponding *lack of women in senior positions* in the political parties, armies and rebel groups, at least at the time of the negotiations. Apparently, patriarchal social structures and power relations are a significant barrier in meaningful and qualitative participation of women in the region's peace processes. Table 4.9 presents an extremely low level of women's official participation as members of peace negotiating teams in South Asia.

In *Afghanistan*, three decades of armed conflict brought an end to Taliban regime in 2001. The Bonn Agreement[94] was signed in December 2001. It was an Agreement that was reached as a result of a round of talks where a number of prominent Afghans met under the auspices of the UN to determine a plan for governing the country. It focused on transformation, reconstruction and development of Afghanistan.

Significantly nine per cent women were on the Peace Negotiation Team according to the UN Peacemaker Database of the Department of Political Affairs. The Agreement provided that the rights of women must be a priority within the reconstruction and peace-building agenda. Though the percentage of women was not very high what is important is that in Afghanistan where women had been pushed behind the doors, they were provided a space—a voice in the post conflict peace process. Women's issues were placed at the top of the agenda. Media were also mobilized to highlight the role of women. During the negotiations, the women representatives fought hard for women's rights, and their achievements included the creation of a Ministry of Women's Affairs. Efforts are still ongoing in Afghanistan to ensure the mainstreaming of gender in various ministries and projects, and ensuring that the new Constitution guarantees equal rights for men and women. However, it is disheartening to note that in the recent Bonn Conference 2011, there was not a single woman in the delegation.

TABLE 4.9
Women in Peace Negotiating Teams

Countries	*Women in Peace Negotiating Teams*	*Number of Women*
1. Afghanistan	Bonn Agreement (2001)	3 women out of 36
	Bonn Conference (2011)	Nill
	National Consultative Peace Jirga (2010)	67 women out of 336 (20%)
2. Bangladesh	Chittagong Hill Tracts Peace Accord (PA), 2 December 1997 with Government of Bangladesh	1 woman (in official capacity as President of Bangladesh)
3. India	- Facilitated the Ceasefire between Govt. of India and National Socialist Council of Nagalim-Isak-Muivah (NSCN-IM) (1997)	Nill
	- Interlocutors for Peace in Jammu and Kashmir (2010)	1 woman out of three Interlocutors
4. Nepal	Ceasefire Negotiation between government and Maoists (2003)	1 woman
5. Sri Lanka	Sub-committee on Gender Issues (SGI) 2002	5

In the case of *Bangladesh*, low-intensity guerrilla warfare, the armed conflict in the *Chittagong Hill Tracts (CHT)*, was ended in 1997 when a peace agreement was signed between JSS/SB (Parbattya Chattagram Jana Sanghati Samiti/Shanti Bahini; Chittagong Hill Tracts People's Coordination Association/Peace Force) and the Government of Bangladesh.[95] Though the Peace Accord was signed by the then woman Prime Minister Sheikh Hasina Wajed of the Awami League, there was no formal women representative in the peace talks.

In *Nepal* a Comprehensive Peace Agreement (CPA)[96] was signed in November 2006 putting an end to the decade long armed conflict. Women's participation in the peace process here too has been negligible. In the first peace talks (in 2001) women were absent on both the sides. In the second peace negotiation (in 2003), a woman minister participated in the government's team[97] but her role was almost limited. The third time (in 2006), no women were involved in drafting the 2006 peace agreement. [98] In the Interim Constitution Drafting Committee, however, women got a significant space as 4 out of 16 members were women.[99]

Similarly, in *India*, every peace negotiation or talk is fully dominated by males. In the North East, be it Assam issue, Manipur issue or Nagaland issue, not a single women has ever been included in peace talks by the Government. Though in 1997, the Naga Mothers Association (NMA) a women's group of Nagaland facilitated the ceasefire between the Government of India and the National Socialist Council of Nagalim-Isak-Muivah (NSCN-IM), there is no recognition of this and the Government had no woman representative on its side.

In Kashmir also a number of times talks have been initiated but no woman from either side found a place on the table. In a meeting called *Sisters for Peace Voices from Kashmir* organized by Women's Initiative for Peace in South Asia (WIPSA) in September 2010, a Resolution was passed demanding fifty per cent representation of women in peace talks. For the first time, in response to women's demand, among the three interlocutors appointed by the Government of India for peace talks in Kashmir, a woman (Radha Kumar) has been included.

Similarly, *Pakistan* has also fully ignored women's participation and their concerns in the negotiations in Baluchistan. Even in the talks held between Pakistan and India from time to time women have not been included in the talks. However, Hina Rabbani Khar has been there in her official capacity as Foreign Minister of Pakistan.

In Sri Lanka in the Ceasefire Agreement with LTTE of 2008 not a single woman was included from either side. Even the LTTE which had a large number of women in their armed rank did not include them in their talks with the Government. Except in 2002 peace talks when a woman was included. However, in 2002, a Gender Sub-committee on Gender Issues (SGI) was constituted that provided space to women representatives both from the government side and the armed opposition group LTTE under the mediation of the

Norwegian Government's adviser to the Sub-committee. The Committee comprised of ten members, five appointed by the Government of Sri Lanka and five from the LTTE.[100] The Committee focused their efforts on the equal representation of women in politics, educational structures and gender bias, violence against women and allegations of sexual harassment, sustaining the peace process, resettlement, personal security and safety, infrastructure and service, livelihood and employment and reconciliation. But as the peace talks were suspended, the fate of the Committee sealed.

(iii) Women's Participation in the Justice and Security Sector in South Asia

The SCR 1325 acknowledges the important role of women in the prevention and resolution of conflicts and in peace-building, and stresses on the importance of their equal participation and full involvement in all efforts for the maintenance and promotion of peace and security in domestic as well as in international arenas. Therefore, SCR 1325 is one of the most important international roadmap for security that mandates all the states to consider it as a guiding principle while working on the security sector reforms.

In general, as seen above, women hold only a small number of ministerial positions throughout the world, an imbalance that is particularly prominent in the areas of defence and justice. In 2010, of the 188 countries assessed, only 11 women headed defence and 40 foreign affairs ministries. A low representation of women to the key security portfolios of defence, police and justice is thus a key challenge to gender justice in conflict situations.[101]

Women's *participation in the Justice and Security Sector is very low* across all countries. The situation is not much different in South Asia. Overall, these sectors are overwhelmingly men dominated.

Currently, in *Afghanistan*, Afghanistan Independent Human Rights Commission (AIHRC) is headed by a woman. There was one woman in the 9-member Regional Security *Jorge*, a body created to decrease the tensions between Pakistan and Afghanistan. Of 1,800 lawyers in the Courts of Afghanistan, 120 of them are women. There are only 4.7 per cent women Judges. Women comprise only of 1 per cent of the police and military forces.[102]

In *India*, the number of women judges in the higher judiciary is less than 10 per cent and the Supreme Court has only one woman Judge. Presently, 3.23 per cent women are in the National Police,

2.44 percent in the Indian Army, 3.0 per cent in the Navy and 6.7 per cent in the Indian Air Force.[103]

Similarly in *Nepal* the representation of women in Armed Police Force is 2.02 per cent.

The National Investigation Department has less than 2 per cent women.[104] One of the most sensitive situations exists in Chief District Officer level that post is considered as chief security official at district level of Nepal government where women representation level is zero.[105]

(iv) Participation of Women in Peace-Keeping Missions

The South Asian countries also contribute female troops to the UN Peace-Keeping Missions all over the world. In fact, the first three positions of highest contributors of female troops are occupied by South Asia.

Women in uniform create more secure conditions for women in the reporting of abuses during armed conflict and post conflict situations. The most well-known example of a laudable role by an all women contingent of 100 is that of Indian police deployed as part of the UN mission in Liberia in 2007. The Unit devoted their personal time and resources to interacting with the community. It focused on meeting the community's needs such as free medical services, clean drinking water and installation of lighting systems. They inspired women and girls to take on non-traditional roles and it led to an increase in the number of women in the security sector in Liberia (including the police and defense forces). Further, the number of girls enrolling in schools rose dramatically and rates of sexual abuse are said to have decreased.[106] The Secretary-General noted in his reporting on Liberia that this deployment—positively contributed to a three-fold increase in the number of applications from women to join the Liberian National Police[107] and their presence helped to get Liberian women to register complaints.[108]

The Indian all women police unit set a precedent and sent strong signals on the potential role of women as peace-keepers. The presence of female peace-keepers and police can help increase the likelihood of women and girls participating in DDR programmes, thus accessing the attached services, which can include things like health care, training, cash incentives and grants for housing or reintegration in the economy.[109]

Table 4.10 reflects the contribution of South Asia of women in the UN Peace-keeping Operation. The data indicate that the overall regional gender composition of peace-keeping forces is 462 women in a total force of 36,541. Bangladesh, India and Nepal stand out with a somewhat greater number of women participating in their country's missions, whereas, Pakistan (34) and Sri Lanka (7) contribute very less number.

Though the South Asian countries are the highest contributors of female troops to the UN Peace Keeping Missions all over the world, still the number is very low. There are multiple reasons for this low female participation. Firstly, it is because of their less strength in *national military and police forces.* Other barriers include *family obligations* and *stereotyped* attitudes and reluctance to go outside the country.

TABLE 4.10

Women in Military and Police Force from South Asia for UN Peace-keeping Operations as of June 30th, 2010

Countries	*Males*	*Females*	*Total*
1. Afghanistan	—	—	—
2. Bangladesh	10465	176	10,641
3. India	8779	141	8,920
4. Nepal	5044	104	5,148
5. Pakistan	10658	34	10,692
6. Sri Lanka	1133	7	1140
South Asia	36079	462	36541

(v) *Participation of Civil Society Organizations in Task Forces on UNSCR 1325 and 1820*

Article 15 of the Resolution 1325 "expresses its willingness to ensure that Security Council missions take into account gender considerations and the rights of women, including through consultation with local and international women's groups".[110] The Resolution acknowledges and endorses the role of civil society in all aspects of the peace process, providing women's organizations and other NGOs formal recognition for their efforts.

The civil society organizations can play a critical role in the implementation of SCR 1325. Their inclusion in the Task Forces (or other similar bodies) on 1325 can greatly help in building peace and preventing SGBV in communities. It is, however, disappointing to note that in the South Asian countries only the Government of Nepal has provided a space to CSOs in the Task Force set-up for the formulation of National Plan of Action. There are 33 per cent women on the High Level Steering Committee on Resolution 1325.

B. Protection and Prevention of Gender-based Violence Against Women and Girls through the Promotion of Women's Rights, Accountability and Law Enforcement

Another area of major focus of UNSCR 1325 is the *protection* of women and girls during and after conflict from sexual and gender based violence. Resolution 1325 obligates the Member-States to improve interventionist strategies for the *prevention* of violence against women, through the *promotion* of women's rights, accountability and law enforcement including strengthening women's rights under national laws, respect for international law of human rights that is reflected in national laws, creating accountability mechanisms within the law, and striving to end impunity. Article 8 (b) of the Resolution underscores the need to support local women's peace initiatives and indigenous processes for conflict resolution, and involve these women in all mechanisms of the peace agreements.

Article 10 of the Resolution 1325 envisages that all parties to armed conflict should take special measures to protect women and girls from gender based violence, particularly rape and other forms of sexual abuse and all other forms of violence in situations of armed conflicts. Article 11 further emphasizes upon the responsibility of all States to end impunity for genocide, crimes against humanity and war crimes, including those relating to sexual and other forms of violence against women and girls and it stresses in this regard the need to exclude these crimes from amnesty provisions where feasible.

Furthermore, Article 12 envisages that all parties to armed conflict should respect the civilian and humanitarian character of refugee camps and settlements, and to take into account the particular needs of women and girls. Similarly, Article 13 layas down that those involved in the planning for disarmament, demobilization and reintegration processes should consider the different needs of female and male ex-combatants and the needs of their dependants.

Even though, as seen in the preceding pages,[111] women in South Asia have been subjected to violence in conflict situations, none of the countries in South Asia has set an exclusive mechanism to deal with the cases of gender-based violence in armed conflict situations. India does not even consider itself technically covered by the term 'armed conflict'.

The Governments, however, have pledged at various national and international fora to improve the status of women and to ensure

TABLE 4.11

International Commitments to Women's Rights by South Asian Countries

Country	*CESCR 1966*	*CCPR 1966*	*1951 Refugees Convention and 967 Protocol*	*CEDAW 1979*	*CRC 1989*	*BPFA 1995*	*OP to CEDAW 2000*	*ICC 2002*	*SAARC Convention on Trafficking*	*2002 UN SCRs-1325, 1820, 1888, 1899*
(1)	*(2)*	*(3)*	*(4)*	*(5)*	*(6)*	*(7)*	*(8)*	*(9)*	*(10)*	*(11)*
Afghanistan	X	✓	2005	2003	✓	✓	X	✓ 2003	✓	✓
Bangladesh	X	X	X	1984	✓	✓	2000		✓	✓
India	X	✓	X	1993	✓	✓	X		✓	✓
Maldives	X	X	X	1993	✓	✓	2006		✓	✓
Nepal	✓	✓	X	1991	✓	✓	2007		✓	✓
Pakistan	X	X	X	1996	✓	✓	X		✓	✓
Sri Lanka	X	✓	X	1981	✓	✓	2002		✓	✓

CEDAW : Convention on the Elimination of All Forms of Discrimination Against Women; *OP CEDAW*: Optional Protocol to Convention on the Elimination of All Forms of Discrimination Against Women; *CRC:* Convention on the Rights of the Child; *CCPR:* International Covenant on Civil and Political Rights; *CESCR:* International Covenant on Economic, Social and Cultural Rights, *BPFA:* Beijing Platform for Action , *UNSCR 1325*, United Nations Security Council Resolution, *ICC*: International Criminal Court ; *SAARC*: South Asian Association for Regional Cooperation.

gender equality in every sphere. Table 4.11 represents the scenario of the Conventions signed by the South Asian Countries. All the States are signatory to CEDAW with some Reservations and Declarations.[112] The Government of Bangladesh, Nepal and Sri Lanka have even ratified the Optional Protocol to CEDAW. The Government of Afghanistan has signed the 1951 Convention on Refugees and its Protocol and the Statute of International Criminal Court.[113] The Convention on the Rights of Child is ratified by all the South Asian Countries.

In addition, the South Asian Governments have adopted various mechanisms to promote gender equality and prevent violence against women and girls in all situations including violence in conflict situations. Some of the key initiatives at the South Asia and at country level are as follows:

(a) Regional Mechanisms

The South Asian Association for Regional Cooperation (SAARC) was established in 1985. Desirous of promoting peace, stability, amity and progress in the region, the South Asian Heads of State/Governments founded the SAARC. It is a regional mechanism to promote the welfare of the peoples of South Asia; to accelerate economic growth and social progress; to promote active collaboration and to contribute to mutual trust and understanding and to cooperate with international and regional organizations. [114] SAARC has not adequately addressed of women's rights. However, a number of initiatives have been taken by the SAARC regarding the concerns of women which are as follows:

(i) A *Technical Committee on Women in Development* which was created under the Integrated Programme of Action (IPA) in 1986. This resulted in the formulation of a *Regional Plan of Action on Women* before its merger in January 2000 into a *Technical Committee on Social Development* under the SAARC Integrated Programme of Action (SIPA). This Committee was again replaced by a new *Technical Committee on Women, Youth and Children* under the revised Regional Integrated Programme of Action (RIPA) in January 2004. Now this Committee oversees the all issues related to women, youth and children at the regional level including *gender-based violence.*[115]

(ii) In 2001, SAARC signed a Memorandum of Understanding with the United Nations Development Fund for Women

(UNIFEM), to help Member-States to strive towards the goals of gender equality based upon the empowerment approach. The memorandum led to the development of the *SAARC Gender Database*: *Mapping Progress of Women in* the South Asia Region and provides the information regarding sexual and gender-based violence and trafficking of women and girls in the region.

(iii) After rigorous campaigning by civil society activists, the SAARC adopted the *SAARC Convention on Preventing and Combating Trafficking in Women and Children for Prostitution* in 2002 to combat the problem of trafficking at regional level in South Asia.[116] The Convention calls for cooperation amongst the Member-States in dealing with various aspects of prevention and suppression of trafficking of women and children for prostitution, and repatriation and rehabilitation of victims of trafficking. It also calls for the prevention of use of women and children in international prostitution networks, particularly where countries of the region are the countries of origin, transit and destination. SAARC has also formed a *Regional Task Force (RTF)* to monitor and assess the implementation of various provisions of the Convention.[117] In 2007, the RTF adopted a Standard Operating Procedure (SOP) on Combating Trafficking in Women and Children for Prostitution by all the Member-States of SAARC.[118]

(iv) Another initiative is the *SAARC Data Pool* a comprehensive data pool on gender issues in South Asia was launched in January 21, 2008 by the SAARC Secretary General, which provides data on trafficking and violence against women, and women's health, including HIV/AIDS and feminization of poverty.[119]

Reference may also be made The SAARC *Autonomous Women's Advocacy Group (SAWAG)* was formed to advocate mainstreaming gender and combat the problem of sexual and gender based violence and make recommendations on gender related issues and programmes in the region. So far the group has aimed to address issues such as women's citizenship, women's political representation, trafficking and sexual exploitation, gender and HIV/AIDS, female education and literacy, legal rights, economic empowerment, impact of globalization on women, etc.[120]

(b) National Mechanisms/Initiatives

A number of institutions, mechanisms and policies have been set up to protect the women and girls from GBV and promote gender equality in the region.

(i) Protection from Gender-based Violence and Promotion of Women's Rights during and post-Armed Conflict Situations

Sexual and gender-based violence is a violation of human rights and in armed conflict situations it has been seen, it has reached epidemic proportions. Several international instruments specifically address sexual and gender-based violence against women and girls. Notwithstanding the *Convention on the Elimination of All Forms of Discrimination Against Women (CEDAW)* and the *Beijing Platform for Action* and the *Rome Statute* that declared violence as a crime against humanity it continues with impunity. Resolution 1325 specifically calls on all member-states to take special measures to protect women and girls particularly from rape and other forms of sexualized violence. In South Asian country, gender-based violence tends to be greatly underreported, particularly in conflict situations and perpetrators commit their crimes safe in the knowledge that they will never face arrest, prosecution or punishment. Impunity contributes to a climate where such acts are seen as normal and acceptable rather than criminal, and where women do not seek justice because they know they will not receive it.

(a) National Machinery for Women's Advancement in South Asia

Resolution 1325 imposes a direct duty on all parties to an armed conflict to take special measures to protect women and girls both from the conflict itself and from gender-based and sexualized violence. Violence against women and girls in South Asia is pervasive because of pre-existing cultural and patriarchal norms which allow the abuse of women. These factors have been further aggravated by war, militarization, poverty, and the lack of social services. There are a few gender responsive institutional mechanisms, laws and policies formulated by South Asian countries which protect the women's rights from sexual and gender-based violence. (Table 4.12)

Afghanistan

The *Ministry of Women's Affairs (MOWA)* was set up in 2002 for women's advancement in *Afghanistan*. The Ministry provides direction, build inter-ministerial collaboration and develop the capacity of government agencies to ensure that policy formulation,

TABLE 4.12
National Machinery for Women's Advancement in South Asia

Country	*National Machinery*
1. Afghanistan	• Ministry of Women's Affairs
	• Afghanistan Independent Human Rights Commission (AIHRC)
	• Women's Rights Unit
2. Bangladesh	• Ministry of Women's and Children's Affairs
	• Central Cell in the Ministry of Women and Children's Affairs to Prevent Violence against Women and Children
	• Ministry of Chittagong Hill Tracts (CHT) Affairs
	• National Council for Women's Development
	• Chittagong Hill Tracts Commission
	• One Stop Crisis Centres (OSCC)
3. India	• Ministry of Women and Child Development
	• National Commission for Women
4. Nepal	• Ministry of Women, Children and Social Welfare
	• National Women's Commission
	• National Rapporteur on Trafficking in Women (NRTW)
	• Gender Responsive Budget Committee
	• Gender-based Violence Unit
	• Ministry of Peace and Reconstruction
	• Local Peace Committees
5. Pakistan	• Federal Ministry for Women Development
	• National Commission on Status of Women
6. Sri Lanka	• Women's Bureau
	• Ministry of Child Development and Women's Empowerment
	• National Committee of Women
	• Child and Women Desks in Police Stations

planning, implementation, reporting and monitoring equitably respond to the differential needs and situations of women and men and it also works to ensure that gender-related commitments made by the government are implemented. These commitments are included in the Constitution of Afghanistan.[121]

Similarly, *Afghanistan Independent Human Rights Commission (AIHRC)* was established pursuant to Bonn Agreement (5 December 2001) and on the basis of decree of the Chairman of the Interim Administration, June 6, 2002. The AIHRC exists independently of the Government, but it cooperates with relevant ministries and officials, carries out research and actively investigates cases of violence against women. It is one institution which is critical to the country's peace-building process and is headed by a woman Dr. Sima Samar, well-known for her work with girls' schools and hospitals that treated women in defiance of the Taliban's edicts against women's education and healthcare.[122] A *Women's Rights Unit* under the Afghanistan Independent Human Rights Commission was also set-up in 2007 to provide legal advice to women.

India

In *India,* the *Ministry of Women and Child Development* came into existence as a separate Ministry in 2006, earlier it was a Department under the Ministry of Human Development and prior to that it was a part of Ministry of Social Welfare. The main objective of the Ministry is to promote social, economic empowerment of women and combat violence against women through cross-cutting policies and programmes, mainstreaming gender concerns, creating awareness about their rights and facilitating institutional and legislative support for enabling them to realize their human rights and develop to their full potential.[123]

The *National Commission for Women* (NCW), a statutory body, established in 1992, has the mandate to safeguard the rights and interests of women by ensuring Constitutional guarantees of equal status to women, review the existing legislations and monitor their effects on women, recommend suitable amendments and provide a forum for women for redressal of their grievances. Many States in India have also established State Commission for Women on the pattern of National Commission for Women.

Nepal

The *Ministry of Women, Children and Social Welfare (MWCSW)* of Nepal was established in 2000.[124] The Ministry is the highest national level machinery which works for the advancement of women's rights and coordinates with other line ministries to incorporate more gender-focused activities in their programmes. It plays an important role in drafting laws and undertaking other activities for elimination of all forms of discrimination and violence against women.

Another potential key actor in promoting and protecting women's rights is the *National Women's Commission*, which was established by statute in 2007. The NWC monitors and investigates cases of violence against women (VAW), providing legal aid, monitor the state obligations to UN reporting under CEDAW, coordinate with government and other agencies for mainstreaming gender policy in national development and recommending and monitoring for the reforms by making research.

Another important mechanism is the *National Rapporteur on Trafficking in Women (NRTW)* under the National Human Rights Commission set-up in 2002 to track and monitor trafficking and address the needs to survivors.

The Office of Prime Minister and Council of Members (OPMCM) has established a separate *Gender-based Violence Unit* to deal with complaints specific to gender-based violence cases so that immediate action can be taken in cases where agencies refuse to register complaints or when they are unresponsive. The Unit is the highest level of request for assistance for the victims outside of the judicial system and will direct the concerned agency to immediately respond to the victims.

To deal with the cases of gender-based violence, the government has also created *Women's Cells* in police offices and has established separate Women and Children Unit at District police offices and Ward/Area police.

In 2005, a *Gender Responsive Budget Committee (GRBC)*[125] was established to promote gender responsive budgeting in Nepal. Most important is the *Ministry of Peace and Reconstruction (MOPR)* which was established in 2007 with the objective of promoting sustainable peace, and addressing the aftermath of conflict through reconstruction efforts. This Ministry is responsible for providing relief and reparation to conflict victims in addition to leading transitional justice efforts and national plan of action on UNSCR 1325 and UNSCR 1820.

Local Peace Committees as district level bodies have been formed under MOPR. This is a local level mechanism to prevent and resolve conflict involving local stakeholders. The Committee members are political party and civil society members, including human rights activists. A 33 per cent representation of women in the LPCs has been made mandatory.

Pakistan

The *Ministry of Women Development* is the national focal machinery for the advancement of women and implementation of CEDAW and Beijing Platform for Action.[126] At the provincial level the Women Development Departments (WDD) have been set-up. The objectives of the Ministry is to formulate public policies to meet specific needs of women including sexual and gender-based violence; to ensure women's interests and needs are adequately safeguarded and met by various organs of the government; to ensure equality of opportunity in education and employment and fuller participation of women in all spheres of national life; and to undertake and promote research on the conditions and problems of women and to undertake and promote programmes and projects for providing special facilities for women.[127]

Similarly, the *National Commission on the Status of Women* was established in 2000 to examine the policies, programmes and other governmental measures for women's development, gender equality and to combat violence against women.[128]

Sri Lanka

In 1978, the *Women's Bureau* was created, under the Ministry of Plan, though it now functions under the Ministry of Women's Affairs. The Women's Bureau focuses mainly on issues of income generation and raising awareness.

A *National Committee on Women (NCW)* was also set-up under the Women's Charter in 1993, to monitor and ensure the implementation of provisions as stated in the Women's Charter. The NCW formulates policies on women's advancement and awareness raising programmes on gender discrimination. A Gender Complaints Unit has also been established under the Committee to receive complaints on gender-based discrimination.

The *Ministry of Child Development and Women's Empowerment* was established in 2005. The primary focus of the Ministry is to implement the policies, plans and programs on women's empowerment. This includes the advancement of the quality of life for women, increased participation in national development policies, and promotion of gender equity and gender justice. The Women's Bureau of Sri Lanka and the National Committee for Women are statutory institutions under the Ministry.

In 60 police stations, *Women and Child Desks* have been established specifically in the war affected areas.

(b) Gender Responsive Laws and Policies

Afghanistan

In Afghanistan, to address the issue of GBV, the Elimination of Violence against Afghan Women (EVAW) passed through a presidential decree in July 2009 but unfortunately this law is still pending for the approval of the Parliament.

The Afghan Constitution, the National Action Plan for Women of Afghanistan (NAPWA), and the Afghan National Development Strategy (ANDS) specifically address the issues of gender equality and women's rights.

Afghanistan's *National Action Plan for the Women of Afghanistan (2007-17)* was formulated in 2007. The Plan is the main resource for gender mainstreaming in Afghanistan's government institutions. It aims to ensure continuity and consistency in government efforts to protect women's citizenship rights in Afghan society through equality and empowerment. Its vision is to build a peaceful and progressive Afghanistan where women and men both enjoy security, equal rights and opportunities in all aspects of life.

These documents and policies reflect the dual nature of the state of women's rights in Afghanistan. Women have their rights protected by official foundational documents, but in reality they are yet to realize their rights for lack of effective enforcement mechanisms.

Bangladesh

In *Bangladesh*, the *National Policy for the Advancement of Women* was adopted in 1997 which includes commitments to eliminating discrimination against women and girls in all spheres and promoting women's equality in areas such as education and training, health and nutrition, housing and shelter, political empowerment and public administration and the economy. A *National Action Plan (NAP)* for implementing the policy as well as meeting commitments under the Beijing Platform for Action (PfA) was approved in 1998.[129] *National Women's Policy* was framed in 2010 and to address the problem of violence against women a *National Action Plan on Violence Against Women* and a *2010* was drafted the same year.

Trafficking is one of the major problems in Bangladesh. To curb this problem a *Joint UN Programme to Address Violence against Women in Bangladesh* (2007-09) was also launched in collaboration with UN Agencies. Another programme which provides for the counselling and psychological care related to VAW, a *Police Reform Project 2005-14* is also running in the country. Furthermore, a *Rehabilitation Programme for Women Survivors of Trafficking* was also launched in 2009 which aims to provide employment support.

In March 2010, an *International Crimes Tribunal (ICT) of Bangladesh* has been established and to convict those who were responsible for the crimes against humanity, genocide, and war crimes in the war of independence from Pakistan in 1971. According to official figures, Pakistani troops, aided by local collaborators, killed an estimated 3 million people, raped about 200,000 women and forced millions more to leave their homes during the bloody nine-month guerrilla war. So far seven people, including two from the main opposition Bangladesh Nationalist Party and five from the Islamist Jamaat-e-Islami party, have been arrested and are facing trial in Dhaka. All of them deny the charges.[130]

India

There is no separate policy or plan of action to deal with violence against women in the country. *The National Policy on Empowerment of Women* adopted in 2001, however, addresses the issue and states "All forms of violence against women, physical and mental, whether at domestic or societal levels, including those arising from customs, traditions or accepted practices shall be dealt with effectively with a view to eliminate its incidence. Institutions and mechanisms/ schemes for assistance will be created and strengthened for prevention of such violence, including sexual harassment at work place and customs like dowry; for the rehabilitation of the victims of violence and for taking effective action against the perpetrators of such violence. A special emphasis will also be laid on programmes and measures to deal with trafficking in women and girls." This Policy is yet to be operationalised into a plan of action.[131]

The *National Alliance of Women (NAWO)* and other women's groups in a Regional North-East Consultation on Engendering the Eleventh Five Year Plan had impressed upon the Planning Commission the need to address the concerns of women affected by the conflict in North-East.[132] The Planning Commission in response to that had recommended in the Eleventh Five Year Plan the setting up of a National Task Force on VAW in Zones of Conflict under the National Commission for Women (NCW) with adequate budgetary allocations to make it effective in monitoring VAW in conflict zones

TABLE 4.13

Gender Responsive Laws and Policies in South Asia

Country	*Gender Responsive Laws and Policies*
1. Afghanistan	• Elimination of Violence against Afghan Women (EVAW) • National Action Plan for Women of Afghanistan (NAPWA) • Afghan National Development Strategy (ANDS)
2. Bangladesh	• National Policy for the Advancement of Women • National Action Plan (NAP) • National Action Plan on Violence Against Women • National Women Policy 2010 • Joint UN Programme to Address Violence against Women in Bangladesh • Rehabilitation Programme for Women Survivors of Trafficking • International Crimes Tribunal, Bangladesh
3. India	• National Policy on Empowerment of Women • National Commission for Women • National Plan of Action to Combat Trafficking and Commercial Sexual Exploitation of Women and Children
4. Nepal	• Gender Equality Act, 2006 • Human Trafficking and Transportation Control Act, 2007 • Human Trafficking and Transportation (Control) Regulation, 2008 • National Plan of Action Against Gender-based Violence • National Plan of Action on Gender Equality and Empowerment of Women • National Action Plan on the Implementation of Security Council Resolutions 1325 and 1820 (2011-16) • National Human Rights Action Plan (2011-13)
5. Pakistan	• National Plan for the Advancement and Empowerment of Women • National Policy for Advancement and Empowerment of Women
6. Sri Lanka	• Women's Charter • National Plan of Action for Women

and facilitating relief and access to justice for affected women.[133] It remains a paper recommendation only as the National Task Force has not been set-up till date. The National Commission for Women members were completely ignorant of this recommendation.

Nepal

Violence against women and girls remains prevalent in Nepal. It has enacted many gender responsive laws and policies to address the problem of gender-based violence that include Gender Equality Act 2006, Human Trafficking and Transportation Control Act, 2007, Human Trafficking and Transportation (Control) Regulation, 2008 etc.[134]

A *National Plan of Action against Gender-based Violence* was prepared by the Government of Nepal in 2010 to control the gender-based violence and to provide security and protection to women and children. The Government also declared the year 2010 as the *Year to End Gender-based Violence.* [135]

In 2011, the *National Action Plan on the Implementation of Security Council Resolutions 1325 and 1820 (2011-16)* was formulated by Nepal. A framework for the Resolutions has been developed in consultation with key stakeholders. The NAP will be crucial in advancing women's representation in decision-making in conflict prevention and resolution, as well as addressing sexual and gender based violence aggravated by conflict.

Similarly, a *National Plan of Action on Gender Equality and Empowerment of Women* has been formulated. This Plan specifically addresses the 12 Critical Areas of Beijing Platform for Action. The section on Armed Conflict includes activities like protecting women from the impact of conflict, providing access to justice for conflict-affected women and making arrangements for relief and rehabilitation.

Furthermore, the *National Human Rights Action Plan (2011-13)* has been formulated in 2011. This Action Plan contains a separate chapter on women focusing on women's rights and social justice.

Pakistan

In *Pakistan*, a *National Plan for the Advancement and Empowerment of Women* was formulated in 1998 as a follow-up of the UN Fourth World Conference on Women through a national participatory process involving the Federal and Provincial Governments, NGOs, women's organizations and individual experts. It lists more than 180 action areas with many sub-actions. The

National Plan of Action identified Women and Armed Conflict as one of the priority areas under which it listed several key actions to combat the problem of armed conflict and to avoid gender-based violence during armed conflict.[136] The Plan identifies strategic objectives and specific actions in the twelve priority areas identified by the Beijing Platform for Action plus a thirteenth area "women and girls with disabilities".[137]

The Ministry of Women Development carried out an audit of the Plan in 2002 to measure the progress. Additionally, it has established an office of the National Plan Coordinator to speed-up and measure progress so that the actions listed in it are completed by 2013—the plan implementation period.[138]

A comprehensive *National Policy for Advancement and Empowerment of Women* was announced by the Government on March 7, 2002. The Policy contains a vision, goal, aims and objectives and lays down key policy measures, specifically addressing the empowerment dimensions in the social, economic and political fields. Cross cutting issues are fully reflected in the key policy measures. These measures have been drawn from the national health policy, education sector reforms, labor policy, access to justice program, police reforms, poverty alleviation program, etc.[139]

Sri Lanka

As mentioned earlier, Sri Lanka is a signatory to CEDAW without reservations. In 1993, a *Women's Charter* was adopted to translate the CEDAW commitments. It has a mandate to both develop policies related to women's issues and investigate areas of gender inequality. The Charter focused on seven areas of concerns which include civil and political rights; the right to education and training; the right to economic activity and benefits; the right to healthcare and nutrition; rights within the family; the right to protection from social discrimination; and the right to protection from gender-based violence.[140]

In 1996, the Ministry of Women's Affairs and the National Committee for Women formulated a *National Plan of Action for Women*. The Plan was based on the critical areas of concern set forth in the Beijing Platform for Action and covered eight areas of concerns, i.e. are violence against women, human rights and armed conflict; political participation and decision-making; health; education and training; economic activities and poverty; media and communication; environment; and institutional strengthening and support. The Plan identifies problems and issues, sets goals for their solution, recommends strategies and activities, and is responsible for the identification of implementing agencies. The Plan was first revised in 1998 and then 2000.[141] In 2011 another Five Year Plan was formulated by the Ministry which covers nine sectors regarding women in Sri Lanka. Chapter 4 of the Plan specifically addresses the concerns about women, war and peace-building. Under this Chapter, the Plan focuses on the protection and ensuring safety of women in welfare centres, providing security and protection for women in the process of rehabilitation, promoting income generation abilities and livelihoods of women whose families affected by war and the resettled and ensuring development and welfare of social strata prone to disasters and difficulties. Developing infrastructure facilities, councelling programmes, awareness programmes on women's rights and prevention of violence against women, training programmes for self-employments, providing loan schemes, etc. are introduced for the implementation of Plan.[142]

(ii) Truth and Reconciliation Commissions

The administration of justice suffers when a country is involved in conflict. The situation of impunity is one of the main challenges for the protection and promotion of human rights. It is necessary to take actions on the crimes committed during conflict, including those that are gender-based and it is essential for social reconstruction to succeed. The transition from war to peace frequently requires the creation of temporary judicial bodies and processes that establish a record of human rights abuses and hold perpetrators accountable.[143]

Governments are confronted with the difficult task of creating transitional justice mechanisms that establish the right balance between ending impunity and facilitating reconciliation. To discover and to reveal past wrongdoing by a government (or, depending on the circumstances, non-state actors also), in the hope of resolving conflict left over from the past, a Truth and Reconciliation Commission[144] can be a very useful.

In South Asia, impunity is the single most important factor contributing to increased human rights violations. The Governments now visualize that without justice and accountability, war crimes will be legitimized and perpetrators currently integrated within the new governance regime will have their crimes silently forgiven, leading to a culture of continuing impunity. This will ultimately encourage instability and renewed conflict, fueling resentment and discontent among the public. There is a perceived strong demand in the South

Asia region for setting up Truth and Reconciliation Commission for different reasons.

Over the past 30 years more than two dozen truth and fact-finding commissions have been established at the international and national level to investigate human rights abuses that occurred during conflict.[145] Women have chaired two of such commissions, the United Nations International Commission of Inquiry, which investigated breaches of international humanitarian law in East Timor and the Sri Lankan Commission on the Western and Southern Provinces.[146]

The *Afghans* have experienced human rights violation since the last three decades. Transitional justice in Afghanistan is not set in a formalized structure under a truth and reconciliation commission (TRC). The civil society has been demanding a Truth and Reconciliation Commission. In 2004, the Afghan Independent Human Rights Commission (AIHRC) produced the report, "A Call for Justice", profiling citizens' desire for national accountability of human rights abusers and violators.[147] Based on the findings of this report, an Action Plan of the Islamic Republic of Afghanistan for Peace, Justice, and Reconciliation was adopted in 2005.[148]

The Action Plan calls attention on five key areas: (1) acknowledgement of suffering through memorial, (2) ensure credible and accountable state institutions and purging human rights violators and criminals from the state institutions, (3) truth-seeking and documentation, (4) promotion of reconciliation and improvement of national unity, (5) establishment of effective and reasonable accountability mechanisms.[149] The Plan has failed and disband illegal armed groups allowed individuals suspected of serious human rights violations to stand for and hold public office.Transitional justice, thus far, has been geared toward reintegrating former fighters into Afghan communities. There has been no significant effort to answer to the crimes committed against civilians by individuals or parties tied to the Communist, mujahideen, or Taliban eras of the conflict.[150]

As far as *India is* concerned, the Chief Minister of *Jammu and Kashmir*, Omar Abdullah has been batting for the formation of a Truth and Reconciliation Commission for Kashmir. Referring to the killing of thousands of people in Kashmir during the past two decades, Omar Abdullah has observed that the Commission in both parts of Kashmir will help check what happened in the last two decades and what had gone wrong.[151]

The Comprehensive Peace Agreement (2006) of *Nepal* that ended the decade long civil war provided an opportunity for the establishment a Truth and Reconciliation Commission to "probe those involved in serious violations of human rights" and to "develop an atmosphere for reconciliation in the society."[152] As a follow-up a Truth and Reconciliation Commission Bill has been drafted in 2007 with a mandate to investigate "incidents of gross violation of human rights and crimes against humanity during the course of armed conflict". The Bill was however never tabled before the Constituent Assembly.[153]

The proposed Commission has a mandate to investigate events surrounding the commission of gross violations of human rights and crimes against humanity but the Act does not contain any definition of these crimes. It does not make any reference of women's experiences in armed conflict and also does not state any recognition of gender-based violence. The proposed TRC in the Comprehensive Peace Agreement lacks specific provision for women's mandatory involvement in the process as stipulated in UNSCR 1325. In addition, there has hardly been any consultation among women's groups or other civil society institutions regarding the mandate and scope of the Act. Women are therefore less likely to be provided leadership positions while designing the TRC. However, some initiatives have been taken by the civil society Accountability Watch Committee and National Human Rights Commission.[154]

Similarly, the alarming escalation of human rights abuses in Sri Lanka over the past years clearly show that existing domestic mechanisms for the protection of civilians and delivery of justice have failed. In response to these human rights violations, the Sri Lankan President Mahinda Rajapaksa set-up a *Lessons Learnt and Reconciliation Commission* (LLRC) in May 2009 to examine the events of the Sri Lankan Civil War between February 2002 and May 2009.

The Commission had eight members including one woman. It had regular public hearings in Colombo and in the former conflict affected areas of Vavuniya, Batticaloa and Kilinochchi. This included field visits to meet people directly affected by the conflict. It received over 1,000 oral submissions and over 5,000 written submissions. The Commission submitted its final Report of the LLRC on December 16, 2011 to the Parliament.[155] The Report contains several recommendations[156] on actions to be taken with regard to detention of suspects, land issues, law and order, administrative and language issues and socio-economic and livelihood issues.

(iii) The Gendered Needs of Internally Displaced Peoples (IDPs) and Refugees due to Armed Conflict in South Asia

As Resolution 1325 recognizes that women and girls have

special needs during repatriation and resettlement and for rehabilitation and reintegration, Article 12 of the Resolution lays down that the needs of women and girls must be considered in the design of refugee camps and in the implementation of humanitarian measures. The protection of refugee population and the reintegration into society of ex-combatants and displaced persons, whether they are internally displaced persons or refugees, is a key challenge for many governments.

Women are estimated to represent 80 per cent of internally displaced persons and refugees and face gender-based challenges.[157] The displacement tends to increase the number of households headed by women, particularly by widows, and changed gender roles. The threat of gender-based violence is always high in refugee camps.

South Asia has been identified as a region that has a large percentage of internally displaced persons. Conflict-related displacement has been a prominent feature of the history of South Asia. The Internal Displacement Monitoring Centre estimates that at least 26 million people were displaced at the end of 2008[158] in the world, a large proportion of whom are thought to have been displaced due to internal conflicts. Of these 26 millions, South Asia alone has around 3 million displaced persons.[159] Table 4.12 gives country-wise distribution of IDPs. Women and girls make up the majority of these internally displaced.

Over the last 25 years, *Afghanistan* has had the world's largest refugee population. According to the UN High Commission for Refugees (UNHCR), approximately 2,97,000 people displaced from their homes in Afghanistan are living in camps in Kabul and Heart.[160] Afghanistan is a party to a variety of international humanitarian and refugee laws that obligate national authorities to guarantee and protect the rights of the population at large.[161] But there is no comprehensive policy or action plan yet developed by the Government of Afghanistan that affirms the human rights of those who are internally displaced or establishes the minimum standards for preventing and responding to situations of internal displacement. However, there are references to IDPs in the Constitution and legal framework of Afghanistan.

For example, the 2004 Constitution obliges the State to respect international human rights standards and "to create a prosperous and progressive society based on social justice, the preservation of human dignity, realization of democracy, attainment of unity, as well as equality between all peoples and tribes..."[162] Presidential Decrees particularly Decrees 104 and 297 make reference to IDPs. Both the Decrees set forth a basic framework for distributing government land to IDPs as well as to returnees as a means of addressing their needs for shelter and also affirms the full panoply of human rights enjoyed by Afghan returning refugees and protects them from discrimination and persecution.[163]

In Bangladesh, the conflict over the Chittagong Hill Tracts (CHT) had displaced more than 50 per cent (approximately 500,000 persons) of the local population. Bangladesh is neither a signatory to the 1951 Refugee Convention nor its 1967 Protocol. The 1997 Peace Accord provided several mechanisms that directly aimed at addressing and resolving the problem of internal displacement including the establishment of a Task Force to coordinate rehabilitation for the internally displaced. However, until now, the Task Force has not made any progress for rehabilitation of the IDPs.[164]

TABLE 4.14

Internally Displaced Persons (IDPs) in South Asia, 2009

	Country	*Estimate*
1.	Afghanistan	2,97,000
2.	Bangladesh	60,000-500,000
3.	India	At least 600,000
4.	Nepal	50,000-70,000
5.	Pakistan	1.25 million
6.	Sri Lanka	Over 800,000

Similarly in India, approximately 600,000 people are displaced due to conflicts and localised violence not only in Kashmir and North East but also in the State of Gujarat and West Bengal.[165] A majority of internally displaced people have not been able to return to their homes for years, due to protracted conflicts or unresolved disputes. The Government's response to displaced people is often *ad-hoc* and largely insufficient, and the IDPs frequently find themselves in an extremely vulnerable situation. A *National Policy on Resettlement and Rehabilitation for Project Affected Families* (NPRR) was launched in February 2004.[166] But this policy applies only to those displaced due to development projects and is primarily meant to safeguard the interests of resource-poor landless agricultural labourers, forest-dwellers, artisans and adivasi groups and ignores those displaced by conflict and/or natural disasters.

The Government of *Nepal* formulated a National Policy on Internally Displaced Persons in 2007. This Policy defined Internally Displaced Persons to include a person who is living somewhere else in the country after having forced to flee or leave one's home or place of habitual residence due to armed conflict or situation of violence or gross violation of human rights or natural disaster or humanmade disaster and situation or with an intention of avoiding the effects of such situations. The Policy seeks to provide relief support to the victims (shelter, food, security, health service, training and appropriate compensation, etc.) and special care to vulnerable groups such as orphan children, widowed women, women with young children, disabled, elderly people, etc. Moreover, it includes the programme of rehabilitation of IDPs to recover their lives at their habitual place of residence.[167]

The largest concentration of refugees in South Asia was recently recorded in Pakistan. It consists of approximately two million people from neighbouring Afghanistan, many of whom first arrived in Pakistan during the Soviet military occupation, but were forced to remain in Pakistan while civil war raged in their country following the Soviet withdrawal. More Afghans have since sought refuge in Pakistan as a result of the American-led war against the Taliban regime.[168] The Pakistan has thus been host to millions of Afghan refugees including women and children since 1979. The UNHCR and other agencies have been providing education, medical care and other services to the refugees and many girls have been educated while in exile in Pakistan.[169]

The Sri Lankan civil war forced 800,000 individuals to flee their homes.[170] Throughout the conflict, no ministry had overall responsibility for welfare of IDPs. In June 2002, the government adopted a National Framework for Relief, Rehabilitation and Reconciliation (NFRRR) to provide a common strategy for needs assessment, planning and delivery of assistance for the IDPs. [171] However, the NFRRR, is neither a binding law nor decree and thus provides no legal protection to IDPs.

In South Asia, only India, Nepal and Sri Lanka have tried to develop national mechanisms for IDPs. However, policies are not sensitive to the needs of all the disadvantaged sections of the population especially women and children and are not adequately address the problems arises due to armed conflict situations.

(iv) Disarmament, Demobilization and Reintegration of Combatants

During the post-conflict period, prevention of new violence depends on the willingness of armed groups to lay down their arms, (disarmament) disband military structures (demobilization), and return to civilian life (reintegration). If armed groups or warlords do not put down their weapons, peace will never be possible.

In South Asia, women and children also have been perpetrators in the armed conflicts. Some of them join armed groups of their own free will, while large numbers are abducted into combat and/or forced to become sexual and domestic slaves. Thus, gender sensitivity is essential in order to fully include all women that were part of fighting forces as beneficiaries of demobilization programs. Resolution 1325 emphasizes that different needs of female and male ex-combatants, their dependents must be taken into consideration in the planning for disarmament, demobilization and reintegration.[172]

In *Afghanistan*, over 7,500 child soldiers went through Disarmament, Demobilization and Reintegration (DDR) programmes between April 2003 and June 2006 under the Afghanistan's post-Taliban peace-building arrangements[173]. The UN leads the DDR process through the Afghanistan New Beginnings Programme (ANBP).

In *Nepal*, the People's Liberation Army (PLA) had a large number of women combatants. According to the United Nations, of the 19,602 people making up the PLA 3,846 were women, that is, approximately 20 per cent of the combatants.[174] The Comprehensive Peace Agreement (CPA) included expressed a commitment from both the Government of Nepal and the CPN Maoists for the rehabilitation of displaced persons within Nepal[175] and the immediate rehabilitation of verified minors.[176] Four years later, the Nepali Rehabilitation Action Plan established the process for release of verified minors from the CPN-Maoist cantonments. Many female ex-combatants are hesitant about reintegration due to stigma associated with their combat duties. Most of the discharged females VMLRs (Verified Minor Late Recruit), refused to return to their communities with such fear. Among those that have returned, there have been reported accounts of experiencing the stigma of "sexual" and "aggressive" women from communities and families.[177]

Similarly, in Sri Lanka LTTE had its women's political wing, which actively participated in combat. Approximately 6,000 female cadres were reportedly killed in combat; although according to the leader of the women's wing, about 5,000 women were killed out of an estimated 18,000 + LTTE cadres killed during the conflict.[178] The Sri Lankan Government with the assistance of the United Nations High Commissioner for Refugees (UNHCR) made a strategy of Confidence Building and Stabilization Measures which will sustain and help the resettlement process by building capacities and confidence between and among key actors in the resettlement process—IDPs themselves, Government officials, Security Forces and host communities in locations of displacement and also in areas of return.

(v) Funding to Civil Society Organisations for Women, Peace and Security Projects and Programs

Article 8(b) of the SCR 1325 calls for measures that support local women's peace initiatives and indigenous processes for conflict resolution.

This Article is hardly implemented. The women's ministries in the region do run a number of schemes for women's empowerment. But there is no data available to indicate the support to women's peace initiatives. Indeed, the intervention with the civil society organizations working on women peace and security revealed that the organizations were severely under-funded and hindered their efforts to build sustainable peace, address sexual violence and gender-based violence and hold their governments accountable.

(c) The Mainstreaming of Gender Perspective in All Peace Operations

Key provisions of SCR 1325 focus on the inclusion of gender perspective in all peace and security operations and mandates. The importance of providing training programmes for military and civilian police personnel on the protection, rights and specific needs of women is stated in paragraph 6 of SCR 1325. The Secretary-General is mandated to provide to Member-States training guidelines and materials on the protection, rights and the particular needs of women, as well as on the importance of involving women in all peace-keeping and peace-building measures.

States are expected to incorporate these elements as well as HIV/AIDS awareness training into their national training programmes for military and civilian police personnel in preparation for deployment. The Resolution further ordains the Secretary-General to ensure that the civilian personnel of peace-keeping operations also receive similar training.[179] These provisions apply both to the United Nations itself and to its Member-States. However, very few countries have taken even the most basic steps such as incorporating a gender perspective into training modules for military personnel or actively encouraging women to serve in peace missions.

The South Asian countries, however, have been quite pro-active in organizing gender sensitization programmes for government officials and the enforcement agencies. For example, the *Afghan* National Police and Afghan National Army train their officers and soldiers with a curriculum that includes seminars and workshops with the Afghan Independent Human Rights Commission (AIHRC) and the Ministry of Interior. The curricula include information and training on international human rights, international humanitarian law, and SCR 1325 and 1820. This training is extended to police academy units in provinces.[180] A Department on Gender and Human Rights has been created in the police academy, but this has not yet been started.

The Afghan Network records in its report on the Implementation of 1325 that the Ministry of Interior did not divulge the specific data on the number and nature of trainings to their researchers.[181]

In *India* a *National Centre for Gender Training and Research* has been set-up in the Lal Bahadur Shastri National Academy of Administration with the objective of sensitizing young administrators and policy-makers on gender-related issues. Similarly, the Police Academies run gender sensitization programmes. The National Commission for Women has also been engaged in organizing gender sensitization programmes for police and judiciary.[182]

Nepal's Administrative Staff College (NASC), a training institute for government officials has a Gender Unit and it has on going programme on gender mainstreaming since 2002.[183] Training of trainers has been provided to government officials on UNSCR 1325 and UNSCR 1820. In 2008 a training of peace-keepers has been organized to sensitize military officials on gender issues related to conflict or related situations.

Pakistan has initiated a gender sensitization programme called Gender Based Governance System (GBG) Project with the collaboration of UNDP to sensitize the bureaucracy and political leaders.[184]

Similarly, the Human Rights unit of the *Sri Lankan* Army has an ongoing programme on Gender, International Convention on Violence Against Women and Women's and Children's Rights in situations of armed conflict.

On the whole it could be said that the Resolution has not made much impact in South Asia. The region is infest with inter and intra-state conflicts. The States have not taken adequate steps to implement the Resolution. While evaluating the progress of the Resolution, it is noted that women's participation in the areas of governance, security, peace and justice has expanded since 1995 but there are wide gaps that need to be addressed. Nearly all the countries have policies on gender equality and empowerment of women but none has addressed the issue of impact of violence on women and girls in conflict and post-conflict situations and framed any specific policy to deal with it and its other consequences like mitigation, trafficking, etc. Women, peace and security is not a priority.

The participation of women in formal peace processes is almost negligible; abuse and violence against women and girls in conflict and post-conflict situations continue with impunity; and inclusion of gender perspective in peace-keeping operations and security sectors is just notional. Nepal is the only country that has framed the National Plan of Action as mandated by Resolution. The UN needs to develop effective monitoring mechanisms to hold the Member-States accountable. It should be made obligatory on the part of the State to submit yearly report on the implementation of the Resolution.

Notes and References

1. Bangladesh, Bhutan, India, Maldives, Nepal, Pakistan and Sri Lanka. The UN Women and SAARC, however include Afghanistan also in south Asia and therefore they may be references in between to Afghanistan.
2. Only Sri Lanka stood in first rank in the region due to the higher level of public commitment towards improving human development of the general population. Levels of public expenditure on health and education in Sri Lanka are higher than that of any other country in the region. Though the rank has fallen from 97 (1995) to 102 (2009). Both Bangladesh and India are still holding the same rank. Pakistan's rank slipped from 128 (1995) to 141 (2009). It is interesting to note that only Nepal has made progress from 151 (1995) to 144 (2009) in the region.
3. *Gender Inequality Index (GII)* is a composite measure reflecting inequality in achievements between women and men in three dimensions: reproductive health, empowerment and the labour market. The 2010 Human development Report shows that in South Asia, only Maldives occupied 59th rank in GII. While Nepal's Rank is 110th, Pakistan's Rank is 112th, Bangladesh's Rank is 116th India's rank is 122, and the Afghanistan has the Worst Ranking in GII and stood at 134th Rank.
4. Mahbub ul Haq Human Development Center (2007), *Human Development in South Asia, 2007: Human Development in South Asia: A Ten Year Review, Islamabad,* Oxford University, p. 39.

(While the number of poor in all other Asian regions declined between 1981 and 2005, South Asia is the only region where they actually increased, from 470 million to 550 million extremely poor ($1.25), and from 709 to 978 million vulnerable poor ($2). There are 212 million people without access to safe water. The number of people without access to basic sanitation is 897 million and the region continues to be the poorest and the most illiterate region in the world).

5. *The Global Peace Index (GPI)* is an attempt to measure the relative position of nations' and regions' peacefulness. The GPI Rankings started in 2007. The number of countries has increased from 121 (2007) to 153 (2011). It is developed by the Institute for Economics and Peace (IEP) in consultation with an international panel of peace experts from peace institutes and think tanks with data collected and collated by the Economist Intelligence Unit. They measured countries' peacefulness based on wide range of indicators, 23. These are: Number of external and internal wars fought; Estimated deaths due to external wars; Estimated deaths due to internal wars; Level of organized internal conflict; Relations with neighbouring countries; Level of perceived criminality in society; Number of refugees and displaced persons as percentage of population; Political instability; Level of respect for human rights (political terror scale); Potential for terrorist acts; Number of homicides; Level of violent crime; Likelihood of violent demonstrations; Number of jailed persons; Number of police and security officers; Military expenditure as a percentage of GDP; Number of armed services personnel; Imports of major conventional weapons; Exports of major conventional weapons; Funding for UN peace-keeping missions; Number of heavy weapons; Ease of access to small arms and light weapons; Military capability or sophistication.
6. Stockholm International Peace Research Institute (SIPRI), (2010), *SIPRI Yearbook, 2010: Armaments, Disarmament, and International Security*, Oxford, Oxford University Press, p. 13.
7. World Bank, (2007), *World Development Report*, Washington, DC, Oxford University Press, p. 56.
8. In 1947, British India was partitioned into two states of India and Pakistan and later in 1971 East Pakistan seceded from Pakistan to become Bangladesh.
9. The first was in 1948 when the fighting was limited to the disputed region of Jammu and Kashmir. The second war was in 1962 between India and China, third in 1965 between India and Pakistan, fourth in 1971 between India and Pakistan and fifth in 1999 known as Kargil war fought again between India and Pakistan.
10. Lakshmi Iyer, (2009), *The Bloody Millennium: Internal Conflict in South Asia*, Working Paper No. 09-086, Harvard, Harvard Business School, *BGIE*, p. 11.
11. Anthony H. Cordesman, (2008), *The Afghan-Pakistan War: A Status Report*, Center for Strategic and International Studies Report, p. 8.
12. Zarin Hamid, (2011), *Report on UNSCR 1325—Implementation in Afghanistan*, Kabul, Afghan Women's Network, p. 9.

13. *Ibid.*, p. 31.
14. For a detail see : Anthony Mascarenhas (1986), *Bangladesh: A Legacy of Blood*, London, Hodder and Stoughton. http://www.alltypesofsmscollection.com/2012/03/history-of-26-march-bangladeshi.html
15. M. Rashiduzzaman (1998), *Bangladesh's Chittagong Hill Tracts Peace Accord: Institutional Features and Strategic Concerns*, Asian Survey, pp. 653-70.
16. Susan, Brownmiller (1975), *Against Our Will: Men, Women, and Rape*, New York, Bantam, p. 81.
17. *Ibid.*
18. *Ibid.*
19. *Ibid.*, p. 83.
20. East Pakistan: Even the Skies Weep, *Time Magazine*, October 25, 1971.
21. Chittagong Hill Tracts Commission, (2003), *Life is Not Ours: The Chittagong Hill Tracts*, Chittagong Hill Tracts, Chittagong Hill Tracts Commission. http://www.chtarchive.com/attachments/003_Life%20is%20not%20ours%20-%20UPDATE%203.pdf
22. Chandra, K. Roy (2004), *Indigenous Women: A Gender Perspective*, Norway, Resource Centre for the Rights of Indigenous Peoples, http://www.galdu.org/govat/doc/indigenous_women_croy.pdf
23. Rita Manchanda (2008), *Kashmiri Women and the Conflict: From Icon to Agency*. In Aparna Rao (ed.), The Valley of Kashmir : The Making and Unmaking of a Composite Culture?, New Delhi, Manohar, pp. 653-712, p. 659.
24. http://www.guardian.co.uk/Archive/ Article /0,4273,3976010,00.html
25. http://www.nytimes.com/2010/09/12/world/asia/12kashmir.html
26. Arunachal Pradesh, Assam, Manipur, Meghalaya, Mizoram, Nagaland and Tripura.
27. The central government and the government of Assam signed accords with the All Bodo Students' Union in 1993 and the Bodo Liberation Tigers (BLT) in 2003, and a ceasefire with the National Democratic Front of Bodoland (NDFB) has been in operation since 2004.
28. Such groups include the People's Liberation Army (PLA), the People's Revolution party of Kangleipak (PREPAK) and the Kangleipak Communist Party (KCP).
29. Speech to the Conference of Chief Ministers on Internal Security, December 20, 2007. http://www.satp.org/satporgtp/countries/india/document/papers/20071220pmspeech.htm
30. Urvashi Butalia , (2000), *The Other Side of Silence : Voices from the Partition of India*, Durham, Duke University Press, p. 3.
31. Urvashi Butalia, (1999), *Gender, Religion And Ethnicity in the Context of Armed Conflict And Political Violence In India*, A briefing note presented at World Bank conference on Gender, Armed Conflict and Political Violence, Washington D.C., June 1999, www.worldbank.org/gender/events/Butalia.doc

32. Indian Army Gang Rape Victims : Testimonies of Young and Old Women of Kunan Pushpora in Kashmir, http://www.kashmir.demon.co.uk/rape/
33. Kashmiri Women's Initiative for Peace and Disarmament, (1994), *Voices Unheard*, Sri Nagar, Kashmiri Women's Initiative for Peace and Disarmament (KWIPD).
34. *Ibid.*
35. Human Rights Watch (1998), *Global Reports on Women's Human Rights*, New Delhi, Oxford University Press, p. 13.
36. http://www.kmsnews.org/archive/all
37. Asha Hans (2000), *Internally Displaced Women from Kashmir: The Role of UNHCR*, Vol. 2, No. 1, South Asian Refugee Watch, p. 22.
38. Persons are picked up on suspicion by some agency and their whereabouts are not revealed leading to mental trauma for the whole family. It is not known whether that person is alive or dead and this practice has led to emergence of new section of society called "half widows", applying to women who do not know whether their husbands are alive or dead. These women go through an identity crisis owing to the disappearances of their husbands which has led them to be designated as "half widows".
39. Meera Khanna (2005), *Women and Armed Conflict (focus on Kashmir),* In Pam Rajput (ed.), NGO Country Report on Beijing + 10, Chandigarh, India Women's Watch, pp. 108-112.
40. Saeed ur Rehman Siddiqui, (2006), *Wailing woes of Kashmiri women,* Sri Nagar, Kashmir Newz, http://www.kashmirnewz.com/a0027.html.
41. http://www.guardian.co.uk/global-development/2010/oct/11/1
42. Saeed ur Rehman Siddiqui, (2006), *Wailing woes of Kashmiri women,* Sri Nagar, Kashmir Newz, http://www.kashmirnewz.com/a0027.html.
43. http://www.youthkiawaaz.com/2010/02/dardpora-the-village-of-widows/
44. Balraj Puri, (1993), *Kashmir Towards Insurgency*, New Delhi, Orient Longman, p. 20.
45. *Ibid.*
46. North-East Network (NEN), (2004), *Violence Against Women in North East*, New Delhi, National Commission for Women
47. http://news.oneindia.in/2007/01/23/un-to-approve-new-political-mission-for-nepal-1169512365.html
48. United Nations, Population Fund (2007), *Priority Areas for Addressing Sexual and Gender Based Violence in Nepal*, Nepal, Human Resource Development Center (*HURDEC*), p. 5.
49. Watchlist on Children and Armed Conflict, (2005), *Caught in the Middle: Mounting Violations Against Children in Nepal's Armed Conflict,* Nepal, Watchlist on Children and Armed Conflict.
50. *Ibid.*
51. *Ibid.*
52. http://www.irinnews.org/report.aspx?reportid=93584.
53. Chris Zambelis, (2009), *Separatists, Islamists and Islamabad Struggle for Control of Pakistani Balochistan,* Washington, DC, The Jamestown Foundation, Terrorism Monitor.
54. Monique Mekenkamp, Paul van Tongeren, and Hans van de Veen, (eds.), (2003), Searching for Peace in Central and South Asia, *An Overview of*

Conflict Prevention and Peace-building Activities, Boulder, Lynne Rienner Publishers, p. 457.

55. http://www.conflictmonitors.org/countries/pakistan/about-the-conflict/conflict-history.
56. Najam U Din (2010), *Internal Displacement in Pakistan : Contemporary Challenges*, Lahore, Human Rights Commission of Pakistan.
57. *Ibid.*, p 24.
58. *Ibid.*, p. 25.
59. http://zeenews.india.com/news/south-asia/tamils-urged-to-mourn-marking-sri-lankan-war-s-end_625744.html
60. *http://www.unhcr.org/*
61. Rita Manchanda (ed.), (2001), *Women War and Peace: Beyond Victimhoodto Agency*, New Delhi, Sage Publications, p. 116.
62. Farah Kabir (2003), *Political Participation of Women in South Asia*, p. 3, http://www.nwmindia.org/articles/links-to-studies-articles.
63. Aristotle (1995), *Politics*, Book 1, Chapter 13, Oxford Worlds Classic, New York, Oxford University Press, p. 35.
64. *Ibid.*, p. 102.
65. Australia (1901), Finland (1906) or Norway (1913) Denmark (1915), Iceland (1915), the Netherlands (1917), Canada (1917), Germany (1918), Sweden (1918), USA (1920) and Italy women got the vote only after WWII in 1945.
66. Convention on the Elimination of All Forms of Discrimination Against Women (CEDAW) General Assembly Resolution 34/180 of 18 December 1979, Article 7.
67. Adopted and opened for signature, ratification and accession by General Assembly resolution 2200A (XXI) of 16 December 1966 *came into force* 23 March 1976, in accordance with Article 49, Article 25.
68. Nairobi Forward Looking Strategies for the Advancement of Women, 1985, adopted at the Third United Nations World Conference on Women, Para 46.
69. United Nations, (1995), *Report of the Fourth World Conference on Women, Beijing (A/CONF.177/2)0*, New York, United Nations.
70. The Outcome Document (OD), adopted by the Twenty-third United Nations General Assembly Session, *Women 2000: Gender Equality, Development and Peace, for Twenty-first Century*, New York, 5-9 June 2000, para 1.
71. *Ibid.*, para G:23.
72. Women in Parliaments: World and Regional Averages, http://www.ipu.org/wmn-e/world.htm
73. *Ibid.*
74. Women in Parliaments: World and Regional Averages, http://www.ipu.org/wmn-e/world.htm
75. *Ibid.*
76. According to the United Nations geographical region classification Southern Asia comprises the countries of Bangladesh, Bhutan, India, the Maldives, Nepal, Pakistan, and Sri Lanka. Afghanistan joined the SAARC organization in 2005.

77. http://www.institute-for-afghan-studies.org/AFGHAN%20 CONFLICT/Bonn%20Meeting/UN/Afghan%20interim%20 government % 20cabinet %20list.htm
78. Inter-Parliamentary Union (IPU), (2002), *Women in National Parliament*, Geneva, Inter-Parliamentary Union, p. 4.
79. This quota system was first introduced by the 1972 Constitution (originally providing for 15 reserved seats for women, out of 315 seats, for a period of 10 years). In 1978 a presidential proclamation enlarged the number of reserved seats to 30 and extended the period of reservation to 15 years The constitutional provision lapsed in 1987 and was re-incorporated in the constitution by an amendment in 1990 to be effective for 10 years. This provision lapsed in 2001. The Parliament elected in October 2001 did not have reserved seats for women. On 2004, the constitutional amendment was passed to reintroduce quotas for women. The 13 percent are reserved for women. The seats are allocated to parties in proportion to their overall share of the vote.
80. Tarayana Foundation (2009), *Alternative Report for Bhutan, Present in the Committee on the Elimination of Discrimination Against Women on 44th CEDAW Session*, Thimphu, Tarayana Foundation, p. 4.
81. Concluding Comments, Bhutan, Committee on the Elimination of Discrimination Against Women, Thirtieth Session, 12-30, January 2004, para 24.
82. http://www.ipu.org/wmn-e/world.htm
83. *Ibid.*
84. http://www.adb.org/Documents/Books/Country_Briefing_Papers/Women_in_Maldives/women_in_maldives.pdf
85. In 1991 elections only 6 (2.9%) women were elected, in 1994 it increased to 7 (3.4%) and in 1999 12 (5.8%) women were elected. http://www.election.gov.np
86. http://www.adb.org/Documents/Books/Country_Briefing_Papers/Women_in_Maldives/women_in_maldives.pdf
87. http://www.quotaproject.org/uid/countryview.cfm?country=166.
88. http://www.ipu.org/wmn-e/world.htm
89. Asian Development Bank, (2008), *Country Gender Assessment : Sri Lanka*, Manila, Asian Development Bank, p. 5.
90. Elizabeth Powley (2005), *Rwanda: Women Hold Up Half the Parliament*, In International IDEA, Women in Parliament: Beyond Numbers, Stockholm, International Institute for Democracy and Electoral Assistance, pp. 142-51.
91. United Nations Development Fund for Women (UNIFEM), (2009), *Women's Participation in Peace Negotiations: Connections between Presence and Influence*, New York, United Nations Fund for Women (UNIFEM).
92. Frerks Bouta and Bannon (2005), *Gender, Conflict, and Development*, Washington, DC: World Bank, p. 49.
93. Elisabeth Rehn and Ellen Johnson Sirleaf (2002), *Women, War and Peace: The Independent Expert's Assessment on the Impact of Armed Conflict on Women and Women's Role in Peace-building—Progress of the World's Women 2002*, Vol. 1, New York, United Nations Development Fund for Women (UNIFEM).

94. The 'Agreement on Provisional Arrangements in Afghanistan Pending the Re-Establishment of Permanent Government Institutions', commonly referred to as the 'Bonn Agreement' was the result of a round of talks where a number of prominent Afghans met under the auspices of the UN to determine a plan for governing the country.
95. The agreement recognised the distinct ethnicity and special status of the tribes and indigenous peoples of the Chittagong Hill Tracts, and established a Regional Council consisting of 22 Members of the local government councils of the three districts of the Hill Tracts which included men and women from the Chakma, Marma, Tripura, Murang and Tanchangya tribes; the delegates would be elected by the district councils of the Hill Tracts.
96. The 5622nd Meeting of Security Council had established United Nations Political Mission in Nepal (UNMIN) by unanimously adopting the resolution 1740 (23 January 2007) as per the request of the Government of Nepal and the CPN (M).
97. Ms. Anuradha Koirala Member, participated in the Peace Talk from the Government side with Maoists.
98. http://www.peace.gov.np/admin/doc/Histroy%20of%20Peace%20Talk-eng-web1.pdf, http://www.realizingrights.org/pdf/UNIFEM_handout_Women_in_peace_processes_Brief_April_20_2009.pdf.
99. http://nepal.unfpa.org/pdf/Media%20kit_final_English.pdf
100. *GOSL:* Dr. Kumari Jayawardena, Dr. Deepika Udagama, Ms. Kumuduni Samuel, Ms. Faizoon Zakariya, Dr. Fazeela Riyas.
    LTTE: Ms. Sivahimi Subramaniyam, Ms. Renuga Sanmugaraja, Ms. Mathimalar Balasingam, Ms. Sridevy Sinnathampi, Ms. Vasanthapireminy Samasundaram.
101. http://www.ipu.org/wmn-e/world.htm
102. UNWomen (formerly Unifem) Factsheet 2010. Last Updated February 2010. Accessible http://www.unifem.org/Afghanistan/media/pubs/factsheet/10/index.html
103. National Institute of Public Cooperation and Child Development (2010), *Statistics on Women in India, 2010,* New Delhi, National Institute of Public Cooperation and Child Development, p. 344.
104. Krishna Hari Pushkar (2010), *Security Sector Reform in Nepal: A Discussion of Gender Dimensions with Reference to UNSCR 1325,* Nepal, http://www.monitor.upeace.org/archive.cfm?id_article=686.
105. *Ibid.*
106. http://www.opendemocracy.net/blog/liberia/kristen-cordell/2009/10/08/liberia-women-peacekeepers-and-human-security.
107. United Nations Security Council, (2009), *Nineteenth Progress Report of the Secretary-General on the United Nations Mission in Liberia* (S/2009/411), New York, United Nations.
108. United Nations Security Council (2008), *Open Debate on Women, Peace and Security,* New York, United Nations.
109. United Nations Development Fund for Women, (2004), *Getting it Right, Doing it Right: Gender and Disarmament, Demobilization and Reintegration,* New York, United Nations Development Fund for Women (UNIFEM), p. 4.

http://www.unifem.org/attachments/products/Getting_it_Right_Doing_it_Right.pdf

110. United Nations Security Council, (2000), *United Nations Security Council Resolution 1325 on Women, Peace and Security* (S/RES/1325), New York, United Nations, para 15.
111. See pages 157-72.
112. Bangladesh: Reservation: Articles 2 and 16.1(c), India: Reservation: 29(1), Declarations: 16.1 and 16.2, Maldives: Reservation: Articles 7(a) and 16, Nepal: Statement: "If provisions of any Convention are inconsistent with national law, national law supercedes, Pakistan: Reservation: Article 29(1) & Declaratory Statement.
113. Afghanistan signed the Rome Statute of the International Criminal Court in 2003.
114. http://www.saarc-sec.org/areaofcooperation/detail.php?activity_id=10
115. *Ibid.*
116. South Asian Association for Regional Cooperation (2002), SAARC *Convention on Preventing and Combating Trafficking in Women and Children for Prostitution*, Kathmandu, Nepal.
http://www.saarc-sec.org/userfiles/conv-traffiking.pdf
117. *Ibid.*
118. *Ibid.*
119. *http://www.saarc-sec.org/*
120. *Ibid.*
121. Zarin Hamid, (2011), *Report on UNSCR 1325–Implementation in Afghanistan*, Kabul, Afghan Women's Network.
122. http://www.nhri.net/NationalData.asp?
123. http://wcd.nic.in/
124. Ministry of Women and Social Welfare was established in September 1995 immediate after Beijing Conference. The ministry has been renamed as Ministry of Women, Children and Social Welfare (MWCSW) in October 2000.
125. The Committee is comprised of Ministry of Finance, Ministry of Women, Children and Social Welfare and UNIFEM.
126. Until 2004, the Ministry was known as the Ministry of Women Development, Social Welfare and Special Education. However, in the reorganization of various ministries, carried out in 2004, the Ministry was re-designated as the Ministry of Women Development.
127. *Ibid.*
128. Government of Pakistan (2005), *Convention on the Elimination of All Forms of Discrimination Against Women : Second and Third periodic report of Pakistan*, Pakistan, p. 16.
129. Government of Bangladesh, (2003), *Convention on the Elimination of All Forms of Discrimination Against Women* : Fifth Periodic Report of Bangladesh, Government of Bangladesh, p. 13.
130. http://criminalisewar.org/?p=687.
The Jamaat-e-Islami is the country's largest Islamist party and it opposed Bangladesh's independence from Pakistan at that time. Some of its members allegedly fought alongside the Pakistani army. However, the

two opposition parties accuse the government of carrying out a vendetta and trying to use the trial to curb their political activities.

131. www.wcd.nic.in
132. *North-East Regional Consultation on Engendering the Eleventh Five Year Plan* organized by National Alliance of Women (NAWO) in 2007, Shillong.
133. Government of India, 2007, Eleventh Five Year Plan (2007-12), New Delhi, Planning Commission of India, p. 194.
134. http://www.lawcommission.gov.np/en/documents/prevailing-laws/prevailing-acts/Prevailing-Laws/Statues—Acts/English/Human-Trafficking-and-Transportation-%28Control%29-Act-2064-%282007%29/
135. http://humanrights.opmcm.gov.np/
136. http://www.mowd.gov.pk/NPA.pdf
137. *Ibid.*
138. Government of Pakistan (2005), *Convention on the Elimination of All Forms of Discrimination Against Women* : Second and Third Periodic Report of Pakistan, Government of Pakistan, p. 17.
139. http://www.mowd.gov.pk/
140. www.childwomenmin.gov.lk/
141. *Ibid.*
142. http://www.priu.gov.lk/Ministries/Min_Child_Dev_womens_empower.html
143. Sanam Naraghi Anderlini, Camille Pampell Conaway, and Lisa Kays, (2005), *Transitional Justice and Reconciliation,* Cambridge, Inclusive Security, Women Waging Peace, p. 1.
144. Truth and Reconciliation Commission are, under various names, occasionally set-up by states emerging from periods of internal unrest, civil war, or dictatorship.Throughout the world, truth commissions have been created under the assumption that getting people to understand the past will somehow contribute to reconciliation between those who were enemies under the ancient regime. A common response to this dilemma is to empanel some sort of "truth commission", often with the power to grant amnesty to those who come forward and confess their illicit deeds Truth commissions are based on the hypothesis that knowledge of the past leads to acceptance, tolerance, and reconciliation in the future, and that learning the "truth" will somehow convince citizens to put the past behind and move on toward a more democratic future. A truth and reconciliation commission is an official form of inquiry into the event or events surrounding a massive abuse of human rights. Usually a truth commission is created by the government of the nation that has undergone the violations, but it can also be formed by a non-governmental organization (NGO) or the United Nations, or a combination of these entities.
145. Inter-Parliamentary Union/IDEA, *Making Reconciliation Work: The Role of Parliaments*, Geneva, Inter-Parliamentary Union, p. 11.
146. Sanam Naraghi Anderlini, Camille Pampell Conaway, and Lisa Kays, (2007), *Transitional Justice and Reconciliation, in Inclusive Security, Sustainable Peace: A Toolkit for Advocacy and Action,* London, International Alert/Women Waging Peace, p. 9.

147. Afghanistan Independent Human Rights Commission (AIHRC), 2004, A Call for Justice, Kabul, Afghanistan Independent Human Rights Commission (AIHRC).
www.aihrc.org.af/Rep_29_Eng/rep29_1_05call4justice.pdf
148. Action Plan of the Islamic Republic of Afghanistan for Peace, Justice, and Reconciliation. Government of Afghanistan. Accessible http://www.norway.org.af/NR/rdonlyres/C9F4CAAC24814924BA760231E37D9BC5/72001/070109TJHandlingsplanenpdf.pdf
149. http://aan-afghanistan.com/index.asp?id=665
150. *Ibid.*
151. Kashmir news, Srinagar, January 15, 2009: http://kashmir.wordpress.com/category/srinagar/
152. http://www.peace.gov.np/admin/doc/TRC-English.doc
153. Asian Centre for Human Rights, (2008), *South Asia Human Rights Index, 2008*, New Delhi, Asian Centre for Human Rights, p. 106.
154. http://www.peace.gov.np/admin/doc/TRC-English.doc
155. The observations : "In evaluating the Sri Lanka experience in the context of allegations of violations of International Humanitarian Law (IHL), the Commission is satisfied that the military strategy that was adopted to secure the LTTE held areas was one that was carefully conceived, in which the protection of the civilian population was given the highest priority. The Commission also notes in this regard that the movement of the Security Forces in conducting their operations was deliberately slow during the final stages of the conflict, thereby evidencing a carefully worked out strategy of avoiding civilian casualties or minimizing them.
156. Following recommendations by the Commission a special committee was appointed in January 2011, to study the cases of detained LTTE suspects and expedite legal action where necessary:
Implementing reconciliation measures suggested by the IIAC the government is gradually releasing lands occupied by the military as High Security Zones (HSZs) in the country, especially in the North; The Sri Lanka Army officially handed over Subash Hotel on Victoria Road in Jaffna town in which the 52 Division Headquarters was established since December 1995, to its owner in March this year; 256 houses surrounding the Palaly HSZ have already been returned to civilians and another 2392 houses have been identified for civilian occupation in more than 2500 hectares of the land that was set apart for HSZs.
157. Tsjeard Bouta and Georg Frerks (2002), *Women's Roles in Conflict Prevention, Conflict Resolution and Post-Conflict Reconstruction*, Washington, DC, World Bank, p. 35.
158. Internal Displacement Monitoring Centre, *Global IDP estimates (1990-2006)*, 2008, http://www.internal-displacement.org/8025708F004CE90B/(httpPages)/10C43F54DA2C34A7C12573A 1004EF9FF? Open Document&count=1000.
159. Internal Displacement Monitoring Centre, 2009, *Global statistics: IDP country figures*.
http://www.internal-displacement.org/8025708F004CE90B/(httpPages)/22FB1D4E2B196DAA802570BB005E787C?OpenDocument&count=1000

160. http://www.unhcr.org/cgi-bin/texis/vtx/country?iso=afg
161. *Ibid.*, Afghanistan is party to the following treaties which make up the core of international human rights law: *International Covenant on Civil and Political Rights* (ICCPR), *International Covenant on Economic, Social and Cultural Rights* (ICESCR), *Convention on the Elimination of All Forms of Racial Discrimination* (CERD), *Convention on the Elimination of All Forms of Discrimination Against Women* (CEDAW), *Convention Against Torture* (CAT), and the *Convention on the Rights of the Child* (CRC). Afghanistan is also a party to the *Geneva Conventions* and the first two additional protocols, and the *Rome Statute of the International Criminal Court*.
162. For details See : *Constitution of the Islamic Republic of Afghanistan*, 2004, Article 6.
163. Brookings-Bern Project on Internal Displacement and Norwegian Refugee Council (2010), *Realizing National Responsibility for the Protection of Internally Displaced Persons in Afghanistan: A Review of Relevant Laws, Policies, and Practices, Bern,* Brookings-Bern Project on Internal Displacement and Norwegian Refugee Council, p. 13.
164. http://bangladeshwatchdog.blogspot.in/2010/12/peacebuilding-in-chittagong-hill-tracts.html
165. www.idpproject.org
166. www.dolr.nic.in/Hyperlink/LRC-status/nprr_2003.htm
167. Nepal Institute of Peace (2007), Internal Displacement: Advocacy Toolkit, Kathmandu (i to xii).
168. Government of Pakistan (2005), *Convention on the Elimination of All Forms of Discrimination against Women* : Second and Third periodic report of Pakistan, Government of Pakistan, p. 91.
169. *Ibid.*
170. http://hrw.org/wr2k2/asia.html.
171. www.erd.gov.lk/publicweb/RRR2002/chapters1-6.doc
172. Article 13.
173. Asian Centre for Human Rights (2008), *South Asia Human Rights Index 2008*, New Delhi, Asian Centre for Human Rights, p. 166.
174. María Villellas Ariño (2008), *Nepal: A Gender View of the Armed Conflict and the Peace Process,* Barcelona, Escola de cultura de pau, p. 7.
175. Nepal, 2006 Comprehensive Peace Accord Concluded Between the Government of Nepal and the Communist Party of Nepal (Maoist), section 5.2.8.
176. *Ibid.*, section 7.6.1.
177. Sarah Dalrymple, 29 July 2010; Interview with Desmond Molloy, 2 August 2010.
178. United Nations Fund for Women (UNIFEM), (2007), *Progress of Women in South Asia, 2007: A Series for the Sixth South Asia Regional Ministerial Conference: Commemorating Beijing*, New York, United Nations Fund for Women (UNIFEM), p. 42.
179. United Nations Security Council (2000), *United Nations Security Council Resolution 1325 on Women, Peace and Security* (S/RES/1325), New York, United Nations, para. 6.

180. Afghanistan; Ministry of Interior (2010), *Working Paper on Convention on the Elimination of All Forms of Discrimination Against Women*, Ministry of Interior, Afghanistan.
181. Zarin Hamid (2011), *Report on UNSCR 1325—Implementation in Afghanistan*, Kabul, Afghan Women's Network, p. 28.
182. www.wcd.nic.in
183. Review of the Implementation of the Beijing Platform for Action an the Outcome Documents of the Twenty-third Special Session of the General Assembly, May 2004.
184. Response to the Questionnaire for Governments on Implementation of the Beijing Declaration and Platform for Action adopted at the Fourth World Conference on Women (Beijing, 1995) and the outcomes of the twenty-third special session of the General Assembly (2000), May 5, 2009 (http://www.unescap.org/ESID/GAD/Issues/Beijing+15/Responds_to_Questionnaire/Pakistan.pdf)

5

Women in Informal Peace Processes in South Asia

Peace processes[1] represent unique opportunities for putting an end to armed conflicts and, furthermore, can be the starting point for profound transformations in the societies that have the chance to make the transition from war to peace through a dialogued manner. Although peace processes are not always successful in putting an end to violence, they allow, at a minimum, certain rays of hope to be maintained, and keep the door open for possible negotiated ends to violence.[2]

Peace processes consist of a complex range of formal and informal activities. The *Formal Peace Processes* may be conducted by governments, political leaders, opposition groups, military, international organizations, such as the United Nations, regional and sub-regional organizations, as well as governmental, non-governmental and humanitarian organizations. Formal peace processes generally comprise early warning, preventive diplomacy, conflict prevention, peace-making, peace-building and global disarmament.[3] The activities in formal peace processes include conflict resolution, peace negotiations, reconciliation, reconstruction of the societies and the provision of humanitarian aid through official channels of governments.[4]

The other method of peace processes is known as *Informal Peace Processes*. This method is very familiar with women's groups or civil society organizations. It refers to peace marches and protests, inter-group dialogue, promotion of inter-cultural tolerance, understanding and the empowerment of ordinary citizens in economic, social, cultural and political spheres. These activities are conducted by a range of actors, such as United Nations entities, international, regional, national and local organizations, and grass-roots organizations, including peace groups, women's groups, religious organizations and individuals.[5]

WOMEN IN INFORMAL PEACE PROCESSES WORLDWIDE

The participation of women in formal peace processes is recognized as the most crucial factor in the establishment of sustainable peace. But in reality, they still do not find fair representation.[6] Thus, women worldwide are engaged in informal peace processes and leading non-violent movements for societal transformation and conflict prevention. Ayo and Suthanthiraraj write, "At the informal level, women have been instrumental in building bridges of dialogue and empathy in polarized societies, forming cross community alliances to address core social concerns and initiating movement beyond ethnic, religious and political stalemates."[7]

In the informal peace processes, women are highly organized and use deliberate strategies to promote peace and democracy. As leaders of non-governmental organizations (NGOs), activists, and mothers, women worldwide mobilize to deter the escalation of conflict and prevent a resurgence of violence through non violence.[8] They come together from all backgrounds and across conflict lines to prevent violence that indiscriminately impacts their constituencies and communities.

Women's involvement in peace building is as old as their experience of violence. There are numerous examples in the history where women in the society have traditionally been active in the conflict prevention and involved in informal peace processes. Beginning perhaps with the sex strike declared by the women of ancient Greece in Aristophanies *Lysistrata* in order to persuade their husbands to end the Peloponnesian War with the Spartans. The Heroine Lysistrata, through her feminist and pacifist ideas convinces the women of Greece to withhold sexual privileges from their husbands and lovers as a means of forcing the men to bring an end to the Peloponnesian War and to negotiate peace.[9] The women also raid the Acropolis to make off with the treasury that is financing the war. The men soon come to their senses and make peace. Spartans and Athenians became friends at a banquet and everyone lives happily ever after.[10]

In the Twentieth Century, women's engagement with pacifist movements dates back to the First World War. Reacting to the carnage of war nearly 1,200 women came together at Hague in April 1915, from warring and neutral countries to protest against the bloodshed and war. They convened the first *International Congress of Women (ICW)* and formed the *Women's International League for Peace and Freedom (WILPF)*, an organization that still continues to advocate internationally for disarmament and human rights.[11] It demanded equality between women and men and among nations, and the creation of a non-partisan international organization to mediate disputes between countries.[12]

Since World War II, women have repeatedly protested against militarism, often drawing on their maternal identities or their strategic positions as outsiders to the military establishment. On November 1, 1961, a group named *Women Strike for Peace (WSP)* called for a one day housewives' strike against Soviet and American nuclear policies. On that day it is estimated that approximately 50,000 women in various countries protested against nuclear testing and in particular, about the hazards posed by such testing to children's health. In the United States, about 1500 women marched in Washington DC. They appealed to abolish nuclear armaments in the US and at the same time protested against the US intervention in Vietnam.[13] WSP remained a significant voice in the peace movement throughout the 1980s and '90s, raising voice against the U.S. intervention in Latin America and the Persian Gulf states. During late 1990s, WSP focused on total international abolition of nuclear armaments by the end of the 20th century.[14]

Women have been active in organising against nuclear weapons and nuclear testing and, by establishing women-only communities have asserted their belief in the peace-loving nature of women.[15] One such community is the *Greenham Common Women's Peace Camp* of United Kingdom. Military order and masculine uniforms and equipment were contrasted with feminine symbols. Photographs of children and families, peace symbols and ribbons were tied to the fences around military bases.[16]

Another movement called *Women in Black* movement with vigils started in the year 1988 in Jerusalem. A group of fifteen women joined hands to raise voice against the Israel occupation of Palestinian territories and to put an end to the continuing cycle of violence and oppression between Israelis and Palestinians. It aimed to raise public awareness regarding this issue.[17] Initially, to attract the attention, it was decided by the protesters that women would wear black clothes and men would wear white. After the men failed to wear the white clothes, the women, who were dressed in black, soon realized that they drew substantial attention from passersby which gradually turned the vigils into a women-only activity.[18] They held weekly demonstrations every Friday every Friday afternoon (between 1- 2 pm) at fixed locations throughout the country. Within weeks following the first vigil in Jerusalem, by word of mouth, women throughout Israel had heard about this form of protest, and launched dozens of vigils. [19] Their protest has remained their trademark—the weekly vigils at major intersections, wearing black clothing and raising a black sign in the shape of a hand with white lettering that reads "End the Occupation", in Hebrew, Arabic and English. [20] It was estimated that during its peak years (1988-91), about 5000 women belonging to this movement (Women in Black) stood at roughly 39 different vigils around the country on a regular basis.[21] This movement has inspired a world-wide Women in Black movement protesting against violence and conflict. It was especially very active in the former Yugoslavia.[22]

It is significant to note that since the early 1990s there has been a revival of practice of protests carried out by social movements all around the globe. A global women's peace movement spread across the world pursuing the goal of global peace, including total elimination of weapons of mass destruction, strengthened controls over the production and sale of conventional arms, the control of missiles, the need to reduce military expenditures and arms exports.[23] The push for peace resulted in all the four UN World Conferences on Women organized in the second half of the last Century as discussed earlier, to include Peace alongwith Equality and Development—the theme of the Conferences.

Apart from these peace movements, women in a number of countries with conflict situations have played a critical role in ending those conflicts and promoting peace. It may be in the fitness of things to refer to some of such conflict situations and the role of women therein.

Reference to a decade long (1989-98) armed conflict in *Bougainville* (*province of Papua New Guinea*) is in order, that left 15,000 dead and thousands displaced between 1989 and the signing of a permanent ceasefire between local factions and the government of Papua New Guinea in 1998,[24] women proved a pivotal force to end the conflict, addressing humanitarian needs of the population, mediating between warring groups, intervening to negotiate disarmament, establishing "peace areas", and observing official peace talks. They continue to work at local and national levels to reintegrate combatants, promote peace education and conflict resolution, and address the ongoing problem of violence against women. When conflict broke out between the Papua New Guinea government and the Bougainville Revolutionary Army (BRA), women intervened as peace builders, landowners, and mothers. Women's groups obtained permission from the village chiefs, the Papua New Guinea government, and the BRA to negotiate with combatants. Women played a substantive role in the peace process and continued to facilitate reconciliation and transitional justice.[25]

They organized peace marches and protested against soldiers who prevented delivery of humanitarian aid. Women also created a "peace area" in 1991 from which they excluded all armed men. As a result of the women's leadership, the community initiated the disarming of the Bougainville Resistance Army and agreed to keep resistance forces away from the area. However, in 1998, despite women's successful efforts to implement a permanent cease-fire, they were left out of national-level negotiations and post-conflict programs.[26] But in 2005, the first autonomous government of Bougainville involved women in the Bougainville Constituent Assembly, an important step forward for women's participation in the political arena.[27]

Colombia's civil war that lasted for forty years, is another example, wherein, the Association of Organized Women of Eastern Antioquia (AMOR), directly negotiated with armed factions to produce tentative humanitarian accords.[28] They developed a complex network of national and local organizations that worked to gain a foothold in peace negotiations and developed a common civil society agenda for peace. Women at the community level directly mediated between the warring factions to avoid escalation, symbolically declaring their villages as "peace communities" and liaising with armed actors to establish informal humanitarian agreements. However, this social activism had to pay a price as 17 per cent of assassinated or disappeared leaders and activists throughout Colombia were women.[29]

Another example is that of *Sierra Leone*. In May 2000, when the RUF (Revolutionary United Front) broke the 1999 Lomé Accord,[30] a group of elderly women came together and demanded a meeting with Foday Sankoh.[31] However, on reaching the RUF compound, they were mistreated and insulted. Frustrated, the women tried a different tactic. They collectively hitched up their skirts, bent over, and bared themselves to Sankoh and his coterie. In Sierra Leone, such an action by women was considered as the worst curse that can be brought upon anyone. The news had a galvanizing effect on the country. Sierra Leoneans felt they had an obligation to uphold the women's honour and support the curse. But the women's actions also gave people the courage to stand up to the RUF. Coinciding with the arrival of the new UN mission and the British Special Forces and coupled with subsequent demonstrations, the women's protest played a pivotal role in the struggle for peace culminating in Sankoh's arrest.[32]

At the same time in May 2000, a group of women from *Guinea, Sierra Leone, and Liberia* came together to advocate for their formal participation in the process of managing conflict and restoring peace in West Africa. This group of women soon became the *Mano River Women's Peace Network (MARWOPNET)* and were recognized for their contributions to peace-building by the UN General Assembly. They were awarded with the 2003 UN Prize for Human Rights. The Network was successful in influencing the three countries and it worked with political, traditional, religious, and civil society leaders to resolve inter-ethnic disputes. It was one of the instrumental forces to end the war in Sierra Leone.[33]

One of the most crucial role for women in most societies is that of a mother. The desire to protect their children from the costs of militarism has also propelled mothers to protest against state-sponsored violence in their own countries. Women's peace activism finds expression in many mothers' movements for peace and justice. The best known mothers movement is perhaps the Argentinean movement known as Las Madres, or the Mothers of the Plaza de Mayo. During the years of military rule in Argentina between 1976 and 1983, a group that called itself "Mothers of the Plaza de Mayo" was formed by women whose children and grandchildren had been kidnapped by the military and disappeared during the Dirty War. The mothers demonstrated regularly in the plaza in front of the presidential palace—in defiance of the military government—to raise questions about the fate of the victims of the disappearances. Their peaceful protest raised awareness and the group garnered support both from within Argentina and the international community. Their efforts played an important role in the process of democratization and post-regime accountability in Argentina.[34]

Burundi suffering from ethnic conflicts, a network *Dushirehamwe*, meaning "Let's Reconcile" was formed by 90 women from 10 provinces across the nation.[35] It played a critical role in inter-ethnic dialogue and trust building. The network emphasized the coming together of women from all ethnic backgrounds. In Gatumba, west of the capital, a *Dushirehamwe* group was formed by displaced women, both Hutu and Tutsi. A member notes: "The Tutsi didn't want to understand the Hutu; the Hutu didn't want to understand the Tutsi. We decided to find some work together. We got some land, and now we work in the field in our group, talking and discussing as we do so."[36] Eventually, this led to the adoption of a new Constitution in February 2005, that provided legal framework for power sharing among ethnic groups.

A good lesson can be learnt from the work of *Women in Black* (a Serbian women's peace group) who organized peace loving women and held peaceful street protests (they silently stood in front of government offices with play cards to denounce violence and calling for peace). Despite the coercive response of the government, they were successful in making the government listen to their voices. UNIFEM in collaboration with other international organizations awarded them Millennium Peace Award, as recognition of their hard work to establish peace in their country. [37]

The *Guatemalan peace process* is another example of the impact informal processes can have on official peace negotiations. The Assembly of Civil Society (ASC) played a central role in advocating the necessity to incorporate women's rights into the agenda of the formal peace process. A highly visible group within the ASC known as the Women's Sector was formed. Universidad Revolucionaria Nacional Guatemalteca (URNG) official Alba Estela Maldonado affirmed that "the Women's Sector, practically the only one with a permanent presence in the Assembly of Civil Society, influenced . the coordination and the content of some of the accords."[38] Once the 1996 accords were signed, the Women's Sector fought to ensure the implementation of the accords, particularly in regard to those provisions concerning women's rights.[39] One of its key achievements was to promote the establishment of the *Foro Nacional de la Mujer*

(National Women's Forum). The *Foro* organized Guatemalan women in defense of the accords.

Throughout *Fiji's* history, women and civil society groups have repeatedly mobilized to call for the release of political hostages, a return to parliamentary democracy and upholding of principles of good governance, democracy, and rule of law. Women have also been instrumental in maintaining a degree of calm and infusing hope during the coups. In May 2000, Fiji experienced a military coup and hostage crisis. Women organized public events to promote peace and protest the situation. A multiethnic group of women, known as "The Blue Ribbon Peace Vigil," to bring different communities and groups together to pray for peace and unity in the country held a daily vigils. Women known as the "Mothers in White" gathered at the parliamentary complex to pray for the hostages[40] and to ensure all Fijians are involved, the NGO Fem'Link Pacific designed a project to bring mobile radios to rural communities so that women could share information, strategies, and testimonies of peace-building activities.[41]

Women's active participation in *'Otpor'* meaning resistance in Yogoslavia provides another example of organizing non-violent resistance. It was against the dictatorial regime of Slobodan Milosevic.[42] Women were on the forefront of the strategic civil disobedience, street demonstrations, and Otpor's campaign whereby 1.8 million stickers were posted noting, "He's Finished".[43] It led to Milosevic's defeat in the elections in 2000 and he eventually stepped down, being unable to suppress the voices of change.

In *Chile* during the 1980s, civil society mobilized against the military junta of General Augusto Pinochet.[44] Women from all backgrounds and political ideologies came together with one common goal: democratic transformation in Chile. Unrelenting public pressure, in which women participated widely, led to a plebiscite in 1988, whereby Chilean citizens would vote "yes" for Pinochet or "no" to military rule. Women were among the key mobilizers for a "no" vote, organizing a massive national campaign that included housewives, academics, feminist activists, professionals, and *campesinas* of all political backgrounds. In their pamphlets, women listed ten different reasons urging people to vote 'no' in the forthcoming plebiscite. "Their pamphlets advocated saying 'no' to the dictatorship, to violence, to a culture of death, to social injustice, to abuse of power, and to repression."[45] The "no" vote won in Chile, and women remained active in the consolidation of democracy long after Pinochet's regime was pushed out from power.

However, conflict management approaches focused mainly on the top leaders of conflicting parties, based on the assumption that a limited number of actors involved in peace negotiations. Though the initiatives of the civil society and non-governmental organizations are not a panacea for peace-building, yet they help to create the conditions for talks, build confidence between parties, shape the conduct of the negotiations and influence the sustainability of peace agreements. They can catalyse public moblisation for peace, whether through demonstrations, petitions or media campaigns.[46]

In *Kenya,* Wajir's movement that started in Wajir district, is a remarkable story of a group of women, normally marginalized in a predominantly Muslim community, who directed their community through an inclusive and effective, non-violent peace process.[47] The women Wajir Peace Group successfully intervened in conflicts between ethnic groups of the Northeast corner of Kenya, engaged in violent warfare over sparse resources and controversial traditional/ colonial geographical boundaries throughout the 1990's and early 2000's.[48]

All these illustrations substantiate that women worldwide are demonstrating their capacity for promoting peace and development through the design and implementation of programs locally and nationally to enhance security, end corruption, increase transparency and accountability, bring reconciliation, and peacefully transform society in their respective countries

SOUTH ASIAN WOMEN : FROM VICTIM TO AGENCY

As seen in the previous chapter, the participation of women in formal peace processes is almost negligible in South Asia. The patriarchal social structures and power relations are the major obstacles in the meaningful and qualitative participation of women in the region's peace processes. Nevertheless, women have been claiming a space in the peace processes in the region. Women may not be the natural allies in peace-building just because they are women but Rita Manchanda rightly points to " the multiplicity of women's roles and creative strategies for peace-building in South Asia—a process that stretches across conflict prevention, conflict mitigation and ceasefire, building reconciliation, sustaining peace and shaping the agenda".[49] They stand for no war, no bloodshed and peace both within the borders and at borders. They have contributed in many ways to conflict resolution and peace-building. Several initiatives have been taken by the women groups through different communication channels and people to people dialogue.

Women's peace activism, observes Rita Manchanda, "is obscured by the fact that women's language of support and resistance flows from their cultural experience of being dis-empowered–that is protest strategies that use symbols of motherhood, mourning, or the culturally recognized strategies of ritual cursing".[50] The resourcefulness of women in peace-building and their leadership skills cannot be underscored. Highlighting women's agency, Rita Manchanda writes, "In the midst of escalating conflict, whether it is in nationalist identity conflicts in India's North-East; Sri Lanka's ethnic and ultra-nationalist conflicts; in Nepal's Maoist civil war or across the border between India and Pakistan, women have been in the forefront of a politics to prevent the outbreak of violent conflict or its recurrence and to mitigate the violence when war breaks out and then to build an inclusive just peace. Women's agency is visible in spontaneous and sporadic interventions to protect their families from immediate violence, to sustained campaigns against human rights abuse and for justice; to build trust and reconciliation across the conflict divide".[51]

In the conflict ridden South Asia, to maintain peace and cooperation use of track diplomacy that is, "Track one"[52], "Track Two"[53] and "Track Three"[54] is frequently resorted to specially between India and Pakistan. "Track Two" and "Track Three" or people to people dialogue has gained tremendous momentum since 1990s. These are generally used for peace-making activities that include hosting of various kinds of meetings, conferences, exchanges, cultural programmes, etc. conducted on both bilateral and multilateral basis. The main objective of these informal processes is to create a conducive environment for interaction and understanding of sensitive issues and to find viable solutions with a shared belief of improving the relations between the countries and the people. The civil society organizations, in particular the women's organizations have been quite involved and active on this front and have led a number of such informal peace processes.

It may be pertinent to mention here that in the *region* women's groups that have long been involved in peace work, and have contributed much to understand the roots of conflicts, the conditions for conflict resolution, human security and human development, have been recognized by the *Peace Women Across the Globe*.[55] It nominated 1000 Women for the Nobel Peace Prize 2005 and among these 1000 nominated women, 157 are from South Asia.[56] This was by far the largest number for any region. Their voices carried forth initiatives in addressing violence against women, land rights of marginalized groups, internally displaced populations, and children in conflict, access to basic health and education services, interfaith and intercultural dialogue.

The selected women were not given the Nobel Peace Prize as such. The objective of the Project was to make women's peace work visible and recognized. Women working at the local, national and international levels on the issues such as promoting political rights, developing peace, supporting health, education, environment, fighting for children's rights or against organized criminality, human trafficking and violence were nominated for this prize. Kamla Bhasin, a woman activist from India is presently the global Co-Chair of Peace Women Across the Globe.

Among the peace groups in the region, there are groups that have *regional outreach,* others work *within* the confines of *their countries.* Different approaches are followed by these groups to maintain peace in the region and their respective countries. Some of these groups use *motherhood ideology,* while others are generic in nature with focus on *prevention of conflicts and conflict resolution.*

The groups which followed the *motherhood ideology* believe that motherhood is a universal category; women share their suffering, pain, bonding and loss as a mother across the region. As such they experience not only greater loss but are also marginalized in power and politics. Yet they present alternative and non-violent ways of negotiating in a conflict situation. As mother and daughter, with their biological and cultural identity, they redefine peace process region and negotiate with the policy-makers in their own way by forging alliances, building networks and articulating their concerns to establish peace and harmony in their respective countries. Women in South Asia have organized and advocated with their cultural roles as mothers, wives, daughters and sisters. The traditional roles of mothers and wives gave women legitimate claim to intervene in the conflict resolution.

The best known example is that of *Naga Mother's Association (NMA)* in Kohima (Nagaland). In *North Eastern India*, Nagaland has been involved in the struggle for independence over decades. The parties to the conflict have failed to negotiate a permanent peace, despite two ceasefire agreements that remain in place. Naga women have played a crucial role in sustaining the ceasefire by mediating among factions and encouraging communities, tribes, and neighboring States to form a broad constituency in support of peace.

In August 1994, 3,000 mothers from various tribes convened in the capital of Nagaland to launch NMA's *"Shed No More Blood Campaign,"* as a way to promote reconciliation between Naga and non-Naga communities. Through these and other many efforts, Naga women have used cultural and tribal traditions to cross-conflict lines and engage in peace activism. They have interceded directly in villages and townships to stop violence among armed actors and have formed coalitions to rescue hostages, provide support for displaced persons, and promote inter-community integration.

The NMA is the only women's group in South Asia that has participated in the ceasefire negotiations in 1997[57] between the Government of India and Nationalist Socialist Council of Nagaland (Issac-Muivah).[58]

In India, *Meira Paibis (or the torch bearers)* is the most prominent group of women in the Manipur who are famous for their campaign against atrocities by the security forces and Armed Forces Special Power Act (AFSPA).[59] Initially they were working for nasha bandi in the towns of Manipur. They would hold Mashaals and roam in the locality to keep a watch on drunkenness and drug-abuse. Gradually they expanded their area of activities.

On July 15, 2004, the *Meira Paibis* shocked the nation by making naked protest against the rape and brutal killing of Thangjam Manorama[60] at the gate of 17 Assam Rifles (Kangla Fort) in Imphal (Manipur), holding up banners that said, "Indian Army Rape Us". They ashamed the authorities and the Indian Army for using women's bodies are used as a weapon in armed conflict between the community and the state. The extreme step taken by the Meira Paibi women is indicative of the level of desperation and frustration among them with repeated incidents of gender-based violence and growing sense of insecurity among the women.

These women raised a number of slogans, questioning how long have they to suffer while their sons and daughters are being trampled, tortured, raped and killed by the security personnel. They also challenged the security personnel to come out and outrage their modesty, if they wished. Holding banners "We are all Manorama's Mother", each of them claimed herself to be Manorama's mother. They are the MOTHERS, they said and like any other mother they can go to any extent to safeguard the lives and interests of their children—their society.

In *Sri Lanka* too the 'Mother' have been very active. Malathi de Alwis records that 1980s and 1990s witnessed the political mobilization of 'motherhood as a counter to violence'.[61] In 1984, women organized themselves into Mothers' Front in Jaffna against the unlawful detention of Tamil youth by the state. Its strength was displayed when it brought women together from all classes. Feminist Rajani Thiranagama who calls this Front as a militant 'Mothers' Front' writes that "it mobilized mass rallies, and picketed public officials demanding the removal of militancy occupation and protesting against arrests. Not only the spirit, but also the enormous numbers that they were able to mobilise, spoke loudly of the high point to which such mass organizations, especially of women can rise."[62] They also inspired the Tamil women in East to form their branch.

In 1990 likewise in Southern Sri Lanka, Sinhale Mothers' Front was formed to protest against the disappearance of 60,000 young and middle-aged men during the Janatha Vimukthi Peramuna (JVP) uprising. It was actually founded by two (male) members of Parliament belonging to the left Naval Sama Plaza de Mayo (The Argentine Mothers Front). Within two years of establishment, the membership of Sinhale Mothers' Front grew to 25,000. These women's only demand was for "a climate where we can raise our sons to manhood, have our husbands with us and lead normal women's lives".[63]

It must however, be noted that both the Fronts could neither network with each other nor be independent of political forces. Jaffna Mothers' Front was disbanded under LTTE pressure and Sinhale Mothers' Front could not free itself from cooption by Sri Lanka Freedom Party (SLFP) which used it against the ruling party—UNP. It is for this reason that feminists, writes Malathi de Alwis, " felt very uncomfortable about working with a political party that not only did not espouse a particular feminist ideology, but in fact, was perceived to be using the Mothers' Front for their own political ends."[64] Southern Mothers' Front had limited agenda and they did not reach to Muslims and Tamil women in the North and East to make a common cause with them and make their movement a mass movement for human rights and against state violence.

In another category fall the prominent women's peace groups and civil society organisations which have been working on the promotion of peace and conflict resolution at the *regional level. South Asia Forum for Human Rights (SAFHR),*[65] *Women's Initiative for Peace in South Asia (WIPSA),*[66] *Women in Security, Conflict Management and Peace (WISCOMP),*[67] *Women's Democratic Association, South Asian*

Network of Gender Activities and Trainers (SANGAT),[68] *Pakistan-India People-to-People Dialogue on Peace and Democracy (PIPFPD),*[69] *Delhi Policy Group*[70] and the *South Asian Social Forum* are among the commendable for their crucial work in the areas of women and peace and human rights.

There are a few *remarkable initiatives* taken by the women's groups to promote peace in the region.

One of the most famous initiative was taken by the *Women's Initiative for Peace in South Asia (WIPSA). It* is the *Women Peace Bus* that journeyed first to Pakistan and later to Bangladesh. In March, 2000, the *Women Peace Bus* with forty one women from India comprising of activists, lawyers, writers, teachers, artists, journalists, film-makers, etc., visited Pakistan. It was a journey of discovery of commonalties, differences, issues that hint on solutions in sight. There they met, interacted with intellectuals, human right activists, politicians, common people and finally with the President of Pakistan Gen. Parvez Musharaf. It was followed by a return visit of Pakistan's women delegation (sixty-one in number) who interacted with intellectuals, minority groups and members of the government.[71] Both the visits attracted wide media coverage. The purpose of this initiative was to demand a war free and nuclear free South Asia and indeed, a nuclear free and war free world.

Veteran peace activist Nirmala Deshpande who led the WIPSA team to Pakistan said, its motto was *goli nahin boli, "dialogue not bullets"*. The accepted norms of nationalism were further challenged when *Nirmala Deshpande* declared that she did not consider herself 'an Indian' but a 'world citizen' who would speak out for peace.[72] Women's groups declared*: "We are not the walls that demarcate the border but rather the crack in the wall."*[73]

Civil society in general and women in particular, wish to claim a space for intervention in the process of normalization of relations between India and Pakistan. No war, no bloodshed and peace at the borders is the major demand. The women's peace initiative has given an impetus to the process of peace. Most women on both sides are committed to peace and reject the prejudices which have partly been state sponsored. WIPSA therefore urges both the governments to end the rhetoric of violence and aggression and it demands an end to violence against women, be it on cultural, political or economic grounds. WIPSA is convinced that in order to restore the peace of mind of the people, there is an urgent need for confidence building among the governments and among the people of both the countries.

A similar Peace Journey was undertaken by WIPSA between Kolkata and Dhaka on May 14, 2005. The Women's Peace Bus carried 34 women peace activists from different walks of life. Even a former member of Parliament and a former judge were among this energetic, motivated group. It was a call to the biggest proponents of peace women—to join hands in the movement to end war in the world.

Women in Security, Conflict Management and Peace (WISCOMP) *is another organization that facilitates gender-sensitive training and research in the areas of conflict transformation, security and peace in South Asia. It is a part of the Foundation for Universal Responsibility of Dalai Lama to foster a culture of coexistence and non-violence. As part of its efforts to build constituencies of peace in the context of violent conflict, WISCOMP supports training programs in Conflict Transformation*[74]*—Engaging South Asian young professionals in non-violent change and strengthening peace-building initiatives in the region. It also facilitates similar initiatives between students, peace activists, educationists and journalists from different regions in South Asia such as Afghanistan and Sri Lanka.*

In *2000*, it organized a *Roundtable titled, "Breaking the Silence: Women and Kashmir"* which brought together Muslim, Hindu and Sikh women from the conflict-torn region of Kashmir in India for the first time. It organized an interface between those who are concerned and those who are affected by the ongoing conflict in Kashmir. The discussion revolved around—"Perspectives on Kashmir" and "Perspectives from Kashmir". The speakers on the Kashmir problem included academicians, activists and journalists. The speakers of second category were exclusively those whose lives have been directly affected by the 12 year old insurgency. The Round Table resulted with the formation of *Athwaas*[75] *and Samanbal.*[76] Both refer to creating safe spaces in the community to explore activities around, active listening, trauma counseling, conflict transformation and articulating concerns of women to policy-makers for initiation of programs that facilitate economic empowerment and political awareness.

Women have also been active in the fora like *Hind-Pak Dosti Manch (India-Pakistan Friendship Forum),*[77] led by Kuldip Nayar (a journalist) and *Pakistan-India People-to-People Dialogue on Peace and Democracy (PIPFPD).*[78] *Hind-Pak Dosti Manch (India-Pakistan Friendship Forum)* gathered more than ten thousand Indians citizens including women on the 47th anniversary of the Independence of India and Pakistan at *Wagah border (Amritsar).* They lighted the candles to express friendship and solidarity with one another.

Reciprocating the festive celebration, few peace groups of Lahore and other Pakistani cities have started lighting the candles from across the border each year are different citizens' groups from Lahore and other Pakistani cities. Similarly, the Pakistan-India People-to-People Dialogue on Peace and Democracy (PIPFPD) has organized peace concerts and peace marches in both countries.

There are some other Initiatives within Borders which have been taken by women in India.

Naga Women's Union of Manipur (NWUM) has been able to work across the boundaries of conflict, and boundaries that exist in post-conflict societies.[79] The Union undertook peace campaigns by conducting seminars in different localities to resolve the Naga-Kuki conflict. NWUM also extended support to women candidates in the Lok Sabha elections running on a platform to uphold the rights and dignity of women and work for equality.

Tangkhul Shanao Long (TSL) is another women group which functions both in Nagaland and Manipur. In 1997, the TSL gained recognition as a serious actor in the peace process. It tackled a traumatic crisis when the Assam Rifles went on a rampage in Ukhrul town after being ambushed by militants.[80] The women persuaded the army to release scores of civilians. They helped the people of the area to return to a normal life by requesting the shopkeepers to open their shops. They appealed to the stranded people to go back home which brought back some semblance of normalcy in the town.

Irom Sharmila Chanu, the *Iron Lady of Manipur* also known as living Gandhi from the North-East is a civil rights activist of Manipur. Sharmila, began her indefinite fast on November 2, 2000, in protest against the Malom Massacre[81] by the army, in which several civilians of a village in Manipur were killed. She demands for a repeal of Armed Forces (Special Powers) Act (AFSPA). [82] AFSPA gives the State agencies unfettered powers including the right to shoot to kill on mere suspicion. Sharmila's protest is remarkable for its insistence upon the Gandhian method of *ahimsa* (non-violence). She is in the 12th year of her fast. There is a growing public support for her non-violent protest. The Save Sharmila Solidarity Campaign (SSSC) has been gathering support for her. Candle vigils at Raj Ghat (New Delhi) and other places and a nation-wide tour was organized recently by the SSSC to raise awareness and elicit support for her. Sharmila is determined and says: "Unless and until they remove the AFSPA, I shall never stop my fasting."[83]

Another significant effort was a two day *Joint Women's Forum For Peace* organized by the Centre for Dialogue and Reconciliation (CDR) and the Women for Peace in September 2011. In the Forum forty-five women participated from all regions of Jammu and Kashmir, as well as Pakistan occupied Kashmir and Gilgit-Baltistan. At the end of the deliberations of this Intra-Kashmir Conference, a statement was issued which said, "We, the women of entire Jammu and Kashmir, from both sides of the LoC desire peace, security, and economic stability to prevail throughout the region and an immediate end to the protracted conflict. We demand the inclusion of women in all peace-building and peace negotiations/dialogue on Kashmir."[84]

Further women also demanded 33 per cent quota for women in the Assemblies, Councils, and local bodies on both sides of the LoC; adequate women's representation in departments dealing with gender issues; representation of women in and the strengthening of autonomous and independent State institutions to monitor and report gender-based issues, such as the State Commission for Women, State Human Rights Commission, Information Commission, the establishment of similar Commissions in other regions and repeal 'draconian' Acts such as the Armed Forces (Special Powers) Act (AFSPA) and the Public Safety Act (PSA).[85]

RESOLUTION 1325 AND NON-GOVERNMENTAL ORGANISATIONS (NGOS) IN SOUTH ASIA

Women's groups were instrumental in getting the Resolution adopted by the Security Council. The Resolution not only acknowledges their role as peace-makers but mandates that measures must be taken that support local women's initiatives and indigenous processes for conflict resolution and involve women in all of the implementation mechanisms of the peace agreements. The Resolution basically enjoins upon the UN, its Agencies and the Member-States—the responsibility of its implementation but it goes without saying that implementation largely rests on the vigilance and active involvement of Civil Society Organisations and NGOs. Their vigilance and advocacy can go a long way in translating the Resolution into action at local level. While NGOs as discussed earlier are quite active in their peace initiatives in South Asia, it is generally believed that most NGOs are not aware of the SCR 1325. To ascertain this, as to how many NGOs are aware of this Resolution and how many actually use it in their work in South Asia, 150 NGOs working on the issue of women and peace were identified for the present study. Of these, 100 NGOs were personally interviewed and the views of another 50 were obtained through an e-mailed questionnaire.

In response to the question regarding their activities, multiple responses were given by the responding NGOs. Table 5.1 provides a snapshot view of those activities of the respondent NGOs. 16.6 per cent NGOs indicated that they were involved in resisting and opposing conflicts by doing demonstrations, signature campaigns, protests and rallies.

TABLE 5.1

NGOs' Activities on Women, Peace and Security in South Asia

Multiple Responses (N=872)		*Particulars*	*Frequency Percentage (%)*
1.	Resistance Activities	145	16.6
2.	Rehabilitation Work and Counselling Services	145	16.6
3.	Capacity Building Programmes on Women's Rights, Political Participation, etc.	142	16.2
4.	Legal Service	140	16.0
5.	Health/Medical Service	130	14.9
6.	Creating Awareness regarding UNSCR 1325	100	11.4
7.	Informal Engagement in Peace Negotiations	35	4.0
8.	Lobby with Governments to Implement UNSCR 1325	35	4.0
9.	Total	872	100

Again 16.6 per cent NGOs work in the region to provide rehabilitation and shelter home services. Along with shelter facilities, these organizations have been providing couselling to the survivors of violence including sexual violence, skill-based trainings, medical support, formal and non-formal education and legal aid services.

16.2 per cent of NGOs are engaged in capacity building for women's rights, political participation and promote women candidates to run for post-conflict elections for increasing their representation. This is especially true of NGOs in Nepal.

To promote the rights and interests of women and children, 16.0 per cent NGOs provide legal aid services and 14.9 per cent provide health-related services to women victims.

It is significant to note that while all the NGOs interviewed focus their work on peace and security, only 11.4 per cent organistaions are engaged in creating awareness regarding Resolution 1325. Again 4.0 per cent of the NGOs are informally engaged in their communities to help peace negotiations and ceasefires between the warring parties and governments. Further, only 4.0 per cent organizations do work related to lobbying with the governments to implement SCR 1325, specially for formulating national action plans.

Table 5.2 reveals that 100 per cent respondents subscribed to the view that armed conflict is highly gendered and women's experiences are different from those of men. Women bear disproportionately the consequences of war and conflicts and suffer violations of human rights, rape, sexual assault, forced prostitution, sexual slavery, forced pregnancy and other forms of sexual violence.

TABLE 5.2
Disproportionate Impact of Violence Against Women in Conflict and Post-Conflict Situations in South Asia

(*N*=*150*)

Particulars	*Frequency*	*Percentage (%)*
1. Yes	150	100%
2. No	—	—
Total	150	100%

The multiple responses, as collated in Table 5.3, depict the various consequences faced by women in the region during and after armed conflicts. 17.1 per cent indicate sexual and gender based violence as the consequence, though it has never been considered a war crime in the region. It has grave social, cultural, domestic, physical and psychological repercussions on women, said the respondents. In addition, women pointed out that they had difficulties in reporting cases of sexual violence to the authorities.

Another form of violence in these situations is torture of women as per 12.5 per cent respondents. Even though most women have no direct participation in the conflict, they still face arrest, and mental and physical torture. Being the close relatives of men involved in the conflict, women are subjected to this form of violence

11.4 per cent respondents felt that girls' education and employment opportunities to women were adversely affected.

TABLE 5.3

Consequences of Armed Conflicts Faced by Women in South Asia

[Multiple Responses (N=877)]

Particulars	*Frequency*	*Percentage (%)*
1. Sexual and Gender-based Violence	150	17.1
2. Arrest and Torture	110	12.5
3. Effects on Education and Employment Opportunities	100	11.4
4. Economic Hardships	90	10.3
5. Displacement	90	10.3
6. Domestic Violence	87	9.9
7. Trafficking and Prostitution	85	9.6
8. HIV/AIDS	85	9.6
9. Sexual Slavery	80	9.1
Total	877	100

Invariably the girls were withdrawn from the schools and colleges in conflict situations.

10.3 per cent respondents referred to economic hardships faced by women. During violent armed conflicts because of the absence of men, bringing up children, taking care of the elderly and earning livelihood for the whole family becomes the sole responsibility of women.

Displacement is another effect in armed conflict situations observed 10.3 per cent respondents. Many women choose to flee from their homes out of fear for their lives and/or in the hope of achieving some level of security elsewhere.

Apart from being prime targets of enemy forces, 9.9 per cent NGOs felt that women were also subjected to increased instances of domestic violence and spousal abuse throughout armed conflict. And this is a leading cause of women's morbidity and mortality and has a negative influence on their physical and psychological well-being.

Women are at risk of certain diseases, including increased exposure to diseases and sexually transmitted infections (STIs), HIV/AIDS according to 9.6 per cent NGOs, followed by threat of trafficking and forced prostitution by another 9.6 per cent.

Sexual slavery is another consequence of gender-based violence experienced by women and girls during armed conflict according to 9.1 per cent. In such instances, women have been abducted and then forced into sexual and domestic labour. Without money or other resources, women and girls may be forced into providing sexual services for men in exchange for safe passage for themselves and their family or to obtain food or other necessary assistance.

Table 5.4 reveals that 100 per cent respondents agree that women should be included in the formal peace processes. Numerous studies have affirmed that the involvement of women in political life significantly enriches policy and decision-making. A review done by the UNIFEM of 21 major peace processes since 1992, indicates that where women have been involved in the peace processes, even as silent observers, they have been able to ensure that a greater number of issues important to them are included in the peace agreements, including human rights guarantees, physical, economic and legal securities and increased participatory rights.[86] But still women's participation in peace processes is marginalized in the world especially in South Asia.

TABLE 5.4
Women's Inclusion in Formal Peace Processes

(N=150)

Particulars	*Frequency*	*Percentage (%)*
1. Yes	150	100%
2. No	—	—
Total	150	100%

Why should women be included in formal peace processes, the multiple responses to this query are tabulated in Table 5.5. According to 26.9 per cent respondents, the rationale for inclusion of the women in formal peace processes is that their conception of peace is different from that of men. Whereas men's outlook of peace is quite narrow in terms of its being only absence of war, women's outlook is broad. They view peace in terms of society being free of structural violence. Hence women should be the part of peace processes.

22.4 per cent considered it important to include women at the highest level of decision making process because they constitute half of the population. Women's exclusion from peace processes restricts their access to equal opportunities in political processes and the benefit of having female perspectives in decision making. Leaving women out of the peace processes would mean their concerns being ignored or bargained away on the negotiation table, observed the respondents.

Another 17.9 per cent believe that women are generally more collaborative than men and thus more inclined towards consensus and compromise. Women often use their role as mothers to cut across the internal divides. Women are motivated to protect their children and ensure security for their families. Because of the harsh experiences of conflict situations, women tend to tilt in favour of peace.

TABLE 5.5

Rationale for Women's Inclusion in Formal Peace Processes

[Multiple responses (N=446)]

Particulars	*Frequency*	*Percentage (%)*
1. Women and Men have Different Concept of Peace	120	26.9
2. Women Constitute Half of the Population	100	22.4
3. Women are more Collaborative than Men	80	17.9
4. Women are Innovative Community Leaders	76	17.0
5. Women have their Fingers on the Pulse of the Community	70	15.7
Total	446	100

More importantly, through the cultural socialization, a legacy that has and continues to teach women to foster relationships and avoid violence. They have been able to prove themselves to be effective change agents. Therefore, their role as mothers, wives, caregivers, etc. coupled with experiences not only with conflicts at all levels but also special relationships with the environment in which they live, women can bring unique insights and values to the peace-building process. Endorsing this, writes Rita Manchanda :

"Traditionally, women have formed the humanitarian front of the war story. But beyond the passivity and powerlessness of victimhood, conflict has seen South Asian women come out and mobilise resistance, confront the security forces, the administration and the courts. Women have formed Mothers' Fronts and coalitions for peace, women have become guerrillas and soldiers and women have emerged as agents of social transformation and conflict resolution."[87]

17.0 per cent support the vital role women play in peace-building processes. The creation of civil society alliances using multi-track approaches right across conflict domains offers them an opportunity for a holistic understanding of peace and security. Similarly, women are able to transcend religious, ethnic, class and socio-economic boundaries to enhance cross community and multi-track interaction in their quest for peace. Naga Mothers' Association (NMA) of India is the living example which adopted this kind of strategy in building peace.

Women in every society are the central caretakers of their families including men and children. In the South Asian context, women are central players in nurturing and enhancing peace, which translates into development in their families, communities and nation. In this regard therefore, everyone suffers when women are oppressed, victimized, and excluded from the complex act of conflict prevention and peace-building

Living and working close to the roots of conflict, women are well positioned to provide essential information about activities leading up to armed conflict and recording events during war, including events of atrocities. They also play a critical role in mobilising their communities to begin post-conflict reconciliation and rebuilding is responded by 15.7 per cent.

The participation of women in the negotiations and implementation of peace agreements is necessary to build a lasting peace. A close examination of the peace negotiations and agreements in South Asia such as Comprehensive Peace Agreement (CPA) in Nepal, Bonn Agreement of Afghanistan and other peace talks show that these peace accords failed to recognize women as actors or change agents. Obviously there are *barriers* to women's inclusion and effective involvement in peace processes. The respondents were asked questions regarding those barriers. The multiple responses received are collated in Table 5.6.

The *patriarchal* construct of power-relations and politics remains all pervasive in South Asia, representing a major barrier in the participation of women in the political sphere feel 16.9 per cent respondents. Security is still considered to be a 'man's world'. The ideology that "women do not 'belong' in political structures

TABLE 5.6
Major Barriers in the Inclusion of Women in Peace Processes in South Asia

[Multiple responses (N=885)]

Particulars	*Frequency*	*Percentage (%)*
1. Patriarchy	150	16.9
2. Economic Limitations	145	16.3
3. Social Limitations (Fear, Violence and Stigma)	140	15.8
4. Lack of Experience, Exposure and Skills in Negotiation, Advocacy and Lobbying Strategies	140	15.8
5. Media	120	13.5
6. Lack of Visibility	100	11.2
7. Ineffective Women's Communication Strategies	90	10.1
Total	885	100

continues to permeate many societies and cultures"[88] and South Asia is no exception. This ideology may manifest itself in social attitudes, or institutionalized discrimination—both of which severely limit the ability and indeed the desire of women to participate in political life at any level. Political participation is often not prioritized by women.[89]

Even where women would consider other forms of political participation, they are often hesitant to be part of the peace process because of their own preconceptions, and the attitudes of their male counterparts. Even where women act in political leadership capacities, they have remained largely absent from peace talks due to marginalization within the government itself, and lack of women in the security sector.

Economic limitations constitute another barrier as recognized by 16.3 per cent respondents. In South Asia, women still do not have control over land and assets, rather these are controlled by men. If they have their earnings, they are more likely to spend them on food and household purchases and on educational and other expenses of children. Women tend to have less access to the funding required to either participate in a negotiation process (for travel expenses, communications, etc.) or to run for an office (campaign finance). The personal meager resources of women put together cannot for instance give them access to even the media networks in order to enhance their peace-building campaigns.

Among the social limitations, the fear of stigmatization is another major barrier in the participation of peace processes. 15.8 per cent women felt that because of the fear of fun remarks or being considered as lewd women, they hesitate to participate in peace processes. Lack of experience, exposure and skills in negotiation, advocacy and lobbying strategies are recognized by 15.8 per cent respondents as limiting factors.

International IDEA conceptualizes the media as "the fourth branch of power" because of their influence on public opinion and on public knowledge of the world around them. The media can contribute to cultivating gender bias and promoting stereotypes; they can objectify women as 'beauty objects' only; and they tend to minimize coverage of issues, events and organizations of interest to women and of areas where women tend to play a leadership role.[90] In the media and in public opinion, leadership is still considered as an inherently male attribute in many cultures.

The media framing process "conveys a decisive impression that women lack appropriate leadership, personal appearance, speech styles, and romantic lives. It deflects attention away from the substantive content of women's ideas, policies, and contributions... [and portrays] them as ill-suited outsiders in public life."[91] About 13.5 per cent identify that women candidates for political office usually receive less media coverage than their male counterparts. It is more focused on personal attributes of women (appearance, style, voice, private and family life) than on their professional qualifications or public policy views.

Lack of visibility during peace negotiations is recognized by 11.2 per cent respondents. Women's conflict resolution activities mostly make use of informal means. Their contributions are often ignored once formal peace negotiations start. The absence of women in the Nepal's Comprehensive Peace Agreement is an example in hand. It is equally true of Naga women whose services were utilized in reaching Naga Peace Accord but they did not find representation at the negotiation table once the talks materialized.

Women's communication strategies (friendship matches for peace, lobbying, plays, poems, stripping naked, etc.) is recognized ineffective by 10.1 per cent respondents. These strategies are confined to the marginalized feminine realm, that is without a strong political strategy. They create no major impact on long-term strategies for securing a seat at formal and official peace negotiations.

Table 5.7 reveals that only *43 organisations* (28.7 per cent) knew about the Resolution 1325, though they have been engaged in peace activities in one form or the other for decades in the region. And significantly among these organizations who knew about the Resolution, they were mostly urban-based organizations. The response from the *grassroots women organizations* was clear and certain that—*none of them had worked on or heard of the Resolution 1325.* Furthermore, none of the grassroot activists look upon the government, police or UN as responsible for maintaining peace; in fact some of them even considered the police and government to be their greatest source of insecurity along with poverty, ignorance and illiteracy.

TABLE 5.7

Awareness of the UNSCR 1325 among the South Asian NGOs

(N=150)

Particulars	*Frequency*	*Percentage (%)*
1. Aware	43	28.7
2. Not Aware	107	71.3
Total	150	100

Out of the 43 organisations, only 17 (39.5%) were fully aware of the provisions of the Resolution, while 20 (46.5%) organisations partially knew about the provisions and six (14%) organizations had just heard about this Resolution. Most of these NGOs, it was observed during the discussions, did not know how to incorporate the Resolution's objectives as an integral part of their work. (Table 5.8)

What are the factors responsible for slow and ineffective implementation of the UNSCR 1325 in South Asia, the multiple responses to this question are reflected in Table 5.9. 9.2 per cent respondents recognized that lack of awareness about this Resolution is one of the major reasons for ineffective implementation of the Resolution. The Resolution was passed in 2000. It is a powerful advocacy tool, but still many actors including the government officials, ministers and civil society organizations remain unaware of it.

TABLE 5.8
Awareness of the Provisions of the SCR 1325

(N=43)

Particulars	*Frequency*	*Percentage (%)*
1. Aware of all Provisions	17	39.5
2. Partially Know	20	46.5
3. Only Heard	6	14.0
Total	43	100

8.8 per cent mentioned that *less funding* specifically for issues related to women, peace and security is the another reason. Though they admitted that there is an increase in the spending on women's issues by the governments of the region with launching of many schemes on women's empowerment and gender equality, yet when it comes to the peace and security issues, the governments are not supportive and consider these as sensitive issues to be meddled with by the NGOs.

In South Asian countries, women are still under represented in politics as well as the defence forces. This severely limits their capacity to participate in decision-making related to peace-building and negotiations say 8.5 per cent of the respondents.

Patriarchal attitudes and practices continue to disadvantage women and adversely affect their opportunities to participate in leadership and decision-making. 8.5 per cent respondents felt that peace processes are still dominated by males. Many women are not involved in issues related to peace and security either because the structures are skewed to exclude them or they exclude themselves. This is described as a major barrier. One of the respondent stated that women don't apply for positions related to peace and security. Jobs like early warning analysts and defence strategists do not attract women primarily because they do not have the skills for these jobs, historically these being men's jobs.

Lack of capacity and advocacy skills is the another barrier for slow implementation of the Resolution as identified by 8.4 per cent. They complained about the training and capacity building programmes which are conducted and supported by various ministries and donor agencies. These programmes did not provide a direct link to women, peace and security issues. Even though trainings are conducted in crisis settings, the skills offered do not include conflict

TABLE 5.9
Reasons for Slow Implementation of SCR 1325 in South Asia

[Multiple Responses (N=1630)]

Particulars	*Frequency*	*Percentage (%)*
1. Lack of Awareness of the Resolution	150	9.2
2. Less Funding/Lack of Sustained Funding	145	8.8
3. Low Representation of Women in Decision-making Bodies	140	8.5
4. Male Domination in Peace Processes	140	8.5
5. Lack of Capacity-building Programmes on 1325	137	8.4
6. Lack of Gender Disaggregated Data on VAW in Conflict and Post-conflict Situations	130	7.9
7. Lack of Cooperation between NGOs and Governments	120	7.3
8. Lack of Political Will	120	7.4
9. Grassroot Organizations always Ignored	117	7.1
10. Non-availability of 1325 in Local Languages	116	7.1
11. Marginalised as Women Issue	110	6.7
12. Lack of Gender Sensitivity	105	6.4
13. Lack of Monitoring Mechanism	100	6.1
Total	1630	100

and gender analysis, scenario assessment, conflict resolution, mediation, negotiation skills, etc. for women that could strengthen their knowledge and capacity to engage effectively.

Gender disaggregated data is an important tool for the formulation of gender sensitive policies and programmes. 7.9 per cent mentioned that lack of gender disaggregation is a serious constraint in implementing the Resolution. Without the availability of disaggregated data, it is very difficult to know how many women are internally displaced due to conflict, number of women refugees, number of women who died in conflict, HIV/AIDS infected women in refugee camps or armed conflict areas etc. The unavailability of disaggregated data can make governments and international institutions less accountable.

The NGOs are not encouraged to intervene in the security and peace issues. The lack of cooperation between the NGOs and the governments is identified by 7.4 per cent for the slow implementation of the Resolution. The NGOs could not build any pressure on the governments to formulate or incorporate the provisions of the Resolution in their policies and plans.

7.3 per cent identified the *lack of political will* as the major obstacle in the way of its full implementation. It is the primary responsibility of the States to implement this Resolution, yet in South Asia, not much attention is being paid by the States. So far only Nepal has formulated National Action Plan on the Resolution.

SCR 1325 calls for "measures that support local women's peace initiatives and indigenous processes for conflict resolution".[92] 7.1 respondents complained that when any UN organization or Government ministry/department organized any consultation or training programmes, they always ignored the grassroot organistions. Only national level or known organisations were invited to these programmes. The grassroot oragnisations, they stated, that have the feel and are closely engaged with the peace issues are ignored.

The unavailability of translated version of the Resolution in their local languages is another barrier as acknowledged by 7.1 per cent. The original text of the Resolution is available in English and other UN recognized languages. It has been translated into Hindi[93] and Punjabi languages but it is yet to be translated into all local languages spoken in the region. Moreover, translation is not enough. The Resolution must be simplified to make it more comprehensible to the grassroot people.

6.7 per cent respondents recognized that without the full involvement of both men and women in peace and security issues, this Resolution cannot be fully implemented. This Resolution is considered as purely for women. It is therefore compartmentalized and marginalized as women's issue. The NGOs pointed out that if they organized any workshop or consultation regarding women, peace and security issues and invited the various ministries to participate in it, only the women representatives of ministries attended such events.

6.4 per cent confessed that the participation of women in peace processes is an important objective but it is not a panacea to all the problems that affect women in relation to conflict resolution and rebuilding peace. According to them that the presence of women in peace processes was no guarantee that gender equality issues will be placed on the peace agenda. Many women participants do not understand gender issues may not advocate women's issues.

Finally, 6.1 per cent respondents felt that lack of monitoring mechanisms for the Resolution in the region constitute another major barrier in its implementation.

For the effective implementation of the Resolution in the region, the respondents offered a few suggestions (Table 5.10). Awareness regarding the Resolution being low among the government officials, the UN personnel and the civil society organizations, 11.6 per cent respondents suggested that more awareness programmes on the provisions and implications of SCR 1325 should be run by the governments and the UN agencies, especially for those actors who are responsible for its implementation. In addition, awareness-raising efforts should not be limited to top-level tiers of leadership, it should also reach down to the grassroots where women's role in peace building is experienced as part of everyday life.

Peace-building cannot succeed if half of the population is excluded from the processes of peace. Despite this fact they are under-represented in official peace processes. The respondents felt that the governments need to recognize the important role women play in peace negotiations, peace building and in conflict resolution. 11.6 per cent respondents stated that the governments must as a policy include at least 50 per cent women in all decision-making bodies and peace negotiating teams. Furthermore, 11.2 per cent respondents suggested that the government and the UN agencies must invest in their capacity-building on SCR 1325, CEDAW and national laws and policies related to women and peace and security so that they can influence the peace processes.

Another important suggestion related to funding. 10.8 per cent respondents said it is imperative that sufficient resources are allocated for work on women, peace and security, including support for the development of *national action plans* on women, peace and security.

10.4 per cent emphaised upon the need for a National Action Plan for the implementation of the UNSCR 1325. Another 10.0 per cent respondents advocated that the translation of the Resolution into all local level is very essential for its full implementation.

TABLE 5.10

Suggestions for Effective Implementation of SCR 1325 in South Asia

[Multiple Responses (N=1290)]

Particulars	Frequency	Percentage (%)
1. More Awareness Programmes	150	11.6
2. Inclusion of Women in All Decision-making Bodies and Peace Negotiating Teams	150	11.6
3. More Capacity Building programmes on Women, Peace and Security Issues	145	11.2
4. More Funding for Peace Activities by Government especially for Grassroot NGOs	140	10.8
5. Formulate Policies/Action Plan on the Resolution	135	10.4
6. Translation	130	10.0
7. Establish Monitoring Mechanism	128	9.9
8. Partnership between Government and NGOs	112	8.6
9. Peace education	110	8.5
10. Protection on the Rights of Women and Girls	90	6.9
Total	1290	100

9.9 per cent respondents favoured a strong monitoring mechanism to oversee the implementation of the Resolution. Another 8.6 per cent suggested that there should be a close cooperation and collaboration between the government and civil society actors with regards to the implementation of Resolutions SCR 1325 and SCR, 1820.

8.5 per cent respondents suggested that the basic education should integrate the concepts of peace, non-violence and gender. 6.9 per cent respondents suggested that there is need to develop effective mechanisms/policies for the protection of rights of women and children in conflict and post-conflict situations.

In *sum* it could be said that while women continue to be marginalized in the formal decision-making structures and peace processes as a result of predominantly patriarchal structures of governance, they do play a critical role as peace-makers in conflict situations and sustaining peace in their communities. In South Asia there are acknowledged initiatives taken by the women's organizations for peace in the region. However, there is lack of awareness of the Resolution among the NGOs in the region. The kind of monitoring and advocacy that is done by the NGOs at the international level is missing at the South Asia level and country level. The Resolution is a critical instrument for strengthening women's rights in conflict and post-conflict situations. The NGOs as stakeholders of the Resolution need to build their capacity for effective monitoring and lobbying with the governments for its effective implementation.

Notes and References

1. A peace process is understood to mean the consolidation of a negotiation scheme, once the agenda, the procedures to be followed, the schedule and facilitation have been agreed. Negotiation is, therefore, just one of the stages in the process. Negotiation is understood to mean a process in which two or more opposing parties (whether they are in government or represent other internal agents in a particular country) agree to discuss their differences within an agreed framework in order to find a satisfactory solution. Negotiations may be held directly or with facilitation from third parties. Usually, formal negotiations include a prior or exploratory stage which is used to establish the framework (format, place, conditions, guarantees, etc.) for the future negotiating process.
2. María Villellas Ariñ, (2008), *Peace Processes, Gendered Processes. Obstacles, Implications and Modalities from a Gender Perspective*, Paper presented at 2008 IPRA Global Conference, Belgium, http://soc.kuleuven.be/iieb/ipraweb/papers/Peace%20Processes,%20Gendered% 20Processes.
3. United Nations Security Council (2002), *Women, Peace, and Security: Study Submitted by the Secretary-General Pursuant to Security Council Resolution 1325 (2000)*, New York, United Nations, p. 53.
4. *Ibid.*
5. Brigitte Sørensen (1999), *Women and post-conflict reconstruction: Issues and sources,* In Dyan Mazurana and Susan R. McKay, Women and Peace-building, Essays on Human Rights and Democratic Development, Vol. 8, Montreal, International Centre for Human Rights and Democratic Development.
6. According to UNIFEM data shows that since 1992, women represented, on average, fewer than 10 percent of official negotiating delegations in peace talks, and only 2.1 percent of signatories to peace agreements. To date, the UN has never appointed a woman as a chief mediator in an UN-supported peace process. Out of 27 United Nations peacekeeping operations, special political missions and peacebuilding support offices, women headed four missions and were deputy heads of five missions.

7. C. Ayo, and K. Suthanthiraraj (2010), *Promoting Women's Participation in Conflict and Post-Conflict Societies*, Global Action to Prevent War, NGO Working Group on Women, Peace and Security, Women's International League for Peace and Freedom.
8. Camille Pampell Conaway and Anjalina Sen (2005), *Beyond Conflict Prevention: How Women Prevent Violence and Build Sustainable Peace*, New York, United Nations, Global Action to Prevent War and Women's International League for Peace and Freedom, p. 13.
9. http://www.pillowrock.com/ronnie/lysistrata.htm
10. *Ibid.*
11. Elisabeth Rehn, and Ellen, Johnson Sirleaf, (2002), *Women, War and Peace: The Independent Expert's Assessment on the Impact of Armed Conflict on Women and Women's Role in Peace-building -Progress of the World's Women 2002*, Vol. 1, New York, United Nations Development Fund for Women (UNIFEM), p. 75.
12. *Ibid.*
13. Amy, G. Swerdlow (1992), *Women's Strike for Peace: Traditional Motherhood and Radical Politics in the 1960s*, Chicago, University of Chicago Press, p. 130.
14. *Ibid.*
15. Greenham Common Women's Peace Camp was established to protest at nuclear weapons at RAF Greenham Common in Berkshire, England. The camp began in September 1981 after a Welsh group, *Women for Life on Earth*, arrived at Greenham to protest against the decision of the British government to allow cruise missiles to be based there. In May 1982 about 250 women protested and blocked the base and then in December 1982, 30,000 women joined hands around the base at the *Embrace the Base* event. The camp became well known when on 1 April 1983, about 70,000 protesters formed a 14 miles (23 km) human chain from Greenham to Aldermaston and the ordnance factory at Burghfield
16. Lynne Segal (1987), *Is the Future Female? Troubled Thoughts on Contemporary Feminism*, New York, Peter Bendrick Books, p. 29.
17. Sara Helman, and Tamar Rapoport, (1997), *Women in Black: Challenging Israel's Gender and Socio-political Orders*, The British Journal of Sociology, Vol. 48, No. 4, pp. 681-700, p. 683.
18. *Ibid.*
19. Gila Svirsky (2003), *The Women's Peace Movement in Israel,* In Jewish Feminism in Israel—Some Contemporary Perspectives, Kalpana Misra and Melanbie S. Rich, (eds.), Hanover, Brandeis University Press, pp. 113-31.
20. *Ibid.*
21. Gila Svirsky (2000), *The Impact of Women in Black in Israel,* In Frontline Feminisms: Women, War and Resistance, Marguerite R. Waller and Jennifer Rycenga, (eds.), New York, Garland Publishing, pp. 235-45, p. 244.
22. *Ibid.*
23. United Nations Security Council (2002), *Report of the Secretary-General on Women, Peace and Security*, (S/2002/1154), New York, United Nations, p. 54.

24. http://www.dfat.gov.au/geo/png/bougainville/
25. femLINKpacific, Interview with Elizabeth Momis (October 2004).
26. http://www.womenwarpeace.org
27. Saovana-Spriggs, Ruth, (2000), *Christianity and Women in Bougainville, quoted in Bougainville: The Homecoming,* Bougainville Updates (http://www.eco-action.org/bougainville/oldarchive/2000-06.html)
28. http://www.usip.org/pubs/specialreports/sr114.html.
29. Jeffrey Neil (2005), *The Impact of War on Women: Current Realities, Government Responses, and Recommendations for the Future*, Memo to US Policy-makers, Washington, DC, United States Office on Colombia, http://www.usofficeoncolombia.org/documents/womenbrief.htm.
30. The Lomé Peace Accord was a peace agreement signed on 7 July 1999 between the President Ahmad Tejan Kabbah and Revolutionary United Front (RUF) leader, Foday Sankoh, of Sierra Leone.
31. Foday Saybana Sankoh was the leader and founder of the Sierra Leone rebel group Revolutionary United Front (RUF) in the 11-year-long Sierra Leone Civil War, starting in 1991 and ending in 2002. An estimated 50,000 people were killed during the war, and over 500,000 people were displaced in neighboring countries.The RUF became notorious for brutal practices such as mass rapes and amputations during the civil war. He was indicted on 17 counts for various war crimes, including use of child soldiers, and crimes against humanity, including extermination, enslavement, rape and sexual slavery.
32. D. Mazurana, and K. Carlson (2004), *From Combat to Community: Women and Girls of Sierra Leone*, Women Waging Peace Policy Commission, Hunt Alternatives Fund.
33. http://www.womenwagingpeace.net/content/articles/SierraLeone FullCaseStudy.pdf.
34. Marguerite Guzman Bouvard (1994), *Revolutionizing Motherhood: The Mothers of the Plaza De Mayo,* Lanham, Rowman and Littlefield, p. 59.
35. "Dushirehamwe". Burundi. London: International Alert, n.d. 25 January 2005, http://www.international-alert.org/fieldwork/wppburundi.htm.
36. http://www.womenscommission.org/pdf/bi.pdf. 9.
37. http://www.womeninblack.net/stats/wibbg10092000.html
38. Ilja A. Luciak (2007), *Joining Forces for Democratic Governance: Women's Alliance Building for Post-war Reconstruction in Central America*, In Donna Pankhurst (ed.), Gendered Peace: Women's Search for Post-war Justice and Reconciliation, Routledge, pp. 229-64, p. 235.
39. *Ibid.*
40. http://csmonitor.com/cgi-bin/durableRedirect.pl?/durable/2000/07/14/fp6s1-csm.shtml
41. http://csmonitor.com/cgibin/durableRedirect.pl?/durable/2000/07/14/fp6s1-csm.shtml.
42. Ackerman, Peter and Jack DuVall (2000), *A Force More Powerful: A Century of Non-violent Conflict,* New York, Palgrave.
43. http://www.pbs.org/weta/dictator/otpor/
44. Augusto José Ramón Pinochet Ugarte was a Chilean army general and leader who imposed military dictatorship that ruled Chile from 1973 to

1990 and was indicted for human rights violations in his native Chile on 10 October 1998.

45. Annie, G. Dandavati (1996), *The Women's Movement and the Transition to Democracy in Chile,* New York, Peter Lang Publishing, p. 90.
46. The World Bank (2006), *Civil Society and Peace-building: Potential, Limitations and Critical Factors,* Washington DC, World Ban, p. 8.
47. http://www.hervoices.org/06Cpresentationswajir.shtml
48. *Ibid.*
49. Rita Manchanda (2005), *Women's Agency in Peace-building: Gender Relations in Post-Conflict Reconstruction,* Economic and Political Weekly, Vol. 40, No. 44, pp. 4737-45.
50. *Ibid.*
51. *Ibid.*
52. Track One pertains to diplomat is efforts to resolve conflicts through official channels of governments.
53. Track Two pertains to policy-related discussions that are non-governmental, informal and unofficial nature, but are close to government agendas and often involve the participation of government.
54. People to people dialoged charectercised as "Track Three" activities involve groups that explicitly functions apart or beyond governments, aiming to build new constituencies for peace.
55. PeaceWomen Across the Globe is an organization that aims to strengthen the influence of Peace Women in all contexts of peace, security and sustainability—because peace is not simply the absence of war.
56. http://www.1000peacewomen.org
57. Paula Banerjee (2008), *The Space Between: Women's Negotiations with Democracy.* In Paula Banerjee (ed.), Women in Peace Politics, Thousand Oaks, CA, Sage, pp. 201-17.
58. The National Socialist Council of Nagaland (NSCN) was formed on January 31, 1980 by Isak Chisi Swu, Thuingaleng Muivah and S.S. Khaplang opposing the 'Shillong Accord' signed by the then NNC (Naga National Council) with the Indian government.
59. The Armed Forces (Special Powers) Act, 1958, gives the armed forces almost a free run and authorities even a no-commissioned officer "to open fire or use force even to causing of death" without any neccessay order from higher authority. Article 4(a) of the Special Power of the Armed Forces Act States :

    Any commissioned officer, warrant officer, non-commissioned officer or any other person of equivalent rank in the armed forces may, in a disturbed area: (a) if he is of opinion that it is necessary so to do for the maintenance of Public order, after giving such due warning as he may consider necessary, fire upon or otherwise use force, even to the causing of death, against any person who is acting in contravention of any law or order for the time being in force in the disturbed area prohibiting the assembly 2 of five or more persons or the carrying of weapons or of things capable of being used as weapons or of fire-arms, ammunition or explosive substances;

Article 6 of the Act also deprives the victim or anyone the right to legal remedies except in the certain circumstances . Protection to Persons acting under Act—No persecution, suit or other legal proceeding shall be instituted, except with the previous sanction of the Central Government, against any person in respect of anything done or purported to be done in exercise of the powers conferred by this Act.

60. On 10 July 2004, Thangjam Manorama, a suspected activist of the banned Peoples Liberation Army, an underground outfit operating in the state, was picked up for interrogation at midnight by a team from Assam Rifles, a paramilitary force. She was brutally assaulted by the Security personnel. The post-mortem in the case, testified before an official commission that Manorama had been shot in her genitals, and that bullets had been lodged in her vagina.
61. Malathi de Alwis (2002), *The changing role of women in Sri Lankan society, Social Research*, Vol. 69, No. 3, pp. 675-91, p. 679.
62. Rajan Hoole, Daya Somasunderam, K. Sntharan and Rajani Thiranagama, (1990), *The Broken Palmyrah,* Claremont, Sri Lanka Studies Institute, p. 320.
63. de Alwis, *op. cit.*, p. 679
64. *Ibid.*
65. South Asia Forum for Human Rights (SAFHR) is a regional network established in 1990. SAFHR is committed to the promotion of the inter-linkages between human rights, peace and substantive democracy. SAFHR is a human rights organization with 'peace as value' as its cornerstone in India, Pakistan and Nepal. Peace is understood as a space for the enjoyment of the rights of all peoples. It is not simply the absence of war or the management of crisis but a fundamental value to be integrated in all programs for realizing peoples' security—that is, security of food, shelter, health and livelihood in a non-hegemonic democratic regional order. It is this perspective which animates SAFHR's flagship program—Human Rights and Peace Studies Orientation Course. It is well known organization to conduct "Peace Audit" exercise, four audits (Chittagong Hill Tracts, Naga Peace Process, Peace Process in Sri Lanka, and the Peace Question in Baluchistan) have brought out the general features of such conflict as predicating their peace processes and settlements, the characteristics of the dynamics of the peace accords, the nature of participation of various actors in the peace process.
66. *Women's Initiative for Peace in South Asia (WIPSA)* was formed in 1999 in the wake of nuclear tests of 1998 and Kargil war between India and Pakistan. And since its formation it has taken a number of initiatives for people to people dialogue through exchange visits to reduce tension.
67. *Women in Security, Conflict Management and Peace (WISCOMP)* was established in 1999, by the Dalai Lama's Foundation for Universal Responsibility with the objective to promote women to positions of leadership in all aspects of peace, security and international affairs, and to work with young people to empower a new generation of peace-builders in South Asia. A key aspect of the organisation's work is peace education. It believes bringing peace education into the mainstream, making it a key

part of the national curriculum, is vital to realising its dream of a South Asia free from violent conflict.

68. *South Asian Network of Gender Activities and Trainers (SANGAT)* is a South Asian feminist network which was established in 1998. The orgainstaion works on issues of gender, sustainable livelihoods, democracy, peace, pluralism and human rights. In addition, the organization also documented women initiatives, from around the globe who have worked towards fostering peace and protecting women's human rights and publicise their work
69. *Pakistan-India People-to-People Dialogue on Peace and Democracy (PIPFPD)* established in 1994. The objective of PIPFPD is to facilitate the common people in both the countries to listen to voices that are different from the belligerent voices of the respective Governments. The Forum was tried to debate the issues related to war, de-militarisation, peace and peace dividends; democratic solution to Kashmir problem; democratic governance; religious intolerance in India and Pakistan regional cooperation between India and Pakistan. The Forum has been acted as a mass-based pressure group. The PIPFPD is an innovative effort that involves activists, women's organizations, trade Unions, artists, journalists, intellectuals, etc. to broaden public awareness regarding the issues related to both the countries. Since 1995, the Forum has held seven conventions, alternately in India and Pakistan, with increasing participation in each meeting. It is without doubt one of the more successful citizen-level initiatives in the region.
70. The *Delhi Policy Group* is an independent think tank founded in 1994 also known as South Asian Women in Peace-making Network. The Group seeks to build a non-partisan consensus on issues of critical national interest. The Group has organized a peace and conflict program through Women's Trialogue in Afghanistan, Pakistan and India. Also formulate a South Asian Peace Charter, which helps in bringing women centre stage for conflict management and peace-building.
71. Meera Khanna (2005), *Women and Armed Conflict,* In Pam Rajput (ed), From shadow to Self, NGO Country Report : Beijing +10, New Delhi, pp. 105-10.
72. Beena Sarwar (2004), 'Women's Role in Building Peace between India and Pakistan', McGill University, Montreal.
73. Richa Singh (2004), *Role of Women in India-Pakistan Peace Process*, a paper presented at a workshop on Women's Role in Building Peace between India and Pakistan, University of McGill's Centre for Research and Teaching on Women), held in July-August 2004.
74. Conflict Transformation was conceptualized as part of the efforts of WISCOMP to empower a new generation of women and men with the motivation, expertise and skills to engage in processes of peace-building between Pakistan and India
75. *Athwaas* is a Kashmiri word, which means a handshake or holding of hands as an expression of solidarity and trust. It is a group comprising Kashmiri Muslim, Sikh and Hindu women, is a unique example of the ways in which women's initiatives can emerge as agencies for personal and

social change. It grew out of aneed to search for non-violent, creative and inclusive approaches for conflict transformation in Kashmir in India.

76. It refers to a Kashmiri term used to describe a meeting point.
77. Hind-Pak Dosti Manch (India-Pakistan Friendship Forum) was founded by prominent journalist Sh. Kuldeep Nayar in 1996. The aim and object of this organisation is to promote peace, friendship and co-operation in the region of South Asia, particularly between India and Pakistan. For this purpose it organises, seminars, meetings and music concerts throughout the year. Every year it organises a Candle Vigil and Cultural Show at Wagah Border.
78. Pakistan-India People-to-People Dialogue on Peace and Democracy (PIPFPD) formed in 1994. The objective of this initiative was to facilitate the common people in both the countries to listen to voices that are different from the belligerent voices of the respective Governments. The Forum was tried to debate the issues related to war, de-militarisation, peace and peace dividends; democratic solution to Kashmir problem; democratic governance; religious intolerance in India and Pakistan regional cooperation between India and Pakistan. The Forum has been acted as a mass-based pressure group. The PIPFPD is an innovative effort that involves activists, women's organizations, Trade Unions, artists, journalists, intellectuals, etc. to broaden public awareness regarding the issues related to both the countries. Since 1995, the Forum has held eight conventions, alternately in India and Pakistan, with increasing participation in each meeting. It is without doubt one of the more successful citizen-level initiatives in the region.
79. NWUM formed the union on 7 January 1994. NWUM comprises all the women's organisations of the Naga Tribes of Manipur. The Union became operational on 5 October 1994 with the approval and adoption of its Constitution on October 1994 at Ukhrul.
80. Banerjee, Paula (2007), *Women in Peace Politics*, South Asian Peace Studies, Vol. 3, London, Sage Publications, p. 209.
81. On November 2, 2000, in Malom, a town in the Imphal Valley of Manipur, ten civilians were allegedly shot and killed by the Assam Rifles, one of the Indian Paramilitary forces operating in the state, while waiting at a bus stop. The incident later came to be known to activists as the "Malom Massacre".
82. The Armed Forces (Special Powers) Act, 1958, gives the armed forces almost a free run and authorities even a no-commissioned officer "to open fire or use force even to causing of death" without any necessary order from higher authority. Article 4(a) of the Special Power of the Armed Forces Act States :

    Any commissioned officer, warrant officer, non commissioned officer or any other person of equivalent rank in the armed forces may, in a disturbed area: (a) if he is of opinion that it is necessary so to do for the maintenance of Public order, after giving such due warning as he may consider necessary, fire upon or otherwise use force, even to the causing of death, against any person who is acting in contravention of any law or order for the time being in force in the disturbed area prohibiting the assembly 2 of five or more persons or the carrying of weapons or of things capable of being used as weapons or of fire-arms, ammunition or explosive substances; Article 6 of the Act also deprives the victim or anyone the right to legal remedies except in the certain circumstances. Protection to Persons acting under Act—No persecution, suit or other legal proceeding shall be instituted, except with the previous sanction of the Central Government, against any person in respect of anything done or purported to be done in exercise of the powers conferred by this Act

83. http://www.situationsasia.com/node/777
84. http://www.thehindu.com/news/national/article2501207.ece *The Hindu*, September 30, 2011.
85. *Ibid.*
86. United Nations Development Fund for Women (UNIFEM), (2009), *Women's Participation in Peace Negotiations: Connections between Presence and Influence*, New York, United Nations Fund for Women (UNIFEM), http://www.realizingrights.org/pdf/UNIFEM_handout_Women_in_peace_processes_Brief_April_20_2009.pdf
87. Rita Manchanda (ed.), (2001), *Where are the Women in South Asian Conflicts? Women, War, and Peace in South Asia: Beyond Victimhood to Agency*, New Delhi, Sage Publications, p. 15.
88. United Nations Fund for Women (UNIFEM), (2006), *Beyond Numbers: Supporting Women's Participation and Promoting Gender Equality In Post-Conflict Governance in Africa*, New York, United Nations Fund for Women (UNIFEM), p. 13.
89. *Ibid.*
90. Julie Ballington, and Azza Karam (eds.), (2005), *Women in Parliament: Beyond Numbers*, Stockholm, Sweden: Institute for Democracy and Electoral Assistance (IDEA), pp. 47-48.
91. Sylvia Bashevkin (2009), *Women, Power, Politics : The Hidden Story of Canada's Unfinished Democracy*, Don Mills, Oxford, pp. 28-29.
92. SCR 1325, Article, 8(b).
93. The Researcher did the translation in Hindi while working as an Intern with Global Action to Prevent War (GAPW).

6

Conclusion

The unanimous adoption of the *United Nations Security Council Resolution 1325* on October 31, 2000 was a milestone in the evolution of international women's rights and in the area of women, peace and security. The concept of equality between men and women is enshrined in the Charter of the United Nations. But it had taken the UN Security Council more than fifty-five years to recognize the relevance of women and gender issues in the maintenance of international peace and security. Resolution 1325 is the first Security Council Resolution that emerged out of its decision to take up women, peace and security as a separate thematic agenda. This was the first time that the Security Council addressed protection of women during armed conflict, calling for an end to impunity for gender-based abuses during and after conflict, as well as the integration of a gender perspective in peace-making and peace-keeping. In addition, the participation of women in all levels of decision-making and issues related to prevention management and resolution of conflict were raised, with a wide range of stakeholders, including the governments, the UN Security Council, UN Secretary-General and all parties to armed conflict required to take action. This was a culmination of several years of campaigns especially by women and peace activists across the world and support of many internal allies within the UN system itself, especially within the Security

Council.

Resolution 1325 builds on earlier UN Resolutions and Conventions including the Convention on the Elimination of All Forms of Discrimination against Women (CEDAW) (1979), the General Assembly's Declaration on the Protection of Women and Children in Emergency and Armed Conflicts (1974), the Statutes of the International Tribunals for the former Yugoslavia and Rwanda, the Vienna Convention on Human Rights (1993), the Beijing Declaration and Platform for Action (1995), the Outcome Document of the 23rd Special Session of the UN Assembly (June 2000), and the Windhoek Declaration and Namibia Platform for Action on Mainstreaming a Gender Perspective in Multi-Dimensional Peace Support Operations (May 2000).

The Resolution spells out roles and obligations of key actors, including the United Nations Secretary General, the Security Council, the Member-States and all the parties to armed conflict. Its core urges for : *Participation* of Women in Decision-making on peace and security issues; Peace Processes; *Protection* and *Prevention* of Gender-based Violence against Women and Girls through the *Promotion* of Women's Rights, Accountability and Law Enforcement and *Gender Mainstreaming* in Peace-keeping Operations.

As a Security Council Resolution, Resolution 1325 is binding on all the UN Member-States. They are mandated to make efforts to protect the human rights of women and girls in conflict-related situations, to increase women's participation in peace processes and to ensure a gender perspective in all levels of activities related to peace building and maintenance.

The present study examines the impact of the Resolution in terms of its implementation in the conflict ridden South Asia in the backdrop of the initiatives and actions taken by the United Nations and other stakeholders to implement the Resolution during the last decade.

The study reveals that on the whole since the adoption of the Resolution, there has been an increased acknowledgement of the disproportionate impact of armed conflict on women and their contribution to peace processes both at the international and national levels. To implement this Resolution, considerable steps have been taken by the UN system and the Member States. The Security Council itself has strengthened Resolution 1325 with a follow-up complementary Resolutions 1820 (2008) and 1888 (2009) on sexual violence during conflict and 1889 (2009) which urges the UN

Member-States and other relevant actors to take further measures to improve women's participation in all stages of peace processes. These Resolution cover a broad range of mechanisms related to improving the status of women in conflict situations. The UN entities individually and in partnerships, have undertaken numerous initiatives to implement this Resolution. The System-wide Action Plans (2005-07 and 2008-09) of the Secretary-General were formulated to track the progress within the UN on the Resolution. In addition, in 2010, the Secretary General presented 26 global indicators against which henceforth the implementation of SCR 1325 will be measured at global level.

An increasing number of countries, it is seen, are developing national action plans on the Resolution. Some countries have integrated strategies and actions on women, peace and security into their existing national policies and strategies on gender equality. In a number of countries various mechanisms have been established to support and monitor the implementation of national strategies and actions on women, peace and security.

The study clearly demonstrates that notwithstanding the efforts of all the stakeholders, the implementation of the Resolution has been slow and uneven, particularly in relation to women's participation in preventing and resolving conflicts across the globe. According to UNIFEM research on 21 major peace agreements it was found that women were signatories to only 2.1 per cent and no woman has been appointed chief or lead peace mediator in the UN sponsored peace talks. Further women made up only 5.9 per cent in negotiation delegation. In addition, no woman has been appointed as the head mediator in the UN-sponsored peace talks. This exclusion has lead to a failure to address concerns such as sexual and gender-based violence, women's rights and post-conflict accountability adequately.

A key constraint in the implementation of the Resolution is that neither there is any lead agency within the UN nor has the Security Council developed any coordinating mechanism to oversee its implementation. There is no formal process for reviewing the progress other than the annual open debates. Mandates explicit in SCR 1325 do not envisage either fixing the responsibility of any particular agency or accountability mechanism. There are several agencies within the UN system that have a mandate and varying degree of responsibility to address women‘s issues and to pursue the implementation of the Resolution. Although a System-wide Action Plan was developed to bring greater coherence to the work of the United Nations on women and peace and security, the performance of the Plan fell short of expectations.

Sexual and gender-based violence (SGBV) is often extremely high both during and after conflict, and impunity remains both at the international and national levels. The prevalence and devastating effects of crimes of sexual violence have been explicitly recognized by the International Criminal Court (ICC), but women and girls continue to be victims of untold gender-based violence, sexual violence and discrimination in the context of armed conflict and its aftermath. There is no progress in the protection of women from acts of sexual violence in armed conflicts. Furthermore, peace-keeping forces are often part of the problem rather than the solution. Continued reports of gender-based violence committed by the UN peacekeepers in conflict and post-conflict societies is one of the major challenges. Even while the Department of Peacekeeping Operations (DPKO) has strengthened its "zero tolerance policy", acts of sexual violence continue in most peacekeeping operations.

The lack of political will of the UN Member-States is another significant factor for the slow implementation of the Resolution. The major responsibility to implement the Resolution is on the Member-States. It is indeed discouraging to note that out of 193 Member-States only 43 Member-States made National Action Plans so far. This is a mere 22%. Most NAPs, it is noted, do not really cover the Resolution in its entirety and lack in providing monitoring mechanisms.

Even after eleven years of the Resolution, the Study reveals that there is in general a limited awareness and understanding of it among the UN country offices, government ministries and civil society oragnsiations. Even the personnel of South Asia who were assigned the responsibly associated with the Resolution is not show much familiarity with the details of the Resolution. Another significant revelation is that the Resolution is mostly considered as a Resolution only for women and the Ministry of Women and Child at country level or UN-women as responsible for its implementation.

In the South Asia region, which is the focus of the present Study, the implementation of the Resolution assumes added significance as it is one of the most conflict ridden region in the world. Caught in various intra-state and inter-state conflicts, it is the most militarized and volatile part of the world—impacting severely the civilian population, especially the women and children.

South Asia, home to one-fifth of world's population, is among the low ranking regions in terms of human development with pervasive gender inequalty. With the exception of Sri Lanka, South Asia presents a poor picture in terms Gender Inequality Index (GII) and Gender Gap (GG-World Economic Survey). Added to this are the problems that women face because of conflict situations like increase in the number of widows, female headed households, displacement, vulnerability to sexual violence, increased level of poverty among the female survivors of conflicts, migration, trafficking, etc.

The Resolution has not made much impact in South Asia. In the first instance there is no effort to develop a comprehensive approach at the SAARC level to implement the Resolution in South Asia and develop indicators to measures the progress. The SAARC countries do have a Convention on Preventing and Combating the Trafficking in Women and Children for Prostitution (2002) but it has a limited purpose. The issues related to sexual and gender-based violence in armed conflicts are not addressed in the Convention.

At the country level, the peace processes are still male dominated. Post-conflict recovery processes continue to be gender-blind. Local and international efforts to reform the security sector, including the police, judiciary and military, still fail to respond to the security needs of women. The study indicates that in South Asia while there has been an increase in women's participation in decision-making and political positions, the participation of women in formal peace processes is extremely low. It is rather notional. Illustrative of this is the fact that in the Bonn negotiations relating to Afghanistan in 2001, there were only three women in a delegation of 36. And in the recent Bonn Conference 2011 on Afghanistan, there was not a single woman in the delegation. Indeed as reported in the media, some quarters tentative steps are being made towards peace talks between the US and Taliban insurgents. Afghan women are worried about about a possible return of the hard line Islamis. Shukria Barakazi, a Parliamentarian has objected and stated that "any talks should be held within Afghanistan and women should have a place at the negotiating table".[1]

In Nepal in 2003, just one woman participated in the ceasefire talks between the Government and the Maoists but in 2006 when Comprehensive Peace Agreement (CPA) was signed, women's representation was nil in the talks. In Sri Lanka in 2002, during the talks between the Government and Liberation Tigers of Tamil Eelam

(LTTE), a Sub-committee on Gender Issues was set-up to elaborate gender-sensitive guidelines for the peace process with the support of Norway but the it failed as the talks were suspended. In India the only instance of formally associating women is that of appointment of a woman interlocutor among the two others for dialogue in Jammu and Kashmir.

All the South Asian countries are signatories to the International Conventions/Conferences on women's rights, including the Beijing Platform for Action which strongly recommends reservation for women to facilitate their entry into the mainstream political processes. Accordingly, women do find spaces through reservation in the decision making bodies both at the national and local levels in Afghanistan, Bangladesh, Nepal and Pakistan. In India 33 per cent reservation is available at the local level and the bill to introduce reservation at the national level is pending. Bhutan, Maldives and Sri Lanka are the exceptions which do not have any quota for women at the local or national level. Even with quota, women are under- represented. Nepal has the distinction of being the only State in South Asia which provides for 33 per cent quota for women at the national level. Patriarchy continues to prevent women from breaking traditional gender norms and staking their claims to public spaces and participating in formal peace-making and peace-building processes.

There are a number of policies and action plans which address the problem of sexual and gender-based violence in South Asia. However, such violence in conflict situations both during and after, does not get addressed in these policies. In addition, there has not been effective implementation of tougher penalties towards perpetrators of sexual and gender-based violence in armed conflicts. SGBV continues unabated with impunity. The study brings forth that in the region, very limited data exists to track the ways in which armed conflicts are impacting women, and the degree to which gender perspectives are being incorporated in all peace and security interventions.

The most discouraging fact is that there is not enough awareness about the Resolution both among the government officials and the civil society organizations. While the women's groups are very active in monitoring and lobbying for the Resolution at the global level, that is missing in South Asia at the country level. Of late women's groups have been very active in demanding a General Recommendation on Women in Conflict and Post-conflict Situations and women's groups from South Asia have made submissions to the CEDAW Committee. If that is adopted by the CEDAW Committee, it will strengthen Resolution 1325 as the Governments will thereby under obligation to report on that in their Reports to the CEDAW Committee.

With the disappointing record of implementation, the Resolution has thus not made much impact, especially in South Asia. To move forward and to ensure that the gains of the Resolution are not lost in its operational terms, it is imperative to take measures for its implementation. First and foremost, the Secretary General should ensure that the countries prepare their National Action Plans. The civil society organizations have demanded that the Secretary General should personally write to the Heads of the States and governments and set a time frame for the Plans. The UN Residents Coordinators should be advised to follow-up this with the respective governments.

The Resolution as such has no accountability mechanism and there is no formal process of its review other than the annual debates. There is need to have a focal point with fixed responsibility to monitor the implementation of the Resolution under direct control and supervision of the Secretary-General of the United Nations.

The Secretary-General should establish an inclusive effective consultative process involving the UN entities and civil society organizations for the implementation of the Resolution.

In the South Asia region, it is suggested that SAARC should also be actively engaged in promoting the Resolution. Like the African Union and the European Union, a Regional Action Plan on Women, Peace and Security should be formulated by the SAARC Secretariat in consultation with the civil society groups working on the issue. To make it more meaningful, the Regional Action Plan should be linked to existing human rights treaties and conventions such as—CEDAW, ICCPR, ICSECR, CERD, CRC, BPFA and ICC. The Action Plan should have SMART (specific, measurable, attainable, relevant and time-bound) objectives with timelines, budgets, indicators attached to activities and outputs, and official annual reporting and review mechanisms. There should be a Focal Point within the SAARC for evaluating the progress of the Resolution and overseeing the implementation of the Action Plan.

Awareness about the Resolution is lacking and this is more true of South Asia. Concerted efforts therefore need to made by the UN, the country level UN offices as well as the Member-States to create the awareness about the Resolution. Capacity Building programmes, local translation, inclusion of the provisions of the Resolution in the curricula of training academies/institutes for military, police and bureaucrats and even curricula of Universities and Colleges and last but not the least the use of media for publicizing the Resolution are some of the steps that can be initiated.

The South Asian Governments must ensure women's participation in formal peace processes and post-conflict reconstruction. Only when women are on the peace table in equal strength that sustainable peace can be achieved.

Ending impunity to perpetrators of violence should be a priority with the governments. The South Asian governments must ensure that gender-based violence is expressly prohibited under the terms of cease-fire agreements, and that peace missions are explicitly mandated to investigate and document such violations within these agreements. Ending impunity must also be part of region's collective efforts. No woman or girl victim of sexual violence can reconstruct her life unless the cycle of recurrence is broken. Beyond a lack of respect for the human being, impunity signals the continuation of a horrendous crime, which has multiplying negative effects on family members and the community as a whole. There must be no impunity for sexual and gender-based violence. For that reason, the South Asian Countries must ratify the Rome Statute and strengthen the crucial role played by the International Criminal Court in ensuring accountability and punishing perpetrators of rape and crimes of sexual violence considered as crimes against humanity.

Incidents of violence against women and girls during war and armed conflicts are often neglected and never documented properly by the State agencies. There is always limited data available to track the ways in which armed conflicts are impacting women, and the degree to which gender perspectives are being incorporated in all peace and security interventions. The South Asian governments should systematise and regularize the collection of sex disaggregated data on WPS (including SGBV) as part of regular monitoring efforts, and make such data accessible for use by all stakeholders. The South Asian governments and the UN entities should support the strengthening of data systems for WPS, including efforts by national statistics offices, gender-responsive budgeting processes, and SGBV data collection and management, this should include both technical and adequate financial support.

Refugee and internally displaced women and children always suffer in situations of conflict and post-conflict. International

Conventions concerning refugees and displaced persons have not been ratified by the South Asian countries except Afghanistan. In most cases, refugee women lack legal protection, and do not enjoy adequate health facilities, educational opportunities, or citizenship rights. Protection to women in camps, economic and relief packages should be provided by the governments for the IDPs and refugees. Medical interventions should include psychosocial support for women in post-conflict areas. In addition health and education programmes should be developed to deal with the effects of sexual violence, such as HIV/AIDS and psychological trauma.

In many disarmament and rehabilitation programs, former female rebels and girl soldiers are entirely overlooked. The special needs of former female combatants, including the stigma that ex-combatants are subjected to in the socio-cultural context of South Asia, must be taken into consideration in all disarmament, demobilisation and reintegration programs. The rehabilitation trainings for former combatants must include the needs of female ex-combatants. Single women and women with dependants must be supported to return to civilian life.

The governments must strengthen their partnership with the civil society particularly women's groups, draw upon their expertise and engage them in the implementation of SCR 1325. As women in South Asia are quite active in informal peace processes, their collective experiences of conflict and their peace work especially at the local level should be documented. Funds should be earmarked for women, peace and security and women organizations should be funded to promote and strengthen their work relating the Resolution.

Finally, it may be said that the S*tudy* affirms the value of SCR 1325 as a tool for galvanizing the participation of women in peace processes, enhancing the protection of women and girls from sexual violence in conflict, and promoting the leadership role of women in the transformation of conflicts. As far as South Asia is concerned, it has come a long way in making its strides for gender equality and empowerment of women but the Resolution is yet to make its impact. Access of justice, equal participation of women in peace-building, economic opportunities for women in post conflict situations and violence are some of the key challenges women continue to face in conflict and post-conflict situations. The conditions that women and girls face even after eleven years of the adoption of the Resolution continue to be abhorrent with lack of effective methods for monitoring its impact.

The CEDAW Committee is in the process of formulating a General Recommendations on Human Rights of Women in Conflict and Post-Conflict Situations. Once that is adopted, the Governments will be under obligation to Report on it in their reports to the Committee. The GR will supplement and enhance the effectiveness of Resolution 1325.

In the meanwhile the South Asian Governments need to pay attention to the measures outlined in his proposal by the architect and champion of the Resolution, Anwarul Chowdhury entitled "Do-able First Track Indicators for Realisng the 1325 Promise into Reality". They need to be pro-active in their advocacy for effectiveness of the Resolution in the United Nations as well as at the country level so as to realize the operational value of the Resolution. Both the Security Council and the Member-States at country level need to internalize gender consideration into the operational behavior of their actions. Though SCR 1325 it not the excusive responsibility of the UN Women, with its enhanced position in the UN, it should take the lead in realizing the true spirit of the Resolution which, as Cora Weiss says, is not to make 'war safe for women' but to achieve sustainable peace and security with women as its active agency.

> *"We should never forget that when women are marginalized there is little chance for the world to get sustainable peace in the real sense."*
>
> —Anwarul K. Chowdhury

Note and Reference

1. *The Tribune*, February 13, 2012.

ANNEXURE

United Nations Security Council Resolution 1325 (2000) on Women, Peace and Security adopted by the Security Council at its 4213th meeting, on October 31, 2000

The Security Council,

Recalling its resolutions 1261 (1999) of 25 August 1999, 1265 (1999) of 17 September 1999, 1296 (2000) of 19 April 2000 and 1314 (2000) of 11 August 2000, as well as relevant statements of its President, and *recalling also* the statement of its President to the press on the occasion of the United Nations Day for Women's Rights and International Peace (International Women's Day) of 8 March 2000 (SC/6816),

Recalling also the commitments of the Beijing Declaration and Platform for Action (A/52/231) as well as those contained in the outcome document of the twenty-third Special Session of the United Nations General Assembly entitled "Women 2000: Gender Equality, Development and Peace for the Twenty-first Century" (A/S-23/10/Rev. 1), in particular those concerning women and armed conflict,

Bearing in mind the purposes and principles of the Charter of the United Nations and the primary responsibility of the Security Council under the Charter for the maintenance of international peace and security,

Expressing concern that civilians, particularly women and children, account for the vast majority of those adversely affected by armed conflict, including as refugees and internally displaced persons, and increasingly are targeted by combatants and armed elements, and *recognizing* the consequent impact this has on durable peace and reconciliation,

Reaffirming the important role of women in the prevention and resolution of conflicts and in peace-building, and *stressing* the importance of their equal participation and full involvement in all efforts for the maintenance and promotion of peace and security, and the need to increase their role in decision-making with regard to conflict prevention and resolution,

Reaffirming also the need to implement fully international humanitarian and human rights law that protects the rights of women and girls during and after conflicts,

Emphasizing the need for all parties to ensure that mine clearance and mine awareness programmes take into account the special needs of women and girls,

Recognizing the urgent need to mainstream a gender perspective into peace-keeping operations, and in this regard *noting* the Windhoek Declaration and the Namibia Plan of Action on Mainstreaming a Gender Perspective in Multidimensional Peace Support Operations (S/2000/693),

Recognizing also the importance of the recommendation contained in the statement of its President to the press of 8 March 2000 for specialized training for all peace-keeping personnel on the protection, special needs and human rights of women and children in conflict situations,

Recognizing that an understanding of the impact of armed conflict on women and girls, effective institutional arrangements to guarantee their protection and full participation in the peace process can significantly contribute to the maintenance and promotion of international peace and security,

Noting the need to consolidate data on the impact of armed conflict on women and girls,

1. *Urges* Member-States to ensure increased representation of women at all decision-making levels in national, regional and international institutions and mechanisms for the prevention, management, and resolution of conflict;
2. *Encourages* the Secretary-General to implement his strategic plan of action (A/49/587) calling for an increase in the participation of women at decision-making levels in conflict resolution and peace processes;
3. *Urges* the Secretary-General to appoint more women as special representatives and envoys to pursue good offices on his behalf, and in this regard *calls on* Member-States to provide candidates to the Secretary-General, for inclusion in a regularly updated centralized roster;
4. *Further urges* the Secretary-General to seek to expand the role and contribution of women in United Nations field-

based operations, and especially among military observers, civilian police, human rights and humanitarian personnel;

5. *Expresses* its willingness to incorporate a gender perspective into peace-keeping operations, and *urges* the Secretary-General to ensure that, where appropriate, field operations include a gender component;
6. *Requests* the Secretary-General to provide to Member-States training guidelines and materials on the protection, rights and the particular needs of women, as well as on the importance of involving women in all peace-keeping and peace-building measures, *invites* Member States to incorporate these elements as well as HIV/AIDS awareness training into their national training programmes for military and civilian police personnel in preparation for deployment, and *further requests* the Secretary-General to ensure that civilian personnel of peace-keeping operations receive similar training;
7. *Urges* Member-States to increase their voluntary financial, technical and logistical support for gender-sensitive training efforts, including those undertaken by relevant funds and programmes, *inter alia*, the United Nations Fund for Women and United Nations Children's Fund, and by the Office of the United Nations High Commissioner for Refugees and other relevant bodies;
8. *Calls on* all actors involved, when negotiating and implementing peace agreements, to adopt a gender perspective, including, *inter alia*:
   (a) The special needs of women and girls during repatriation and resettlement and for rehabilitation, reintegration and post-conflict reconstruction;
   (b) Measures that support local women's peace initiatives and indigenous processes for conflict resolution, and that involve women in all of the implementation mechanisms of the peace agreements; and
   (c) Measures that ensure the protection of and respect for human rights of women and girls, particularly as they relate to the constitution, the electoral system, the police and the judiciary;
9. *Calls upon* all parties to armed conflict to respect fully international law applicable to the rights and protection of

women and girls, especially as civilians, in particular the obligations applicable to them under the Geneva Conventions of 1949 and the Additional Protocols thereto of 1977, the Refugee Convention of 1951 and the Protocol thereto of 1967, the Convention on the Elimination of All Forms of Discrimination against Women of 1979 and the Optional Protocol thereto of 1999 and the United Nations Convention on the Rights of the Child of 1989 and the two Optional Protocols thereto of 25 May 2000, and to bear in mind the relevant provisions of the Rome Statute of the International Criminal Court;

10. *Calls on* all parties to armed conflict to take special measures to protect women and girls from gender-based violence, particularly rape and other forms of sexual abuse, and all other forms of violence in situations of armed conflict;
11. *Emphasizes* the responsibility of all States to put an end to impunity and to prosecute those responsible for genocide, crimes against humanity, and war crimes including those relating to sexual and other violence against women and girls, and in this regard *stresses* the need to exclude these crimes, where feasible from amnesty provisions;
12. *Calls upon* all parties to armed conflict to respect the civilian and humanitarian character of refugee camps and settlements, and to take into account the particular needs of women and girls, including in their design, and recalls its resolutions 1208 (1998) of 19 November 1998 and 1296 (2000) of 19 April 2000;
13. *Encourages* all those involved in the planning for disarmament, demobilization and reintegration to consider the different needs of female and male ex-combatants and to take into account the needs of their dependants;
14. *Reaffirms* its readiness, whenever measures are adopted under Article 41 of the Charter of the United Nations, to give consideration to their potential impact on the civilian population, bearing in mind the special needs of women and girls, in order to consider appropriate humanitarian exemptions;
15. *Expresses* its willingness to ensure that Security Council missions take into account gender considerations and the

rights of women, including through consultation with local and international women's groups;

16. *Invites* the Secretary-General to carry out a study on the impact of armed conflict on women and girls, the role of women in peace-building and the gender dimensions of peace processes and conflict resolution, and *further invites* him to submit a report to the Security Council on the results of this study and to make this available to all Member-States of the United Nations;
17. *Requests* the Secretary-General, where appropriate, to include in his reporting to the Security Council progress on gender mainstreaming throughout peace-keeping missions and all other aspects relating to women and girls;
18. *Decides* to remain actively seized of the matter.

Bibliography

Primary Sources

Asian Centre for Human Rights (2006), *South Asia Human Rights Index, 2006*, New Delhi, Asian Centre for Human Rights.

Asian Centre for Human Rights (2008), *South Asia Human Rights Index, 2008*, New Delhi, Asian Centre for Human Rights.

Asian Women's Human Rights Council (AWHRC) (1994), *In the Court of Women II : Asia Tribunal on Women's Human Rights in Tokyo: Proceedings of the International Public Hearing on Traffic in Women and War Crimes Against Women*, Manila, Philippines, Asian Women's Human Rights Council.

Brahimi, Lakhdar (2000), *Report on the Panel on United Nations Peace Operations* (A/55/305 –S/2000/809), New York, United Nations.

Gobierno de Chile (2009), *Plan de Acción Nacional Para la Implementación de la Resolución del Consejo de Seguridad de la Organización de las Naciones Unidas 1325/2000, Mujeres, Paz y Seguridad*, Santiago de Chile.

Gobierno de España (2008), *Plan de acción del gobierno de España para la aplicaciónde la Resolución 1325 del consejo de seguridad de las naciones unidas (2000),sobre mujeres, paz y seguridad*, Madrid, Gobierno de España.

Government of Nepal (2004), *Convention on the Elimination of All Forms of Discrimination against Women* : Second and Third periodic report of Nepal, Government of Nepal.

Government of Sri Lanka (2002), *Convention on the Elimination of All Forms of Discrimination against Women* : Second and Third Periodic Report of Sri Lanka, Government of Sri Lanka.

Government of Austria and Federal Ministry for European and International Affairs (2007), *Austrian Action Plan on Implementation UN Security Council Resolution 1325 (2000)*, Vienna, Federal Ministry for European and International Affairs.

Government of Bangladesh (2003), *Convention on the Elimination of All Forms of Discrimination Against Women* : Fifth Periodic Report of Bangladesh, Government of Bangladesh.

Government of Belgium, Federal Public Service Foreign Affairs and Foreign Trade and Development Cooperation (2009), *Women, Peace and Security, Belgian National Action Plan on the Implementation of UN Security Council Resolution1325*, Brussels, FPS Foreign, Affairs, Foreign Trade and Development Cooperation.

Government of Côte d'Ivoire and Ministry of Women and Social Affairs (2007), *National Action Plan for the Implementation of Resolution 1325 of the Security Council (2008-12)*, Abidjan, Ministry of Women and Social Affairs.

Government of Denmark, Ministry of Foreign Affairs of Denmark and the Ministry of Defence (2005), *Denmark's Action Plan on Implementation of Security Council Resolution 1325 on Women and Peace and Security*, Copenhagen, Ministry of Foreign Affairs of Denmark and the Ministry of Defence.

Government of Finland and the Ministry of Foreign Affairs, 2008, *UN Security Council Resolution 1325, Finland's National Action Plan, 2008-11*, Helsinki, Ministry of Foreign Affairs.

Government of Iceland and the Ministry of Foreign Affairs, 2008, *Women, Peace and Security: Iceland's Plan of Action for the Implementation of United Nations Security Council Resolution 1325 (2000)*, Reykjavik, Ministry of Foreign Affairs.

Government of Norway and the Ministry of Foreign Affairs (2006), *The Norwegian Government's Action Plan for the Implementation of UN Security Council Resolution 1325 (2000) on Women, Peace and Security*, Oslo, Norwegian Ministry of Foreign Affairs.

Government of Pakistan (2005), *Convention on the Elimination of All Forms of Discrimination against Women* : Second and Third Periodic Report of Pakistan, Government of Pakistan.

Government of Portugal (2009), *Plano Nacional de Acção para implementação da Resolução CSNU 1325 (2000) sobre Mulheres, Paz e Segurança (2009-2013)*, Government of Portugal.

Government of Sweden and the Ministry of Foreign Affairs (2006), *The Swedish Government's Action Plan to Implement Security Council Resolution 1325 (2000) on Women, Peace and Security*, Stockholm, Ministry of Foreign Affairs.

Government of Switzerland and the Federal Department of Foreign Affairs (2007), *Switzerland's National Action Plan for the Implementation of UN Security Council Resolution 1325 (2000) on Women, Peace and Security*, Bern, Federal Department of Foreign Affairs.

Government of the Netherlands and the Ministry of Foreign Affairs (2007), *Dutch National Action Plan on Resolution 1325, Taking a Stand for Women, Peace and Security, Policy Department, DSI/SB*, The Hague, Ministry of Foreign Affairs.

Government of the Republic of Liberia and the Ministry of Gender and Development (2009), *The Liberian National Action Plan for the Implementation of United Nations Resolution 1325*, Monrovia, Ministry of Gender and Development.

Government of the United Kingdom (2006), *United Kingdom National Action Plan to Implement UNSCR 1325*, London, Government of the United Kingdom.

Government of Uganda, Ministry of Gender and the Labour and Social Development (2008), *The Uganda Action Plan on UN Security Council Resolutions 1325 and 1820 and the Goma Declaration*, Goma, Ministry of Gender, Labour and Social Development.

Human Development in South Asia (2007), *A Ten-year Review*, The Mahbub ul Haq Human Development Centre, Karachi, Oxford University Press.

Human Rights Watch (1998), *Global Reports on Women's Human Rights*, Delhi, Oxford University Press.

International Criminal Tribunal for Rwanda (ICTR) (1998), *ICTR-96-4-0001, Akayesu, Jean-Paul* (International Criminal Tribunal for Rwanda).

International Criminal Tribunal for the Former Yugoslavia (ICTY), (1999), *Tadic, Dusko IT-94-1-A*, (International Criminal Tribunal for the Former Yugoslavia).

Ministry of Human Resource Development and Department of Women and Child Development (2005), India's Second and Third Periodic Report on the Convention on the Elimination of All Forms of Discrimination Against Women, New Delhi.

National Institute of Public Cooperation and Child Development (2010), *Statistics on Women in India, 2010,* New Delhi, National Institute of Public Cooperation and Child Development.

NGO Working Group on Women, Peace and Security (2006), *SCR 1325 and the Peace-building Commission: Security Council Resolution 1325 on Women, Peace and Security—Six Years Report*, New York, NGO Working Group on Women, Peace and Security.

Protocol Additional to the Geneva Conventions of 12 August 1949, and relating to the Protection of Victims of International Armed Conflicts (Protocol I), 8 June 1977.

Protocol Additional to the Geneva Conventions of 12 August 1949, and relating to the Protection of Victims of International Armed Conflicts (Protocol II), 8 June 1977.

Rome Statute of the International Criminal Court (1998), U.N. Diplomatic Conference of Plenipotentiaries on the Establishment of an International Criminal Court, July 17, 1998, UN Doc. (A/CONF.183/9).

Rehn, Elisabeth and Johnson Sirleaf, Ellen, 2002, *Women, War and Peace: The Independent Expert's Assessment on the Impact of Armed Conflict on Women and Women's Role in Peace-building—Progress of the World's Women 2002*, Vol. 1, New York, United Nations Development Fund for Women (UNIFEM).

Report of the World Conference of the United Nations Decade for Women: Equality, Development and Peace, held in Copenhagen from 14 to 30 July 1980, A/CONF.94/35.

Stockholm International Peace Research Institute (SIPRI), (2010), *SIPRI Yearbook 2010: Armaments, Disarmament, and International Security,* Oxford, Oxford University Press.

The World Bank's New Poverty Data (2008), *Implications for the Asian Development Bank*, Manila, Asian Development Bank.

The Nairobi Forward-looking Strategies for the Advancement of Women from the World Conference to Review and Appraise the Achievements of the United Nations Decade for Women: Equality, Development and Peace, held in Nairobi from 15 to 26 July 1985, A/Conf.116/28/Rev. 1, 1986.

United Nations (2012), *2011-12 : Progress of World's Women,* New York, United Nations.

United Nations Development Programme (2011), *Human Development Report, 2011*, New York, Oxford University Press.

United Nations Commission on the Status of Women (2011), *Agreed Conclusions of the Commission on the Status of Women on the Critical Areas of Concern of the Beijing Platform for Action, 1996-2011,* New York, United Nations.

United Nations Security Council (2010), *Presidential Statement on Women, Peace and Security,* 2010 (S/PRST/2010/22), New York, United Nations.

United Nations Secretary General (2010), *Secretary General-Report on Women, Peace and Security,* (S/2010/173), New York, United Nations.

United Nations Secretary General (2010), *Secretary General-Report on Women, Peace and Security,* (S/2010/498), New York, United Nations.

United Nations Security Council (2010), *Open Debate on Women, Peace and Security,* New York, United Nations.

United Nations Security Council, 2010, *Open Debate on Sexual Violence in Conflict,* New York, United Nations.

United Nations Development Programme (2010), *Human Development Report, 2010,* New York, Oxford University Press

United Nations Security Council Report (2010), *First Cross-Cutting Report on Women, Peace and Security.*

United Nations Security Council (2009), *United Nations Security Council Resolution 1888 on Women, Peace and Security* (S/RES/1888), New York, United Nations.

United Nations Security Council (2009), *United Nations Security Council Resolution 1889 on Women, Peace and Security* (S/RES/1889), New York, United Nations.

United Nations Secretary-General (2009), *Secretary General-Report on Women, Peace and Security* (S/2009/465), New York, United Nations.

United Nations Security Council (2009), *Open Debate on Women, Peace and Security,* New York, United Nations.

United Nations Security Council (2009), *Open Debate on Sexual Violence in Conflict,* New York, United Nations.

United Nations Development Programme (2009), *Human Development Report 2009,* New York, Oxford University Press

United Nations Fund for Women (UNIFEM) (2009), *Who Answers to Women? Gender and Accountability, Progress of the World's Women 2008/2009,* New York, United Nations.

United Nations Development Fund for Women (UNIFEM) Handouts (2009), *Women's Participation in Peace Negotiations:*

Connections between Presence and Influence, New York, United Nations Fund for Women (UNIFEM).

United Nations Development Fund for Women (2004), *Getting it Right, Doing it Right: Gender and Disarmament, Demobilization and Reintegration*, New York, United Nations Development Fund for Women (UNIFEM).

United Nations Security Council (2008), *Presidential Statement on Women, Peace and Security*, 2008 (S/PRST/2008/39), New York, United Nations.

United Nations Secretary General (2008), *Secretary General-Report on Women, Peace and Security*, (S/2008/622), New York, United Nations.

United Nations Security Council (2008), *United Nations Security Council Resolution 1820 on Women, Peace and Security* (S/RES/1820), New York, United Nations.

United Nations Security Council (2008), *Open Debate on Women, Peace and Security*, New York, United Nations.

United Nations Security Council (2008), *Open Debate on Sexual Violence in Conflict*, New York, United Nations.

United Nations Development Programme (2008), *Human Development Report, 2008*, New York, Oxford University Press.

United Nations Security Council (2007), *Presidential Statement on Women, Peace and Security*, 2007, (S/PRST/2007/40), New York, United Nations.

United Nations Secretary General (2007), *Secretary General-Report on Women, Peace and Security*, (S/2007/567), New York, United Nations.

United Nations Fund for Women (UNIFEM), (2007), *Progress of Women in South Asia, 2007: A Series for the Sixth South Asia Regional Ministerial Conference: Commemorating Beijing*, New York, United Nations Fund for Women (UNIFEM).

United Nations Security Council (2007), *Open Debate on Women, Peace and Security*, New York, United Nations.

United Nations Security Council (2006), *Presidential Statement on Women, Peace and Security* 2006, (S/PRST/2006/42), New York, United Nations.

United Nations Secretary General (2006), *Secretary General-Report on Women, Peace and Security* (S/2006/770), New York, United Nations.

United Nations Security Council (2006), *Open Debate on Women, Peace and Security*, New York, United Nations.

United Nations (2006), *The Millennium Development Goals Report, 2006*, New York, United Nations.

United Nations International Research and Training Institute for the Advancement of Women (UN-INSTRAW),(2006), *Securing Equality, Engendering Peace: A Guide to Policy and Planning on Women, Peace and Security*, Costa Rica, United Nations International Research and Training Institute for the Advancement of Women.

United Nations Fund for Women (UNIFEM) (2006), *CEDAW and Security Council Resolution 1325: A Quick Guide*, New York, United Nations Fund for Women (UNIFEM).

United Nations (2006), *The World's Women, 2005: Progress in Statistics*, New York, United Nations.

United Nations Security Council (2005), *Presidential Statement on Women, Peace and Security* 2005 (S/PRST/2005/52), New York, United Nations.

United Nations Secretary General (2005), *Secretary General-Report on Women, Peace and Security*, (S/2005/636), New York, United Nations.

United Nations Security Council (2005), *Open Debate on Women, Peace and Security*, New York, United Nations.

United Nations Development Programme (2005), *Human Development Report, 2005*, New York, Oxford University Press.

United Nations Security Council (2004), *Presidential Statement on Women, Peace and Security, 2004*, (S/PRST/2004/40), New York, United Nations.

United Nations Secretary General (2004), *Secretary General-Report on Women, Peace and Security*, (S/2004/814), New York, United Nations.

United Nations Security Council (2004), *Open Debate on Women, Peace and Security*, New York, United Nations.

United Nations Commission on the Status of Women (2004), *Agreed Conclusions of CSW: Women's Equal Participation in Conflict Prevention, Management and Conflict Resolution and in Post-conflict Peace-building*, New York, United Nations Commission on the Status of Women.

United Nations Security Council (2003), *Open Debate on Women, Peace and Security*, New York, United Nations.

United Nations Secretary-General's Bulletin (2003), *Special Measures for Protection from Sexual Exploitation and Sexual Abuse*, (UN Doc ST/SGB/2003/13), New York, United Nations.

United Nations Office for the Coordination of Humanitarian Affairs (OCHA), (2003), *Glossary of Humanitarian Terms in Relation to the Protection of Civilians in Armed Conflict,* New York, United Nations Office for the Coordination of Humanitarian Affairs (OCHA).

United Nations Security Council (2002), *Presidential Statement on Women, Peace and Security,* (S/PRST/2002/32), New York, United Nations.

United Nations Secretary-General (2002), *Secretary General-Report on Women, Peace and Security,* (S/2002/1154), New York, United Nations.

United Nations Security Council (2002), *Open Debate on Women, Peace and Security,* New York, United Nations.

United Nations Security Council (2001), *Presidential Statement on Women, Peace and Security,* (S/PRST/2001/31), New York, United Nations.

United Nations Security Council (2001), *Open Debate on Women, Peace and Security,* New York, United Nations.

United Nations Security Council (2000), *Press Release on International Women's Day Statement,* (S/6816, 2000), New York, United Nations.

United Nations Security Council, 2000, *United Nations Security Council Resolution 1325 on Women, Peace and Security* (S/RES/ 1325), New York, United Nations.

United Nations Security Council (2000), *Open Debate on Women, Peace and Security,* New York, United Nations.

United Nations Development Programme (UNDP), (2000), *Women's Political Participation and Good Governance: 21st Century* Challenges, New York, United Nations Development Programme.

United Nations, *The Peoples' Millennium Forum Declaration and Agenda for Action Strengthening the United Nations for the 21st Century (May 2000), (A/54/959),* New York, United Nations.

United Nations Department of Peacekeeping Operations (2000), *Windhoek Declaration and Namibia Plan of Action on Mainstreaming a Gender Perspective in Multidimensional Peace Support Operations* (A/55/138- S/2000/693), New York, United Nations.

United Nations (1995), *Beijing Declaration and Platform for Action* (A/CONF.177/20 and A/CONF.177/20/Add.1), New York, United Nations.

United Nations (1995), *United Nations and the Advancement of Women, 1945-95*, The United Nations Blue Book Series, Volume VI, New York, United Nations.

United Nations General Assembly (1982), General Assembly Declaration on the Participation of Women in Promoting International Peace and Cooperation of 3 December 1982, (A/RES/37/63), New York, United Nations.

United Nations General Assembly, 1979, *The Convention on the Elimination of All Forms of Discrimination against Women (CEDAW)*, New York, United Nations.

United Nations, *Report of the World Conference of the International Women's Year*, 19 June-2 July 1975, Mexico City, 1976, (CONF.66/34, 76/IV.1), Mexico.

United Nations World Plan of Action for the Implementation of the Objectives of the International Women's Year. Report of the World Conference of the International Women's Year, Mexico City, 19 June-2 July 1975.

United Nations General Assembly Declaration on the Protection of Women and Children in Emergency and Armed Conflict 3318 (XXIX) of 14 December 1974.

United Nations General Assembly (1948), *Universal Declaration on Human Rights*, New York, United Nations.

United Nations Economic and Social Council (1946), ECOSOC Resolution establishing the Commission on the Status of Women, (E/RES/2/11), 21 June 1946, New York, United Nations.

United Nations (1945), *Charter of the United Nation*, San Francisco, United Nations.

World Conference on Human Rights (1993), *Vienna Declaration and Programme of Action*, A/CONF.157/23, Vienna.

World Bank (2007), *World Development Report*, Washington, DC, Oxford University Press.

Secondary Sources

Books

Aafijes, Astrid (1998), *Gender Violence: Hidden War Crime*. Washington DC, Women, Law and Development International.

Allen, Beverly (1996), *Rape Warfare: The Hidden Genocide in Bosnia-Herzegovina and Croatia*, Minneqpolis, University of Minnesota Press.

Anderlini, Sanam Naraghi (2000), *Women at the Peace Table. Making a Difference*, New York, United Nations Fund for Women.

Anderlini, Sanam Naraghi (2007), *Women Building Peace, What They Do, Why it Matters*, London, Lynne Reiner Publisher.

Antrobus, Peggy (2004), *The Global Women's Movement: Origins, Issues and Strategies*, London, Zed Books.

Archer, John and Barbara Lloyd (1985), *Sex and Gender*, Cambridge, Cambridge University Press.

Ackerman, Peter and Jack DuVall (2000), *A Force More Powerful: A Century of Non-violent Conflict*, New York, Palgrave.

Ariño, María Villellas (2008), *Nepal: A Gender View of the Armed Conflict and the Peace Process*, Barcelona, Escola de cultura de pau.

Bouvard, Marguerite Guzman (1994), *Revolutionizing Motherhood: The Mothers of the Plaza De Mayo*, Lanham, Rowman and Littlefield.

Baksh, Rawwida, Linda Etchart and Elsie Onubogu (eds.) (2005), *Gender Mainstreaming in Conflict Transformation: Building Sustainable Peace*, New Gender Mainstreaming Series on Development Issues, London, Commonwealth Secretariat.

Banerjee, Paula (2007), *Women in Peace Politics*, South Asian Peace Studies, Vol. 3, London, Sage Publications.

Bassiouni, M. Cherif (1999), *Crimes Against Humanity in International Criminal Law*, The Hague, Kluwer Law International.

Beauvoir, Simone de (1949), *The Second Sex*, New York, Alfred A. Knopf, Inc.

Breines, Ingeborg, Dorota Gierycz, and Betty Reardon (1999), *Towards a Women's Agenda for a Culture of Peace*. Paris, UNESCO.

Brill, Marlene Targ (1997), *Women for Peace*, New York, Franklin Watts.

Brock-Utne, Birgit (1985), *Educating for Peace: A Feminist Perspective*, the Athene Series, New York, Pergamon Press.

Brock-Utne, Birgit (1989), *Feminist Perspectives on Peace and Peace Education*, New York, Pergamon Press.

Brownmiller, Susan (1975), *Against Our Will. Men, Women and Rape*, Penguin, Middlesex.

Butalia, Urvashi (ed.) (2002), *Speaking Peace: Women's Voices from Kashmir*, New Delhi, Kali for Women.

Butalia, Urvashi (1998), *The Other Side of Silence*, New Delhi,

Penguin.

Cabrera-Balleza, Mavic, Krista Lynes, and Gina Torry (2005), From Local to Global: Making Peace Work for Women, New York, *NGO Working Group on Women, Peace and Security.*

Caldicott, Helen (1989), *Women and Peace*, Amherst, MA, The Center for Community Access Television.

Chandhoke, Neera (2003), *The Conceits of Civil Society,* Delhi, Oxford University Press.

Chandhoke, Neera (2007), *From Where We Stand : War, Women's Activism and Feminist Analysis*, London, Zed Books.

Chenoy, Anuradha (2002), *Militarism and Women in South Asia*, New Delhi, Kali for Women.

Cockburn, Cynthia and Dubravka Zarkov (2002), *The Postwar Moment : Militaries, Masculinities, and International Peace-keeping*, London, Lawrence and Wishart.

Cockburn, Cynthia (1998), *The Space Between Us: Negotiating Gender and National Identities in Conflict*, London, Zed Books.

Cockburn, Cynthia (2007), *From Where We Stand: War, Women's Activism and Feminist Analysis*, London, Zed Books.

Cohn, Carol (ed.), (1993), *Wars, Wimps and Women: Talking Gender and Thinking War*, Princeton, Princeton University Press.

Connell, Robert W. (1995), *Masculinities*, Cambridge, Polity Press.

Conaway, Camille Pampell and Sen, Anjalina (2005), *Beyond Conflict Prevention: How Women Prevent Violence and Build Sustainable Peace*, New York, United Nations, Global Action to Prevent War and Women's International League for Peace and Freedom.

Coomaraswamy and Dilrukshi Fonseka (eds.) (2004), *Peace Work: Women Armed Conflict and Negotiation*, New Delhi, Women Unlimited.

Cooper, Davina (1995), *Power in Struggle: Feminism, Sexuality and the State,* Buckingham Open University Press.

Cronin, Bruce and Ian Hurd (eds.), (2008), *The UN Security Council and the Politics of International Authority*, London, Routledge.

Dandavati, Annie G. (1996), *The Women's Movement and the Transition to Democracy in Chile,* New York, Peter Lang Publishing.

De Mel, Niloufer (2001), *Women and the Nation's Narratives: Gender and Nationalism in Twentieth Century Sri Lanka*, New Delhi, Kali for Women.

El Jack, Amani (2003), *Gender and Armed Conflict: Overview Report,* Brighton, BRIDGE.

Enloe, Cynthia (1993), *The Morning After: Sexual Politics at the End of the Cold War*, Los Angeles, University of California Press.

Elshtain, Jean Bethke (1987), *Women and War*, New York, Basic Books.

Ferdousi, Priyabhashini (1999), *Ekattorer Duhsaha Smriti*, Dhaka, Ekattorer Ghatok Dalal Nirmul Committee.

Galtung, Johan (1996), *Peace by Peaceful Means: Peace and Conflict, Development and Civilization*, London, Sage.

Goldstein, Josuah (2001), *War and Gender: How Gender Shapes the War System and Vice-versa,* Cambridge, Cambridge University Press.

Gordon Peake, Cathy Gormley-Heenan and Mari Fitzduff (2004), *From Warlords to Peacelords : Local Leadership Capacity in Peace Processes,* Londonderry, INCORE.

Hamid, Zarin (2011), *Report on UNSCR 1325—Implementation in Afghanistan, Kabul,* Afghan Women's Network.

Jain, Devaki (2005), *Women, Development, and the UN: A Sixty-Year Quest for Equality and Justice*, Bloomington, Indiana University Press.

Kaldor, Mary (1999), *New and Old Wars: Organized Violence in a Global Era*, Cambridge, Polity.

Kapadia, Kiran (ed.) (2002), *The Violence of Development*, New Delhi, Kali for Women.

MacFarlane, Neil S. and Yuen Foong Khong (2006), *Human Security and the UN: A Critical History*, Bloomington, Indiana University Press.

Maçhel, Graca (1996), *Impact of Armed Conflicts on Children,* New York, United Nations.

Manchanda, Rita (ed.), (2001), *Women, War and Peace: Beyond Victimhood to Agency*, New Delhi, Sage.

Mazurana, Dyan, Angela Raven-Roberts and Jane Parpart (eds.), (2005), *Gender, Conflict and Peace-keeping,* Oxford, Rowman and Littlefield.

Meghna Guhathakurta (2001), *Women's Narratives from Chittagong Hill Tracts*, New Delhi, Sage.

Mekenkamp, Monique, Paul van Tongeren, and Hans van de Veen (ed.) (2003), *Searching for Peace in Central and South Asia An Overview of Conflict Prevention and Peace-building Activities,* Boulder, Lynne Rienner Publishers.

Meintjies, Pillay and M. Turshen, (eds.), (2001), *The Aftermath: Women in Post-Conflict Transformation*, London, Zed Books.

Moser, Caroline and Fiona C. Clark (eds.), (2001), *Victims, Perpetrators or Actors? Gender, Armed Conflict and Political*

Violence, London, Zed Books.

North East Network (NEN) (2004), *Violence Against Women in North East*, New Delhi, National Commission for Women.

Pietila, Hilkka and Jeanne Vickers (1994), *Making Women Matter: The Role of the UN*, London, Zed Books.

Pietilä, Hilkka (2007), *The Unfinished Story of Women and the United Nations*, New York, United Nations Non-Governmental Liaison Service.

Reardon, Betty A. (1993), *Women and Peace: Feminist Visions of Global Security*, Albany, State University of New York Press.

Reardon, Betty A. (1996), *Sexism and the War System*, New York, Syracuse University Press.

Roy, Chandra K. (2004), *Indigenous Women: A Gender Perspective*, Norway, Resource Centre for the Rights of Indigenous Peoples.

Sajor, Indai Lourdes (ed.), (1998), *Common Grounds: Violence Against Women in War and Armed Conflict Situations*, Quezon City, Asian Center for Women's Human Rights.

Sharma, Kalpana (2002), *Making Peace: Women in Communal Conflicts in Mumbai*, New Delhi, Kali for Women.

Sharoni, Simona (1995), *The Politics of Alliances Between Palestinian and Israeli Women*, New York, Syracuse University Press, Syracuse.

Shepherd, Laura J (2008), *Gender, Violence and Security : Discourse as Practice*, London, Zed Books.

Sjoberg, Laura and Gentry Caron, E. (2007), *Mothers, Monsters and Whores*, London, Zed Books.

Skjelsbaek, Inger and Smith Dan (eds.), (2001), *Gender, Peace and Conflict*, London, Sage Publications.

Steans, Jill (1998), *Gender and International Relations: An Introduction*, New Brunswick, Rutgers.

Tanaka, Yuki (2002), *Japan's Comfort Women: Sexual Slavery and Prostitution During World War II and the US Occupation*, London, Routledge.

Thakur, Ramesh (2005), *The United Nations, Peace and Security*, Cambridge, Cambridge University Press.

Tickner, J. Ann (1992), *Gender in International Relations: Feminist Perspectives on Achieving Global Security. New Directions in World Politics*, New York, Columbia University Press.

Tickner, J. Ann (2001), *Gendering World Politics: Issues and Approaches in the Post-Cold War Era*, New York, Columbia University Press.

Walikhanna, Charu (2004), *Women Silent Victims in Armed Conflict: An Area Study of Jammu and Kashmir*, India, New Delhi, Serials

Publications.

Zambelis, Chris (2009), *Separatists, Islamists and Islamabad Struggle for Control of Pakistani Balochistan,* Washington, DC, The Jamestown Foundation, Terrorism Monitor.

United Nations (2002), *Gender Mainstreaming: An Overview*, New York, United Nations.

United Nations Security Council (2002), *Women, Peace, and Security: Study Submitted by the Secretary-General Pursuant to Security Council Resolution 1325 (2000)*, New York, United Nations.

United Nations Division on the Advancement of Women (2005), *Short History of the Commission on the Status of Women*, New York, United Nations Division on the Advancement of Women, 2005.

Articles

Abeysekera, Sunila (2008), *Organizing and Mobilizing Women for Peace,* In Dubravka Zarkov (eds.), Gender, Violent Conflict and Development. New Delhi, Zubaan, pp. 96-112.

Abrahamsen, Rita and Michael C. Williams (2009), *Security Beyond the State: Global Security Assemblages in International Politics*, International Political Sociology, Vol. 3.1, pp. 1-17.

Akuve, Tsahe Dzigdobi (1997), The *Reality of Rwanda's Genocide,* Women's World, pp. 4-6.

Alwis, Malathi de (2008), *Motherhood as a Space of Protest: Women's Political Participation in Contemporary Sri Lanka*, In Paula Banerjee (ed.), *Women in Peace Politics*, Thousand Oaks, CA, Sage, pp. 152-60.

Anderlini, Sanam B. Naraghi, Rita Manchanda and Shereen Karmali (2000), *Women, Violent Conflict and Peace-building: Global Perspectives*, Report of the Conference Women, Violent Conflict and Peace-building, London, International Alert.

Anderlini, Sanam Naraghi, Camille Pampell Conaway, and Lisa Kays (2007), *In Transitional Justice and Reconciliation, Inclusive Security, Sustainable Peace: A Toolkit for Advocacy and Action,* London, International Alert/Women Waging Peace.

Ballington, Julie, and Azza Karam (eds.) (2005), *Women in Parliament: Beyond Numbers,* Stockholm, Sweden: Institute for Democracy and Electoral Assistance (IDEA), pp. 47-48.

Banerjee, Paula (2002), *The Space Between: Women's Negotiations with Democracy*, In C. Joshua Thomas and Gurudas Das (eds.), *Dimensions of Development in Nagaland*, New Delhi, Regency, pp. 187-97.

Banerjee, Payal and Moushumi Shabnam (2006), *Ten Years After Beijing: A Conference on Collective Reflections about Gender Justice,* International Feminist Journal of Politics, Vol. 8, No. 3, pp. 430-37.

Bashevkin, Sylvia *(2009), Women, Power, Politics : The Hidden Story of Canada's Unfinished Democracy,* Don Mills, Oxford UP, pp. 28-29.

Behera, Navnita Chadha (2002), *Forging New Solidarities: Non-Official Dialogues,* In Searching for Peace in Central and South Asia, (eds.), Monique Mekenkamp, Paul van Tongeran and Hans van de Veen, Boulder, Lynne Rienner, pp. 226-31.

Binder, Christina, Karin Lukas and Romana Schweiger (2008), *UN Security Council Resolution 1325, Gender and Transitional Justice,* In Chima J. Korieh and Philomina Okeke-Ihejirika (eds.), Gendering Global Transformations, London, Routledge, .pp. 201-19.

Blanchard, Eric M. (2003), *Gender, International Relations, and the Development of Feminist Security Theory,* Journal of Women in Culture and Society, Vol. 28, No. 4, pp. 1289-1312.

Brock-Utne, Birgit (1994), *Listen to Women, for a Change.* In Robert Elias and Jennifer Turpin (eds.) Rethinking Peace, Boulder (CO), Lynne Rienner, pp. 205-09.

Butalia, Urvashi (2001), *Women and Communal Conflict: New Challenges for the Women's Movement in India,* In Fiona Clark, and Caroline Moser (ed.), Victims, Perpetrators or Actors? Gender Armed Conflict and Political Violence, London, Zed Books, pp. 99-114.

Byrnes, A. (2002), *The Convention on the Elimination of All Forms of Discrimination against Women,* In W. Benedek, G. Oberleitner and E. Kisaakye (eds.), The Human Rights of Women—International Instruments and African Experiences, London, Zed Books, pp. 119-223.

Carlsnaes, Walter (1992), *The Agency-Structure Problem in Foreign Policy Analysis,* International Studies Quarterly. 36.3, pp. 245-70.

Carpènter, R. Charli (2002), *Gender Theory in World Politics: Contributions of a Non-Feminist Standpoint, International Studies Review,* Vol. 4, No. 3, pp. 153-65.

Charlesworth, Hilary (1994), *Transforming the United Mens Club: Feminist Futures for the United Nations,* Transnational Law and

Contemporary Problems Vol. 4, No. 2, pp. 421-54.

Charlesworth, Hilary (2005), *Not Waving but Drowning: Gender Mainstreaming and Human Rights in the United Nations*, Harvard Human Rights Journal, Vol. 18, pp. 1-18.

Charlotte Bunch and Roxanna Carillo (1998), *Global Violence against Women: The Challenge to Human Rights and Development*, In Michael Klare and Yogesh Chandrani (eds.), *World Security: Challenges for a New Century*, New York, St. Martin's Press.

Chenoy, Anuradha (1998), *Militarization, Conflict, and Women in South Asia*, In Lois Anne Lorentzen, and Jennifer Turpin (eds.), The Women and War Reader, New York, New York University Press, pp. 101-10.

Cockburn, Cynthia (2001), *The Gendered Dynamics of Armed Conflict and Political Violence,* In Caroline Moser and Fiona Clark (eds.), Victims Perpetrators or Actors: Gendered Armed Conflict and Political Violence, London, Zed Books, pp. 13-29.

Cockburn, Cynthia (2004), *The Continuum of Violence*, In Jennifer Hyndman and Wenona Giles (eds.), A Gender Perspective on War and Peace, in Sites of Violence, University of California Press, Berkeley, pp. 24-44.

Cohn, Carol (1993), *Wars, Wimps, and Women: Talking Gender and Thinking War*, In Miriam Cooke and Angela Woollacott *(eds.),* Gendering War Talk, Princeton University Press, pp. 227-48.

Cohn, Carol (2004), *Feminist Peacemaking*, The Women's Review of Books, Vol. 21, No. 5, pp. 8-9.

Cordesman, Anthony H. (2008), *The Afghan-Pakistan War: A Status Report*, Center for Strategic and International Studies Report.

Costin, Lela B. (1982), *Feminism, Pacifism, Internationalism and the 1915 International Congress of Women,* Women's Studies International Forum, Vol. 5, No. 3, pp. 301-15.

D'Antonio, Patricia (2002), *Nurses in War,* The Lancet, Vol. 360, No. 1, pp. 7-8.

Desai, Manisha (2005), *Transnationalism: The Face of Feminist Politics Post-Beijing*, International Social Science Journal, Vol. 57, No. 184, pp. 319-30.

Donald, Dominick (2002), *Neutrality, Impartiality and UN Peacekeeping at the Beginning of the 21st Century, International Peacekeeping*, Vol. 9, No. 4, pp. 21-38.

Ellis, Mark S. (2006), *Breaking the Silence: Rape as an International Crime,* Case Western Reserve Journal of International Law 38, pp. 227-47.

Etchart, Linda (2005), *Progress in Gender Mainstreaming in Peace Support Operations*. In Rawwida Baksh Linda Etchart and Elsie Onubogu (eds.), Gender Mainstreaming in Conflict Transformation: Building Sustainable Peace, London, Commonwealth Secretariat, pp. 56-81.

Fitzsimmons, Tracy (2005), *The Post-conflict Post-script: Gender and Policing in Peace Operations*. In Dyan Mazurana, Angela Raven-Roberts and Jane Parpart (eds.), Gender, Conflict and Peace-keeping, Oxford, Rowman and Littlefield, pp. 185-201.

Fraser, Arvonne S. (1995), *The Convention on the Elimination of All Forms of Discrimination Against Women* (The Women's Convention). In Anne Winslow (ed.) Women, Politics and the United Nations, Westport, Greenwood Press, pp. 77-94.

Fujio, Christy (2008), *From Soft to Hard Law: Moving Resolution 1325 on Women, Peace and Security Across the Spectrum*, Georgetown Journal of Gender and the Law, Vol. 9, No. 1, pp. 215-36.

Galtung, Johan (1969), *Violence, Peace and Peace Research*, Journal of Peace Research, Vol. 6, No. 3, pp. 167-91.

Gardam, J., 1997, *Women and the Law of Armed Conflict: Why the Silence?*, International and Comparative Law Quarterly, Vol. 46, p. 55.

Gardam, Judith and Hilary Charlesworth (2000), *Protection of Women in Armed Conflict*, Human Rights Quarterly, Vol. 22, No. 1, pp. 148-66.

Gardam, Judith and Michelle J. Jarvis (2000), *Women and Armed Conflict: The International Responses to the Beijing Platform for Action*, Columbia Human Rights Law Review, Vol. 32, pp.1-65.

Gierycz, Dorota (2001), *Women, Peace and the United Nations: Beyond Beijing*. In Inger Skjelsbaek and Dan Smith (eds.), Gender, Peace and Conflict, London, Sage, pp. 14-31.

Goetz, Anne-Marie (1988), *Feminism and the Limits of the Claim to Know: Contradictions in the Feminist Approach to Women in Development*, Millennium, Journal of International Studies, Vol. 17, No. 3, pp. 477-96.

Goswami, Roshmi (2000), *Women and Armed Conflict—Ground Realities from North-East*, New Delhi, WISCOMP.

Handrahan, Lori (2004), *Conflict, Gender, Ethnicity and Post-Conflict Reconstruction*. Security Dialogue, Vol. 35, No. 4, pp. 429-45.

Hans, Asha (2000), *Internally Displaced Women from Kashmir: The*

Role of UNHCR, Vol. 2, No. 1, South Asian Refugee Watch.

Hill, Chris (1994), *Academic International Relations: The Siren Song of Policy Relevance*. In Christopher Hill and Pamela Beshoff (eds.), Two Worlds of International Relations: Academics, Practitioners and the Trade in Ideas, London, Routledge, pp. 3-45.

Iyer, Lakshmi (2009), *The Bloody Millennium: Internal Conflict in South Asia*, Working Paper No. 09-086, Harvard, Harvard Business School, *BGIE*.

Jacobson, Ruth (2008), *Gender, Development and Conflict in Mozambique*, In Dubravka Zarkov (eds.), Gender, Violent Conflict and Development, New Delhi, Zubaan, pp. 75-95.

Jansen, Golie G. (2006), *Gender and War: The Effects of Armed Conflict on Womens Health and Mental Health*. Affilia, Journal of Women and Social Work, Vol. 21, No. 2, pp. 134-45.

Joachim, Jutta (1999), *Shaping the Human Rights Agenda: The Case of Violence against Women*. In Mary K. Meyer and Elisabeth Prügl (eds.), Gender Politics in Global Governance, Oxford, Rowman and Littlefield, pp. 142-60.

Karam, Azza (2001), *Women in War and Peace-building*, International Feminist Journal of Politics, Vol. 3, No. 1, pp. 2-25.

Kate Nahapetian (1999), *Selective Justice: Prosecuting Rape in the International Criminal Tribunals for the Former Yugoslavia and Rwanda*, Berkely Women's Law Journal, Vol. 14, pp. 126-30.

Kelly, Liz (2000), *War Against Women : Sexual Violence, Sexual Politics and the Militarised State*, In Susie M. Jacobs, Ruth Jacobson and Jen Marchbank (eds.) States of Conflict: Gender, Violence and Resistance, London, Zed Books, pp. 45-65.

Kirleis, Edda (2008), *Rethinking Gender, Violent Conflict and Development*. In Dubravka Zarkov (eds.), Gender, Violent Conflict and Development, New Delhi, Zubaan, pp. 41-59.

Klot, Jennifer (2002), *Women and Peace Processes—An Impossible Match*?, In Louise Olsson (ed.), Gender Processes–an Impossible Match?, Uppsala, Collegium of Development Studies, pp. 17-23

Krasno, Jean E. (2004), *Founding of the United Nations: An Evolutionary Process*. In Jean E. Krasno (eds.), The United Nations : Confronting the Challenges of a Global Society, Boulder (CO), Lynne Rienner, pp. 19-46.

Mackay, Angela (2005), *Mainstreaming Gender in United Nations Peace-keeping Training: Examples from East Timor, Ethiopia and*

Eritrea, In Dyan E. Mazurana, Angela Raven-Roberts and Jane Parpart (eds.), Gender, Conflict and Peace-keeping, Oxford, Rowman and Littlefield, pp. 265-79.

Manchanda, Rita (2001), *Ambivalent Gains in South Asian Conflicts*, In Meintjies, Pillay and M.Turshen (ed.), Aftermath: Women in Post-Conflict Transformation, London: Zed Books, pp. 97-120.

Manchanda, Rita (2001), *Guns and Burqua: Women in the Kashmir Conflict*, In Rita Manchanda (ed.), Women,War and Peace in South Asia: Beyond Victimhood to Agency, New Delhi, South Asia Forum for Human Rights, pp. 42-101.

Mazurana, Dyan (2004), *Gender and the Causes and Consequences of Armed Conflict*, In Dyan E. Mazurana, Angela Raven-keeping. Oxford, Rowman and Littlefield, pp. 66-86.

Meidzian, Myriam (1994), *Real Men, Wimps, and National Security*, In Robert Elias and Jennifer Turpin (eds.), Rethinking Peace, Boulder, Lynne Rienner, pp. 17-25.

Meyer, Mary K. (1999), *The Women's International League for Peace and Freedom: Organizing Women for Peace in the War System*, In Mary K. Meyer and Elisabeth Prugl (eds.), Gender Politics in Global Governance, Oxford, Rowman and Littlefield, pp. 107-21.

Miller, Carol (1994), *The Key to Equality: Inter-war Feminists and the League of Nations, Geneva—Women's History*, Review Vol. 3, No. 2, pp. 218-45.

Mitchell, David S. (2005), *The Prohibition of Rape in International Humanitarian Law as a Norm of Jus Cogens: Clarifying the Doctrine*, Duke Journal of International and Comparative Law, Vol. 15, pp. 219-57.

Moghadam, Val (2001), *Globalization, Militarism, and Women's Collective Action*, National Women Studies Association Journal, Vol. 13, No. 2, pp. 60-67.

Moser, Caroline (2001), *The Gendered Continuum of Violence: An Operational Framework in Caroline Moser and Fiona Clark* (eds.), Victims Perpetrators or Actors: Gendered Armed Conflict and Political Violence, London, Zed Books, pp. 30-52.

Neil, Jeffrey (2005), *The Impact of War on Women: Current Realities, Government Responses, and Recommendations for the Future*, Memo to US Policy-makers, Washington DC, United States Office on Colombia.

Neuwirth, Jessica (2002), *Women and Peace and Security: The*

Implementation of U.N. Security Council Resolution 1325, Duke Journal of Gender Law and Policy, Vol. 9, pp. 253-60.

Nikolic-Ristanovic, Vesna (1996), *War and Violence against Women.* In Jennifer Turpin and Lois Ann Lorentzen (eds.), The Gendered New World Order: Militarism, Development, and the Environment, London, Routledge, pp. 195-210.

Olivera Simiæ (2010), *Does the Presence of Women Really Matter? Towards Combating Male Sexual Violence in Peacekeeping Operations, International Peace-keeping,* Vol. 17, No. 2, pp. 188-99.

Olsson Louise and Torunn L. Tryggestad (eds.), (2001), *Gender Mainstreaming in Practice: The United Nations Transitional Assistance Group in Namibia,* Cass Series on Peace-keeping, London, Frank Cass, pp. 97-110.

Pearson, Michael (2001), *Humanizing the Security Council,* In Fen Osler Hampson, Norman Hilmer, Mareen Appel Molot. (eds.), Canada Among Nations, 2001, The Axworth Legacy, Oxford University Press, pp. 127-51.

Porter, Elisabeth (2003), *Women, Political Decision-making, and Peace-Building.* Global Change, Peace and Security, Vol. 15, No. 3, pp. 245-62.

Powley, Elizabeth (2005), Rwanda: Women Hold Up Half the Parliament, In International IDEA, *Women in Parliament: Beyond Numbers,* Stockholm, International Institute for Democracy and Electoral Assistance, 142-51.

Puechguirbal, Nadine (2003), *Women and War in the Democratic Republic of Congo. Signs,* Journal of Women in Culture and Society, Vol. 23, No. 4, pp. 1272-81.

Rashiduzzaman, M.,(1998), *Bangladesh's Chittagong Hill Tracts Peace Accord: Institutional Features and Strategic Concerns,* Asian Survey, pp. 653-70.

Reilly, Niamh (2007), *Seeking Gender Justice in Post-conflict Transitions : Towards a Transformative Women's Human Rights Approach,* International Journal of Law in Context, Vol. 3, No. 2, pp. 155-72.

Ruane, Joseph and Jennifer Todd (2005), *Communal Conflict and Emancipation : The Case of Northern Ireland.* In Ken Booth (ed.), Critical Security Studies and World Politics, London, Lynne Rienner, pp. 237-55.

Ruddick, Sara (1990), *The Rationality of Care.* In Jean Bethke Elshtain and Sheila Tobias (eds.), Women, Militarism and War, Savage (MD), Rowman and Littlefield, pp. 229-54.

Rupert, Mark (1998), *(Re-) Engaging Gramsci : A Response to Germain and Kenny*, Review of International Studies, Vol. 24, No. 3, pp. 427-34.

Sandler, Joanne (2008), *Implementing Security Council Resolution 1325*, Disarmament Times, Vol. 31, No. 1, pp. 2-3.

Skjelsbaek, Inger and Dan Smith (2001), *Introduction.* In Inger Skjelsbaek and Dan Smith (eds.), Gender, Peace and Conflict, London, Sage, pp. 1-13.

Sorpong Peou (2002), *The United Nations, Peacekeeping and Collective Human Security: From An Agenda for Peace to the Brahimi Report*, International Peace-keeping: Special Issue on Recovering from Civil Conflict, Vol. 9, No. 2, pp. 52-54.

Spees, Pam (2003), *Women's Advocacy in the Creation of the International Criminal Court: Changing the Landscapes of Justice and Power, Signs*, Vol. 28, No.4, pp. 1234-54.

Stephenson, Carolyn M. (1982), *Feminism, Pacifism, Nationalism, and the United Nations Decade for Women*, Women's Studies International Forum, Vol. 5, No. 3, pp. 287-300.

Stienstra, Deborah (1999), *Of Roots, Leaves and Trees : Gender, Social Movements, and Global Governance,* In Mary K. Meyer and Elisabeth Prugl (eds.), Gender Politics in Global Governance, Oxford, Rowman and Littlefield, pp. 260-72.

Strickland, Richard and Duvvury, Nata (2003), *Gender Equity and Peace-building, From Rhetoric to Reality: Finding the Way*, Gender Equity and Peacebuilding Workshop, International Centre for Research on Women

Summerfield, Penny (1997),*Gender and War in the Twentieth Century*, The International History Review, Vol. 19, No. 1, pp. 2-15.

True-Frost, Cora, 2007, *The Security Council and Norm Consumption*, NYU Journal of International Law and Politics, Vol. 40, No. 115, pp. 115-217.

United Nations, Population Fund (2007), *Priority Areas for Addressing Sexual and Gender-based Violence in Nepal*, Nepal, Human Resource Development Center *(HURDEC)*.

Usta, Farver and Lama Zain (2008), *Women, War and Violence: Surviving the Experience*, Journal of Women's Health, Vol. 17, No. 5, pp. 793-804.

Watchlist on Children and Armed Conflict (2005), *Caught in the*

Middle: Mounting Violations Against Children in Nepal's Armed Conflict, Nepal, Watchlist on Children and Armed Conflict.

Key Websites

http://www.amnesty.org
http://www.un.org
http://www.un.org/womenwatch/feature/wps/
http://www.aihrc.org.af
http://www.genderandsecurity.umb.edu/
http://www.iansa.org/
http://www.international-alert.org/
http://www.isanet.org/
http://www.haguepeace.org
http://www.womenpeacesecurity.org
http://www.peacewomen.org
http://www.securitycouncilreport.org
http://www.un.org/Depts/dpko/dpko/dpko.shtml
http://www.womenwarpeace.org
http://www.un-instraw.org/
http://www.womensrefugeecommission.org/
http://www.peacewomen.org
http://www.kmsnews.org/archive/all
http://www.guardian.co.uk/global-development/2010/oct/11/1
http://www.youthkiawaaz.com/2010/02/dardpora-the-village-of-widows/
http://www.ploughshares.ca/libraries/ACRText/ACR-Nepal.html
http://watchlist.org/reports/pdf/nepal.report.20050120.pdf
http://www.nwmindia.org/articles/links-to-studies-articles
http://www.ipu.org/wmn-e/world.htm
Error! Hyperlink reference not valid.
http://www.aihrc.org.af/2010_eng/
http://www.unhcr.org/cgi-bin/texis/vtx/country?iso=afg
http://hrw.org/wr2k2/asia.html.
Error! Hyperlink reference not valid.
www.wcd.nic.in

Index